Educational Wastelands

# EDUCATIONAL WASTELANDS

The Retreat from Learning
in Our Public Schools

## ARTHUR BESTOR

Second Edition

*with Retrospectives by*
Clarence J. Karier
and Foster McMurray

University of Illinois Press
*Urbana and Chicago*

First published by the University of Illinois Press in 1953
© 1985 by the Board of Trustees of the University of Illinois
Manufactured in the United States of America

*This book is printed on acid-free paper.*

Library of Congress Cataloging in Publication Data

Bestor, Arthur Eugene, 1908–
  Educational wastelands.

  1. Bestor, Arthur Eugene, 1908–    . 2. Education—
United States—Aims and objectives.   3. Education—
Philosophy.   I. Karier, Clarence J.   II. McMurray, Foster.
III. Title.
LB875.B345   1985          370'.973          85-1014
ISBN 0-252-01226-7

To my sons, BILL, TOM, and TED,
whose generations will need to know more
and think harder than ours.

# Contents

# Publisher's Note on the Second Edition

The first edition of Arthur Bestor's *Educational Wastelands* created a considerable stir in educational circles, before as well as after its publication in 1953. Bestor's assertion that "the men and women who are professionally engaged in education . . . have allowed themselves to become confused about the purpose of education [and] have sponsored school and college programs which make no substantial contribution to knowledge or to clear thinking" quite naturally drew fire from the nation's schools and colleges of education, from none more than from the one at his own institution, the University of Illinois. When the decision was made to reissue the book, at a time when there is once again much concern about the quality of American education, it seemed fitting to ask two members of the faculty of the College of Education at the University of Illinois to place the work in its proper historical perspective and to provide contemporary readers with frank discussions of both its merits and its inadequacies. The retrospectives by Clarence J. Karier and Foster McMurray, which appear at the back of this edition, not only represent very well the general viewpoints of the book's supporters and detractors but also constitute in and of themselves significant contributions to the ongoing debate about how American children should be educated.

# Preface to the Second Edition

Some writings are first received as polemics, only later to be recognized as affirmations. No doubt King George III saw in the Declaration of Independence merely an impertinent and disloyal diatribe. We read it differently.

It is my hope that this book, on its republication after some thirty years, will be read as a statement of what the writer is *for*, and only incidentally as a statement of what, in consequence, he must needs be against.

The book was written as a defense of public education. The gravest threats, as the writer sees it, are always those from within. They consist in a confusion about the purposes of education, a consequent lessening of its aims and its standards, and an under-valuing of the intellectual capacities of the nation's young people, whose highest expectations (rather than whose immediate gratifications) it is the responsibility of educators to arouse and to foster. Erosion of the ideals of an institution, like erosion of the soil, means the creation of wastelands.

Writing as one member of the faculty of a university, I attempted in this book to explain the views that prevail in the world of scholarship and science concerning the nature and purpose of education. Writing as a historian, I pointed out that this conception of education was one that was shared, at least until well into the twentieth century, by those conscientious educators who devised, for every level of the educational system, programs of study that would carry students forward, progressively and cumulatively, from the initial stages of learning to mature intellectual achievement.

Finally, writing as a citizen and parent, I argued that a commitment to democracy requires a concomitant commitment to the maintenance of a public educational system in which the talents and efforts of all students would be steadily channeled into the mainstream of intellectual effort, not diverted into the eddies and stagnant pools of mere vocationalism or condescendingly paternalist programs of "life adjustment."

Fads, in education as elsewhere, come and go. Sampled in the chapters that follow are some of the trivialities that intruded into school programs in the 1950s. Were this book simply a criticism of these, it would serve no higher purpose than as a guidebook to a museum of already faded absurdities. But educational innovation, healthful and necessary as it ever must be, raises constantly the question, What things are of unchanging value? That this book may keep so vital a question alive in the public mind is the hope of

THE AUTHOR

Department of History,
University of Washington, Seattle
20 September 1984

# 1

## The Vanishing Sense of Purpose
## in Education

Americans have unbounded faith in schools, but they seem to distrust the results of schooling. We send, at public expense, an ever-increasing proportion of the population to school and college, yet we are suspicious of the highly educated man who offers to make some return by devoting his special training to the public service. At graduation we are proud to see our sons and daughters march forward in cap and gown, but in the morning newspaper we recognize the very same cap and gown as the cartoonist's accepted symbol for folly and ineffectiveness.

Universal, free, public education is part of the democratic creed, which Americans accept but which they would find it hard to explain in rational terms. It does not appear that many of them seriously expect society to get its money's worth out of the process. We pay our school taxes, but we rarely conceive of ourselves as making thereby an investment in the intellectual advancement of the nation. Our motive seems to be little more than warm-hearted benevolence. We hate to think that any child should be deprived of his fair share of anything so costly, so orna-

mental, and so well-regarded as education. To put the matter
bluntly, we regard schooling as a mere experience, delightful to
the recipient but hardly valuable to society. The school or college
has become, to our minds, merely a branch of the luxury-purvey-
ing trade. Like the club car on a passenger train, it dispenses
the amenities of life to persons bound on serious errands elsewhere.

Now, public opinion is not so perverse as to adopt such a view
without cause. It is fully aware of the traditional claims of education. It is prepared to believe that knowledge is a good thing
both in its own right and for the practical uses to which it can
be put. It sees a connection between good citizenship and the
ability to think. What it is skeptical about is the ability of our
schools and colleges to impart these qualities of mind to their
graduates. Responsibility for this disbelief rests squarely upon
the men and women who are professionally engaged in education. They have allowed themselves to become confused about
the purposes of education, and they have transmitted that confusion to the public. They have sponsored school and college
programs which make no substantial contribution to knowledge
or to clear thinking, and which could not conceivably make such
a contribution. The public, seeing no point in much of what is
done under the name of education, have developed a justifiable
skepticism toward education itself. They are willing to keep on
playing the game, but they refuse to think of it as much more
than a game.

The founders of our nation and of our school system betrayed
no such confusion of purpose. "If a nation expects to be ignorant
and free," wrote Thomas Jefferson, ". . . it expects what never was
and never will be." Jefferson intended his words to be taken
literally. He knew, moreover, what he meant by education. It is,
first of all, the opposite of ignorance. Its positive meaning is indicated by the synonyms which Jefferson employs in his letters.
The kind of schooling that is vital to a democratic society is the
kind that results in the "spread of information" and the "diffusion
of knowledge"; the kind that regards "science . . . [as] more important in a republican than in any other government"; the kind
that recognizes that "the general mind must be strengthened by
education"; the kind that aims to make the people "enlightened"

and to "inform their discretion." [1] These are the ends which the schools must serve if a free people is to remain free. These, be it noted, are intellectual ends. Genuine education, in short, is intellectual training.

The founders of our public school system meant by education exactly what Jefferson meant by education and exactly what thoughtful men had always meant by it. They believed, quite simply, that ignorance is a handicap and disciplined intelligence a source of power. A democracy, they argued, should make intellectual training available to every citizen, whether poor or rich. So great would be the benefit to the state from such a diffusion of knowledge and intelligence that it was legitimate to support the educational system by taxation, and even to use the coercive authority of law to compel every future citizen to secure an education by attending school for a substantial period of time.

The American people, more than a century ago, committed themselves to this program, and they have invested heavily in the effort to bring it to full realization. By every quantitative measure—time, effort, numbers, money—we should be well on the way toward achievement of the noble ends in view. Enrollment has steadily increased until today four out of every five American children between the ages of five and seventeen, inclusive, are in school. We talk so much about overcrowding that we are apt to forget the significant fact that the equipment and resources of the public schools have increased far more rapidly than attendance. Approximately four times as many children as in 1870 are now in school, but we spend more than ninety times as much on their education. The child of today enjoys a school year twice as long. The proportion of teachers to pupils is greater, and the teachers are required to have spent far more time in training. Compared with 1870 (*after* adjustments have been made for the changed value of the dollar), we find that nine times as much money is spent per year on the education of *each* child, and nearly thirteen times as much is invested in the buildings and equipment which each one is privileged to use.[2] Inequalities and inadequacies persist, of course, and these must be eliminated. But the fact remains that the American people have generously and faithfully supported their schools. They have a right to ask whether the qualitative educational achievement of our public schools is commensurate with the money and effort that have been invested in them. In effect this is to ask whether school administrators have been as faithful to the ideal of democratic education as have the American people.

Admittedly it is a complicated task to measure the effectiveness of a school system. But on almost every count there is general dissatisfaction with the results of the twelve years of education currently provided by most of our public schools. And it is an exceedingly important fact that the criticisms come with greatest intensity from those who believe most strongly in the value and importance of education, and who, by their professions, are best qualified to judge what sound education consists in. Discontent with the training which the public schools provide is all but unanimous, I discover, among members of the liberal arts and professional faculties of our universities and colleges. It is almost equally widespread among doctors, engineers, clergymen, lawyers, and other professional men throughout the nation. Business men are dismayed at the deficiencies in reading, writing, arithmetic, and general knowledge displayed by the high school and college graduates they employ. Parents are alarmed at the educational handicaps under which their children are obliged to labor as they enter upon the serious business of life.

In every community, searching questions about present-day educational policy are being raised by intelligent, responsible, disinterested citizens. The criticism is not that of "reactionaries." Among my acquaintances and correspondents, the liberals in political and social matters are just as outspoken in their denunciation of current trends in the public schools as are the men and women whose views can be labelled conservative. Upon college and university faculties the criticism does not come primarily from classicists in the older "traditional" branches of learning; it comes with perhaps greatest intensity from professors in the sciences, in mathematics, and in the other disciplines directly connected with the problems of a modern technological world.

The defense of their stewardship that is offered by public school administrators and by their allies in university departments of education is so feeble as to amount to a confession of failure. They quote criticisms of earlier date to show that discontent in the past was as great as it is today.[3] The logic is that of Looking-Glass Land, where, the Red Queen explained to Alice, "it takes all the running you can do, to keep in the same place. If you want to get somewhere else, you must run at least twice as fast as that!" In every other area of American life progress is measured in terms of defects overcome. Only the professional educationists take pride in the fact that, though they run several times as hard, they can always be found by their critics in pretty much the same spot.

Some improvement, indeed, the professional educationists do claim, but the evidence they adduce is exceedingly slight and scattered, and it never gives weight to the vastly increased time, effort, and money which have gone into producing the results described. Typical of the evidence which school administrators offer is this: "Arithmetic tests given to ninth-grade pupils in Springfield, Massachusetts, in 1845, were administered to Minneapolis eighth-graders in 1926. The percent of correct answers in 1845 was 29.4 as compared to 67.1 in 1926." [4] If these figures could be accepted as a valid statistical sample, they would merely prove that when the elementary schools stick to their traditional tasks they do a job appreciably better than the ill-equipped and financially impoverished schools of a century ago, with their short school terms and their inadequately trained teachers. In weighing this evidence let us remember (as a previous paragraph has pointed out) that by the time a pupil has finished a given grade today, he will have spent twice as many days in school as a comparable student would have spent eighty years ago. He will have received a greater share of the personal attention of a better trained teacher. Nine times as much money will have been expended in his education, and he will have used buildings and equipment at least thirteen times as good. A comparison with 1845, could it be made, would show an even greater increase in resources. If the achievement of a present-day student is only a little greater than that of his predecessor, instead of several times as great, there has been an alarming decline in the efficiency of public school instruction.

To choose such a standard of comparison in the first place is evidence that professional educationists have all but forgotten the high aims and ideals of American public education. We did not set out to make a fourth-rate educational system into a third-

5

rate one. We have invested more money in education than any other nation because we want the best education for our children that money can buy. No serious critic of modern American education is asserting that the public schools enjoyed a golden age in the past. It is the shortcomings of the schools today that concern us. If we are to have improvement, we must learn to make comparisons, not with the wretchedly inadequate public schools of earlier generations, but with the very best schools, public or private, American or foreign, past or present, of which we can obtain any knowledge. The failure of virtually all professional educationists to make such comparisons is one of their gravest derelictions of duty. Their measuring-rod seems always to be what poor schools used to do, never what good schools have done, can do, and ought to do.

The present effectiveness of the schools, measured against the best that can possibly be achieved, is the only valid measure of our educational accomplishment. If some other nation designs a better military plane, our aeronautical engineers do not point smugly to the fact that our own aircraft are better than they were in 1920 or 1930 or 1940. They accept the challenge of equalling or bettering the best that any other nation can produce. We would take them grimly to task if they adopted any lesser aim, for we are realistic enough in these matters to know that a lesser aim would be no aim at all but an invitation to national disaster. If we take education seriously, we can no more afford to gamble our safety upon inferior intellectual training in our schools than upon inferior weapons in our armory.

If we propose to make American schools the world's finest, we cannot avoid studying, and perhaps borrowing from, the best educational systems of other places and times. We must demand that our schools be superior to the less adequately financed educational systems of other countries—superior in the intellectual discipline which they provide in languages, history, mathematics, and science. We must welcome comparisons between the graduates of our public schools and the graduates of the best private schools of the present and the past. If we cannot equal the achievement of these other schools, then we should know why. If it is lack of money, then the people should be realistically informed of the cost of giving all our children the truly best in education. If, as I suspect, it is a difference in method or aim, then we should adopt as a guide in these matters, not the methods and aims that present-day educationists have spun out of their own heads, but the methods and aims that have proved themselves in the practice of the best educational systems of the world.

We must, moreover, measure the achievement of our schools against an even more rigorous standard. Are they giving to the people and to the nation the values which were the promised result of universal public education? If the schools are doing their job, we should expect educators to point to a significant and indisputable achievement in raising the intellectual level of the nation—measured perhaps by larger per capita circulation of books and serious magazines, by definitely improved taste in movies and radio programs, by higher standards of political debate, by increased respect for freedom of speech and of thought, by a marked decline in such evidences of mental retardation as the incessant reading of comic books by adults. We should expect superintendents to report that because of improved methods of instruction, longer school years, and better trained teachers they have been able to teach successfully in the high school many of the fundamental disciplines to which students were formerly introduced only in college. We should expect school administrators to produce testimonials from employers, professional men, college professors, and officers of the armed services to the effect that young men and women are coming out of high school with sounder intellectual background and greater skill and competence than ever before.

No such claims are being advanced and no such comparisons are being made by the men and women to whom we have entrusted the control of our public schools. They do not ask that the American public schools be judged by such standards. They do not ask it, because, by and large, they no longer accept these as valid standards. There are many honorable exceptions, of course, but the most influential men in the field of elementary and secondary education have, for a generation, been redefining the purposes of the public schools in a fashion that amounts to a repudiation of these objectives. The charge which this book advances is that professional educationists, in their policy-making role, have lowered the aims of the American public schools. And because the sights have been lowered, no possible increase in pedagogical efficiency can ever enable our schools as currently administered to reach the target which the American people originally set up for them.

In the last analysis, it is not lack of effort but lack of direction that has resulted in the mediocre showing of our public high schools. Where educational aims have been well conceived, as in many fields of higher education and professional training, the money and the effort that Americans have poured into education have produced unmistakable progress. Seventy-five years ago American public schools were poor, but so too was American training for medicine, for law, and for research in the sciences and arts. All these fields have shared in the great American effort for educational improvement. But how different are the results! Would we be satisfied to hear the dean of a medical school assert merely that doctors today are just as well prepared as when they learned the theory of medicine in a few months of lectures and picked up the practice in the back office of an old-fashioned sawbones?

The difference is not a matter of money. It is a matter of adequate aims. In the sciences, in scholarship, in the learned professions, the men responsible for educational progress have been scholars and scientists in their own right. They have begun by accepting the traditional aims of their respective disciplines and professions, and they have defined their task as the carrying out of these recognized aims in a manner more effective than ever before. They have deliberately measured their achievement, not in terms of some slight improvement over the past, but in terms of the best that could possibly be done by any man, in any place, at any time. Until public school educationists can learn to think in this same way—until they acquire sufficient intellectual humility to accept the guidance of past experience and of the considered judgment of the modern learned world—no amount of financial support can possibly raise our schools above mediocrity. And mediocrity, given the possibilities which America offers to public education, is nothing else than downright failure.

Since I am critical of current practices in American education, I shall be automatically branded an enemy of the public schools by those who have a vested interest in the educational status quo. This charge has been used before by educational administrators to silence criticism, and it will be used again. It is a curiously perverse argument, which belongs to dictatorship, not to democracy. When the citizen of a free state criticizes the policies of a political party in office, he is not attacking government itself. When he denounces a bureaucrat as incompetent, he is not saying that the work of the bureau ought not to be done and done well. In point of fact, he is reaffirming his faith in an institution every time he insists upon holding its responsible managers to strict accountability. In the same manner, he is reaffirming his faith in public education whenever he insists that it *be* education and not something else. We are fools if we allow a politician to tell us that we cannot attack him without undermining government. We are no less fools if we permit professional educationists to tell us that we cannot criticize their policies without becoming enemies of the public schools.

To dispel any doubts about my position, however, let me offer at the outset a full and frank confession of faith. I am a firm believer in the principle of universal, public, democratic education. As a professor in a state university I am part of an institution dedicated to that very principle, and I am proud to be so. I believe that publicly financed education from the nursery school through the highest levels of graduate and professional instruction is essential to American democracy as we know and value it. I have no sympathy whatever with anyone who proposes to cut school appropriations in such a way as to limit educational opportunity or impair the quality of instruction. That is the road not to reform but to ruin. I believe in doing away with every barrier that race, religion, or economic status interposes to prevent any American from pursuing to the highest levels any form of study for which he has the intellectual capacity, the desire, and the will.

I believe that the United States is wealthy enough to afford the best education for its future citizens. I believe, moreover, that the American people are ready to pay the price, if only they are assured that what they are buying is genuinely good public education. One of the gravest charges that can be made against the professional educationists is that they have undermined public confidence in the schools by setting forth purposes for education so trivial as to forfeit the respect of thoughtful men, and by deliberately divorcing the schools from the disciplines of science and scholarship, which citizens trust and value. The treasure of public confidence that the educationists have frittered away can be garnered again, I am convinced, once the public schools set for themselves goals that are worthy of such confidence.

I believe, finally, in academic freedom. I conceive it to be the scholar's duty to resist every effort to stifle the free and responsible investigation and discussion of public issues. And I stand ready to oppose to the uttermost any group that seeks to limit or pervert the curricula of schools and colleges so as to impose upon them its own narrow and dogmatic preconceptions concerning matters that are properly the subject of free and objective inquiry.

These are not merely my personal convictions. They are, it seems to me, part and parcel of the ideal of liberal education which I am defending. It is because liberal education is synonymous with intellectual freedom that it needs to be constantly defended. And part of my criticism of professional educationists is that they, by misrepresenting and undervaluing liberal education, have contributed—unwittingly perhaps, but nevertheless effectually—to the growth of an anti-intellectualist hysteria that threatens not merely the schools but freedom itself.

I trust that my position is clear. I stand for an American public school system that shall be free and democratic. I stand also for an American public school system that shall be *educational*. There is an antique play on words that still seems to tickle the fancy of professional educationists. "We do not teach history," they say, "we teach children." The implication that those who teach history teach it to no one is a manifest impossibility, no classrooms being located in the empty desert. But it *is* a distinct possibility, alas, that educationists, following their own maxim, may succeed in teaching children—*nothing*.

The thesis of this book is that schools exist to teach *something*, and that this something is the power to think. To assert this, of course, is to assert the importance of good teaching. Professional educationists are fond of beclouding the issue by suggesting that those who believe in disciplined intellectual training deny the importance of good teaching. Nothing could be farther from the truth. It is sheer presumption on their part to pose as the only persons in the academic world with a concern for good teaching. Disciplined intellectual training depends on good teaching, and scholars and scientists in American universities have shown as much genuine concern with good teaching as professors of education, many of whom betray an amazing disregard of its principles in the conduct of their own classes.

The issue in American education today is not drawn between those who believe in scholarship but are indifferent to good teaching, and those who believe in good teaching but are indifferent to scholarship. The issue is drawn between those who believe that good teaching should be directed to sound intellectual ends, and those who are content to dethrone intellectual values and cultivate the techniques of teaching for their own sake, in an intellectual and cultural vacuum.

# 2

# The Ideal of Disciplined Intelligence

As a people we believe that education is vital to our national welfare and to the security of our democratic institutions. But to believe this is not enough. We must understand why and in what way education is vital. Otherwise we cannot distinguish between the kind of schooling that truly protects and advances the well-being of the country, and the kind that merely provides decorous amusements to while away the time of young men and women not yet ready to engage in the serious work of the world.

Education is vital to American democracy for reasons that can be clearly specified. In the first place, a republican system of government requires citizens who are highly literate, accurately informed, and rigorously trained in the processes of rational and critical thought. If the schools fail to raise up a nation of men and women equipped with these qualities of mind, then self-government is in danger of collapse through the sheer inability of its electorate to grapple intelligently with the complex problems in science, economics, politics, and international relations that constantly come up for public decision.

In addition to this, the American public schools—working in close harmony with the colleges, universities, and professional schools—have the responsibility of training scientists, physicians, scholars, engineers, and other professional men equal in competence to the best which any educational system is capable of producing. If the schools fail to do their part in this, the nation is threatened with the loss of intellectual strength and, as a direct consequence, the loss of industrial prosperity and military security.

Less tangible, but no less real and significant, are the cultural values of a nation, which must likewise be safeguarded through intellectual training in its schools. With a decline of respect for cultural and intellectual values in and for themselves comes a decline of faith on the part of a people in its own higher purposes. Degradation of the spirit proceeds step by step: the undermining of genuine loyalty, the destruction of freedom of thought and of speech, and finally the loss of that self-respect which, to a man or a nation, is the ultimate source of courage and hope and virtue and will.

The economic, political, and spiritual health of a democratic state depends upon how successfully its educational system keeps pace with the increasingly heavy intellectual demands of modern life. Our civilization requires of *every* man and woman a variety of complex skills which rest upon the ability to read, write, and calculate, and upon sound knowledge of science, history, economics, philosophy, and other fundamental disciplines. These forms of knowledge are not a mere preparation for more advanced study. They are invaluable in their own right. The student bound for college must have them, of course. But so must the high school student who does not intend to enter college. Indeed, his is the graver loss if the high school fails to give adequate training in these fundamental ways of thinking, for he can scarcely hope to acquire thereafter the intellectual skills of which he has been defrauded.

Throughout history these intellectual disciplines have rightly been considered fundamental in education for practical life and for citizenship, as well as in training for the professions. The modern world has made them more vital than ever. Every vocation has grown more complicated. The artisan of an earlier century might make his way in the world even though illiterate and all but unlearned in elementary arithmetic. Today even the simplest trades require much more. The responsibilities of the citizen, too, have grown more exacting year by year. Intelligent citizenship does not mean merely a simple faith in American democracy. It calls for a thorough knowledge of political principles and institutions, of history, and of economics. It demands a clear understanding of the various sciences, for the voter must help decide public policy on such intricate matters as the development and control of atomic energy. Above all, intelligent citizenship requires an ability to read, to understand, and to test the logic of arguments far more complicated than any hitherto addressed to the public at large.

The nation depends upon its schools and colleges to furnish this intellectual training to its citizenry as a whole. Society has no other institutions upon which it can rely in the matter. If schools and colleges do not emphasize rigorous intellectual training, there will be none. This is not true of the other services that educational agencies may incidentally render. It is well for the schools to pay attention to public health, for example, but if they are unable to do so, the health of the nation will not go uncared for. The medical profession and the existing welfare agencies remain unimpaired. But if the schools neglect their vital function of intellectual training, the loss to society is an irreparable one.

Intellectual training may seem a formidable phrase. But it means nothing more than deliberate cultivation of the ability to think. It implies no unnatural distinction between the mind and the emotions, for men can think about emotional and aesthetic problems, and can be taught to think more clearly about them. It implies no opposition between the intellectual and the moral realm, for ethics is applicable to the thinking process itself, and rationality is a constituent of every valid ethical system. Morality enters the classroom and the study as it enters all the chambers of life. It assumes special form as intellectual honesty and as that species of reflectiveness which converts a mere taboo into an ethical imperative.

Least of all is there a sharp contrast between the intellectual and the practical. Knowledge does, of course, become more abstract and reasoning more intricate as one proceeds farther into each of the fields of science and learning. But this does not mean that knowledge becomes less practical or less applicable to human affairs as it advances. Quite the contrary. It becomes more practical because it becomes more powerful. A formula is abstract not because it has lost touch with facts but because it compresses so many facts into small compass that only an abstract statement can sum them up. Simple forms of knowledge can accomplish simple tasks; complex forms of knowledge can accomplish complex tasks. One does not need higher mathematics to build a workable waterwheel or an oxcart, but one does need it to build a dynamo or a jet plane.

The modern scientist or the modern scholar knows the delight of intellectual endeavor for its own sake, and he rightly resents the undervaluing of this motive. But when all is said and done he knows that the principal value to society of a man's cultivating the power of abstract thought is that he is thereby enabled to deal more effectively with the insistent problems of modern life. If he prefers to work with differential equations instead of a screwdriver and a pair of pliers, it is not because he thinks the work of the hands ignoble, but because he thinks the work of the brain more powerful. The basic argument for the intellectual disciplines in education is not that they lift a man's spirit above the world, but that they equip his mind to enter the world and perform its tasks.

A school that sticks to its job of intellectual training is not thereby indifferent to the vocational needs of its students, to their physical development, or to the problem of moral conduct. Such a school merely recognizes that it must deal with these matters within the context provided by its own characteristic activity. By knowing its capabilities and its limitations, a school can make a more effective contribution to vocational training, to physical education, and to ethics than if it cherishes the delusion that it is a home, a church, a workshop, and doctor's office rolled into one.

An educational institution contributes in a specialized, not an all-inclusive, way to these areas of human life. Schooling is better than apprenticeship as preparation for a job, but only if it leads a man to grasp the theory behind the practice. Physical education makes sense in the school, but only if it is linked with a knowledge of physiology. Training in ethics is a responsibility of the school, but it must meet that responsibility, not by offering a course in "How to be good," but by seeing to it that morality permeates the regular activities of the school. Work in the classroom must be honestly done; rewards must be based upon performance; prestige must be attached to the activities that are serious and worthy, and trivia must be treated as trivia; athletics must be honorably conducted in accordance with the professed aim of producing physical fitness for all. A school administrator may talk about morality, but if he permits the intellectual ideal of the school to be debased, he contributes to the debasement of all ideals. And if he permits the physical education program of a school to degenerate into a subsidized gladiatorial contest between muscular mercenaries, he furnishes the community with a living example of fraud, and thus turns the school itself into an active teacher of *im*morality.

The school has a contribution to make to every activity of life. But it makes that contribution by doing its own particular job honestly and well. That job is to provide intellectual training in every field of activity where systematic thinking is an important component of success. As a *public* school, its responsibility is to offer such training to every young man or woman who has the capacity and the will to apply intellectual means to the solution of the problems that confront him. And as an agency of general influence in society, its duty is to encourage intellectual effort and respect for intellectual effort on the part of every citizen, whatever his background or occupation.

To say that the primary purpose of the school is intellectual training is not at all the same thing as saying that intellectual activity is the most important thing in human life. One can say that the primary function of the medical profession is to safeguard the health of the nation, without either affirming or denying that good health is the most important thing in human life. Men have a multitude of needs, and society provides specialized agencies and professions to deal with each. Individuals rate their needs differently, and therefore attach varying importance to different social agencies. But no one has a right to redefine the purposes of an institution or a profession simply because he thinks he has no present need for the services it was created to render.

The school exists to serve the needs of men. But, like the

hospital or the post office, it is not designed to provide all kinds of services indiscriminately. There are many needs of mankind which are exceedingly important in themselves, but which education has little to do with. On the other hand, many of the most vital needs of individuals and of society cannot be met at all except through the extensive and rigorous application of intellectual means. No agency but the school can possibly provide the comprehensive, systematic, disciplined, intellectual training required. The school was devised for the very purpose of doing this job effectively. The overriding responsibility of the school, the responsibility it cannot shirk without disaster and may not sacrifice to any other aim, however worthy, is its responsibility for providing intellectual training.

But in what does intellectual training consist?

No misconception is so prevalent and so deceptive as the notion that liberal education is merely the communicating of factual information. The widespread use of so-called objective examinations—"true-false" tests and the like—is an alarming symptom of the prevalence of this fallacy in educational circles. At a popular level, the quiz program on the radio is another symptom. Men who are anxious to undermine disciplined intellectual training deliberately foster this misconception of liberal education. According to a recent article by a professor of education, the scientists and scholars on university faculties

visualize the mind as a sort of cold storage warehouse, which is empty at birth. The process of learning consists in hanging on the walls of the warehouse chunks of fact and information. . . . The chunks hang there in the same condition in which they were first stored until some day the student needs one or more of them; then he can go into the warehouse, unhook the right chunk, and use it for some mature purpose which he could not have conceived in the immature condition of his mind when he first acquired the material. . . . The conception that new learnings become part of the learner through their digestion and assimilation into other previously acquired material is quite foreign to this idea of learning.[1]

This is an outsider's view of intellectual life. No one who knows at first hand what goes into the training of a mathematician or a biologist or an historian could ever imagine that the process follows any such absurd pattern as this. Nowhere in the writings

17

of responsible scientists or scholars is there a single sentence propounding a theory of learning so fantastic as this.

The difference between this caricature of liberal education and the true nature of its purposes and methods can be illustrated by a difference in terminology. The difference may seem trivial at first glance, but it is actually portentous. What I have hitherto called the fundamental "disciplines"—history, chemistry, mathematics, philosophy, and the like—have become, in the jargon of secondary school educationists, "subject-matter fields." But a discipline is by no means the same as a subject-matter field. The one is a way of thinking, the other a mere aggregation of facts.

The liberal disciplines are not chunks of frozen fact. They are not facts at all. They are the powerful tools and engines by which a man discovers and handles facts. Without the scientific and scholarly disciplines he is helpless in the presence of facts. With them he can command facts and make them serve his varied purposes. With them he can even transcend facts and deal as a rational man with the great questions of meaning and value.

The scholarly and scientific disciplines won their primacy in traditional programs of education because they represent the most effective methods which men have been able to devise, through millennia of sustained effort, for liberating and then organizing the powers of the human mind. It is nonsense to say that they occupy their position in intellectual life because some clique of men have agreed to confer an arbitrary prestige upon them. The reverse is true. It is the disciplines that have conferred prestige—and more than prestige, power—upon mankind.

Consider how the disciplines of science and learning came into being. The world enters the consciousness of the individual—and it first entered the consciousness of mankind—as a great tangle of confused perceptions. Before man could deal with it at all he had to differentiate one experience from another and to discover relationships among them: similarity and diversity, cause and effect, and the like. Gradually he discovered that one kind of relationship could best be investigated in one way (by controlled experiment, it may be), and another in another way (by the critical study of written records or of fossil remains, perhaps). Thus the separate disciplines were born, not out of arbitrary invention but out of evolving experience. The process of trial and error, prolonged over centuries, has resulted in the perfecting of these tools of investigation. The methods can be systematized and taught, hence the intellectual power that mankind has been accumulating throughout its entire history can be passed on to successive generations. Thereby each generation is enabled to master the new environment and to solve the new problems that confront it. This ability to face unprecedented situations by using the accumulated intellectual power of the race is mankind's most precious possession. And to transmit this power of disciplined thinking is the primary and inescapable responsibility of an educational system.

The disciplines represent the various ways which man has discovered for achieving intellectual mastery and hence practical power over the various problems that confront him. He lives in a world of quantity and relationship, and he has put four thousand years of ingenuity into creating the mathematical tools by which he handles quantity and relationship. He knows that the wisdom of mankind has been set down in a multitude of languages, and he has cultivated the linguistic disciplines so that he may unlock this storehouse, and so that he may add to it his own ideas, expressed with precision and vigor. He realizes that his present is influenced by his past, and he has therefore devised, through unremitting effort, the historical techniques which provide the maximum of reliable knowledge concerning this aspect of his environment. He works every day with matter, and he has subdued matter to his purposes by sorting out its various characteristics in his mind and eventually creating the sciences of physics and chemistry, which have grown more useful to him in proportion as they have grown more abstract and theoretical. There is nothing arbitrary or fortuitous in any of this. The older disciplines have emerged, and newer ones are emerging, as responses to man's imperious need for that wide-ranging yet accurate comprehension which means power—power over himself and over all things else.

It is this concentrated intellectual power for which the scholarly and scientific disciplines are respected. A man is educated in them that he may gain the powers which they confer. Note, however, one curious thing: to be given only the *results* of the exercise of this species of power is to be given nothing. A man may be given wealth or he may inherit social position, each the product of another's exertions, and thereafter he can exercise whatever power appertains to either. If, however, a man is given merely the answer to a complex mathematical calculation, or the narrative that results from a critical investigation of historical sources, he shares in no slightest way the power of the mathematician or the historian. Some poor inert formula, some poor inert fact, is all that is left in his hand.

Liberal education, in other words, is essentially the communication of intellectual power. That it cannot be communicated by someone who does not possess it—by a teacher who is not also a scholar—is self-evident. But neither can it be communicated by scholars and scientists if they pay too much attention in their classes to what they have learned and too little to how they have learned it. Courses may bear the respected labels of academic disciplines and yet be, in reality, no more than the subject-matter fields about which the educationists talk. In my own field of history, there are college textbooks and "survey" courses which would suggest to even an intelligent student that the discipline of history consists in the memorization of facts rather than in the weighing of evidence and the investigation of relationships. In the field of English literature many anthologies published for college use would seem to imply that a student's literary comprehension is measured by the number of different authors he can remember by name. One of my professors of mathematics used to complain that certain of his colleagues were content to turn their students into machines that would grind out answers according to formula with no more comprehension of the mathematical reasoning involved than a mechanical computer would have.

Academic courses which teach men to manipulate laboratory apparatus but not to think scientifically, to carry out intricate computations but not to think mathematically, to remember dates but not to think historically, to summarize philosophical arguments but not to think critically—these advance no man toward liberal education. To be perfectly honest, one must admit that higher education has lost repute because so many offerings in the liberal arts and sciences have failed to provide the intellectual discipline which they promise. But the answer, surely, is not to abandon the ideal of disciplined intelligence in favor of an educational program that even on the surface offers nothing to liberate and strengthen men's minds. The answer is not to banish the scholarly and scientific disciplines, but to hold them rigorously to their task.

Liberal education means deliberate cultivation of the power to think. Because clear thinking is systematic thinking, liberal education involves the logical organization of knowledge. Students must be brought to see the structure of the science they are learning. To know a few facts about lines and angles and triangles is not to know plane geometry; the essential thing is to grasp the orderly process by which a group of postulates can be made to reveal their implications in theorems of increasing complexity. To know a few episodes in the past is not to know history; the essential thing is to comprehend the forces that are at work through a long sequence of events, and to incorporate the perspective of time into one's day-to-day judgments. Instruction need not always follow a strictly logical or chronological order. But to leave a subject without having understood the order inherent in it, is to leave it without seizing hold of the most significant and the most useful of its characteristics.

Liberal education may well commence with an examination of familiar things. Perhaps in an ultimate psychological sense it cannot begin otherwise. The distinction between liberal education and its opposite is the spirit in which that examination is conducted. Is it directed toward increasingly higher generalization? Does it seek through rigorous comparison to gain perspective? Is it constantly concerned with developing those powers of mind whose potency lies in their very abstractness? If so, it is liberating and liberal. If not, not. A hundred and sixteen years ago Ralph Waldo Emerson stated the matter in his Harvard address on "The American Scholar":

What would we really know the meaning of? The meal in the firkin; the milk in the pan; the ballad in the street; the news of the boat; the glance of the eye; the form and the gait of the body; . . .

So much of the quotation is familiar. So much of it would seem

21

to argue for that involvement in the immediate and the petty which I am condemning. But Emerson did not stop here. The passage continued, without break in the sentence:

. . . show me the ultimate reason of these matters; show me the sublime presence of the highest spiritual cause lurking, as always it does lurk, in these suburbs and extremities of nature; let me see every trifle bristling with the polarity that ranges it instantly on an eternal law; and the shop, the plough, and the ledger referred to the like cause by which light undulates and poets sing;—and the world lies no longer a dull miscellany and lumber-room, but has form and order; there is no trifle, there is no puzzle, but one design unites and animates the farthest pinnacle and the lowest trench.[2]

Here is our clue. The study of what is near at hand and familiar—the study of contemporary problems, for example,—is an easy door. But it must be, not a door into a dull miscellany and lumber-room, but a door opening outward upon the universe of human endeavor and natural process.

Such a door opening outward upon freedom is what I conceive a liberal education to be. This is true to the etymology of the phrase: liberal education is the education worthy of a free man. More than that, it is the education by which a man achieves freedom. But what can achieving freedom possibly mean except liberation from some form or other of slavery? To make himself truly free, a man must break the intellectual chains that keep him a serf by binding him to his parish, by binding him to his narrow workaday tasks, by binding him to accept the authority of those placed over him in matters temporal and spiritual. A liberal education frees a man by enlarging and disciplining his powers. He is no longer bound to his parish, because education makes him spiritually a citizen of all places and all times. His workaday tasks no longer subdue his mind to their narrow demands, for he is large enough to cope with them and with the great intellectual tasks of a free man as well. He is no longer obliged to accept blindly the authority of those above him, for they are above him no longer. In the things of the mind he is their peer, and he can decide for himself, on as good grounds as they, the great human issues that confront him. Thereby he is entitled to be the citizen of a free state, participating in its highest decisions, and obeying no political mandates save those that derive their ultimate sanction from his own consent.

The test of every educational program is the extent to which it trains a man to think for himself and at the same time to think painstakingly. Originality and rigor, imagination and discipline—these are not pairs of mutually exclusive qualities. They are qualities that must be welded together in a liberal education. The aim is expressed most broadly and clearly in the requirement laid down for the highest university degree: that a student shall make an original contribution to knowledge. I am aware of the paltry substitutes that are frequently accepted: dissertations which show merely that the candidate has read his sources or his dials faithfully and has performed his critical or his statistical manipulations in approved fashion. The real questions are too rarely asked, I know, but they are at least implicit in the requirement.

Has the student developed in the process of doing research the penetrating mind that will make him more than an accredited technician? Does he see the world bristling with unsolved problems?—historical problems if he is an historian, biological problems if he is a biologist. Does he seize with a kind of instinct upon the ones that are crucial to the determination of even larger issues? Does his imagination range over all the possible, and even the impossible, avenues to a solution before he selects the most promising? Having chosen, does he possess the ingenuity to construct, as they are required, the little bridges and the narrow but necessary stairways that will enable him to cross successfully the unforeseen obstacles lying between him and his destination? And does he, finally, possess the toughness of intellectual fibre to carry through a hard task to a really definitive conclusion? If the answers are affirmative, then the student has done more than make a contribution to knowledge. He has given assurance that he can think and act with power and precision when completely new problems confront him. To him has been communicated not merely factual information and craftsmanship, but intellectual discipline.

This is not the ideal of graduate instruction alone. It is, or it should be, the ideal of liberal education at every level. It can direct the first steps in instruction, and it can guide a man's quest for knowledge to the end of his life. A man whose formal education has strengthened these qualities in him is equipped for life in the present and in the future as no merely vocational training could possibly equip him. His is a disciplined mind. And because his mind is disciplined, he himself is free.

# 3

## Is a Good Education Undemocratic?

The American public school system, like the nation itself, is dedicated to the proposition that all men are created equal. Public education is an effort to carry that principle upward into the most complex and exalted realms of human life, those of the mind and spirit.

"We are told," said William Ellery Channing in 1837, "that this or that man should have an extensive education; but, that another, who occupies a lower place in society, needs only a narrow one: that the governor of a state requires a thorough education, while the humble mechanic has need only to study his last and his leather. But why should not the latter, though pursuing an humble occupation, be permitted to open his eyes on the lights of knowledge? Has he not a soul of as great capacity as the former? Is he not sustaining the same relations as a parent, a citizen, a neighbor, and as a subject of God's moral government?"

Democracy, according to this argument, implies the right of every citizen to develop his intellectual powers to the fullest extent possible. It also assumes that intellectual ability is independent of the accidents of wealth and social position. "The poor man," Channing asserted, "as to his natural capacity, does not differ from others. He is equally susceptible of improvement, and would receive as great advantages as others from a well-bestowed education."

Society itself has a stake in education. American institutions, Channing continued, "are for the common mass of the people; and unless the people are educated, they both lose the benefit of these institutions and weaken their power. Liberty requires that every citizen, in order to its proper enjoyment, should have the means of elevation."

Nothing that Channing says suggests that the nature, the quality, or the purpose of education should be altered in the process of extending its privileges to the whole body of citizens. To alter, limit, or debase it, in fact, would be to defeat the very object of democratization. Popular education is designed to endow the people as a whole with precisely the kinds of intellectual power that have hitherto been monopolized by an aristocratic few. "In other countries," Channing pointed out, "the class in power have the principal means of knowledge, and, in order to keep the civil power in their hands, their object is to withhold from others the means of mental improvement. But, according to the genius of our government, education must bring all conditions and classes together," until "society, by its general culture, is raised to a higher state of refinement and happiness." [1]

This is the authentic ideal of American democratic education. It inspired the great educational reformers of the nineteenth century, who strove to create for the United States a "single educational ladder," which rich and poor might climb together. "A Public High School," said Henry Barnard in 1848, "is not . . . a public or common school in the sense of being cheap, inferior, ordinary. . . . It must make a good education common in the highest and best sense of the word common—common because it is good enough for the best, and cheap enough for the poorest family in the community." [2]

Today, however, many public school administrators and professors of education are repudiating the position taken by these founders of our public school system. A school which concen-

trates its effort upon intellectual training, they assert, is an aristocratic school. The views that I am expressing in this book are
accordingly said to have "a 'class' character." [3] This curious line
of argument can be summed up as follows: Because intellectual
training was once monopolized by an aristocracy, it retains its
aristocratic character even when extended to the masses of men.
To so extend it would be to undermine democracy.

Now it is perfectly true that in a stratified society the only
individuals who can hope to receive sound training in the sciences,
mathematics, history, and languages—the only ones who can cultivate a knowledge and appreciation of literature, philosophy, and
the arts—are those who belong to the aristocratic or wealthy
classes. It is equally true, let us remember, that the only persons
in such a society who can live in warm and comfortable houses,
who can eat and dress well, who can travel freely, and who can
enjoy leisure time are men of means or of aristocratic birth. Does
it follow from this that democratic housing ought to be drafty
and cramped, that a democratic diet should be meagre, that
democratic clothing should be shabby and mean, that in a democracy men ought not to have automobiles or time in which to
drive them?

In America we have attempted to furnish to every man and
woman the advantages and opportunities that were once enjoyed
only by an aristocracy. We have supposed that in doing so we
were *building* a democratic society, not *undermining* it. The test
we have accepted of our achievement in spreading democracy is
whether we have given to the many the things that none but the
few could once possess.

Why should intellectual values be the exception to this rule?
If a privileged class once monopolized for itself the kind of education we call liberal, we are not perpetuating aristocracy but
destroying it if we make the same education available to all the
people. The way to perpetuate aristocracy is to give sound intellectual training to a minority and to offer the people generally a
cheap and shoddy substitute. In a society where only the upper
classes can ride, a carriage or an automobile is a symbol of aristocracy. In a society where the masses of men can afford the
means of transportation, a crowded parking lot is a symbol of
democracy. Now a personal library of good books is a symbol also.

27

If only a few possess and can use one, we have a "class" society. When every family possesses and can use one, we have a democratic society.

Whether our intellectual life is in reality democratic or aristocratic depends on whether the masses of the people, or only a select minority, are reading mature books and handling complex ideas and revealing a profound comprehension of history and science and the arts. The school is not creating a democratic structure of intellectual life merely by gathering all the nation's children within its walls. It becomes an agency of true democratization only if it sends them forth with knowledge, cultural appreciation, and disciplined intellectual power—with the qualities, in other words, that have always distinguished educated men from uneducated ones.

To create a truly democratic cultural and intellectual life is a tremendously difficult task. It requires an organization of economic life so efficient that children can be released from toil and adults can enjoy abundant leisure. This we have at last achieved in the United States. It also requires heavy and continuing expenditures for school buildings, for teachers, and for a host of administrative and auxiliary services. The American people have shown their willingness to underwrite these costs. The preconditions necessary for a democratic school system have been met. But we shall never create a genuinely democratic intellectual and cultural life if, as victory comes almost within our grasp, we repudiate the very purposes we set out to achieve.

When present-day educationists assert that the ideal of rigorous intellectual training throughout the public schools is a false or unattainable ideal, they are taking (whether they realize it or not) precisely the position that was occupied a century ago by the *opponents* of public education. Let us re-examine briefly the traditional anti-democratic arguments against mass education.

Partisans of an aristocratic philosophy of education in the early nineteenth century insisted that literature, philosophy, history, mathematics, science, art, and foreign languages were of concern only to an élite class. Disciplined intellectual training should be reserved for the minority who planned to do advanced study and to enter the learned professions. Such training would be beyond the grasp of the ordinary man, and would be utterly

28

useless to him. The common man should receive only such an education as would fit him for a trade, furnish him with a rudimentary skill in reading, writing, and arithmetic, and give him some helpful guidance, moral, practical, and miscellaneous, in adjusting himself to the way of life he was destined to live. To offer to the masses of men an education which went beyond their immediate practical and personal needs would be futile and wasteful. The common man would see no purpose in it. He would not put the requisite effort into acquiring it. If compelled to master the great intellectual disciplines, he would not appreciate them. He could not use them. And the few who might try to do so would thereby unfit themselves for their practical callings and for a happy life in the station to which society might assign them.

One of the Fourth of July toasts offered in 1830 in Philadelphia contained this sentiment: "May the day soon come when in point of literary acquirements the poorest peasant shall stand on a level with his more wealthy neighbors." Commenting on these sentiments, a conservative newspaper said:

It is our strong inclination and our obvious interest that literary acquirements should be universal; but we should be guilty of imposture, if we professed to believe in the possibility of that consummation. . . . There will ever be distinctions of condition, of capacity, of knowledge and ignorance, in spite of all the fond conceits which may be indulged, or the wild projects which may be tried, to the contrary. The "peasant" must labor during those hours of the day, which his wealthy neighbor can give to the abstract culture of his mind; otherwise, the earth would not yield enough for the subsistence of all: the mechanic cannot abandon the operations of his trade, for general studies; if he should, most of the conveniences of life and objects of exchange would be wanting; languor, decay, poverty, discontent would soon be visible among all classes.

The common man, the paper went on to assert, is in fact indifferent to the values of liberal education for himself or his children. "We do know that it has been found extremely difficult to induce the poorer classes of Philadelphia to avail themselves, for their children, of our Common Schools; and that they neglect the benefit in a degree that would be deemed almost incredible."

Finally, the diffusion of educational opportunity would mean the degradation of education itself, according to the opponents of the public schools. "Universal Equal Education is impossible, . . . unless the standard of education be greatly lowered and narrowed," said the newspaper just quoted. It would "pull down what is above, but never much raise what is below." [4] Alexis de Tocqueville in 1840 reported the same view as prevalent among educated men abroad. "It must be acknowledged," he wrote, "that in few of the civilized nations of our time have the higher sciences made less progress than in the United States. . . . Many Europeans, struck by this fact, have looked upon it as a natural and inevitable result of equality; and they have thought that if a democratic state of society and democratic institutions were ever to prevail over the whole earth, the human mind would gradually find its beacon lights grow dim, and men would relapse into a period of darkness." [5] Tocqueville, one should note, did not accept this conclusion, he merely reported it. But it was a view widely held, and the proponents of democratic education in the nineteenth century knew that they had to disprove it.

The great American educational reformers committed themselves, in both argument and action, to the view that genuine education, in the sense of intellectual training, was both appropriate and valuable for the common man. They were not inventing something new to which they applied the old and honored name of education. They understood by education what had always been understood by education. They believed in it, and they were anxious that its unquestioned powers should be the possession of every citizen. These democratic writers differed from their aristocratic opponents not because they defined education differently, but because they proposed, quite simply, to make this kind of education available to the many instead of confining it to the few.

Horace Mann summed the matter up in his last annual report as Secretary of the Massachusetts Board of Education:

According to the European theory, men are divided into classes,—some to toil and earn, others to seize and enjoy. According to the Massachusetts theory, all are to have an equal chance for earning, and equal security in the enjoyment of what they earn. . . . [But] If one class possesses all the wealth and the education, while the residue of society is ignorant and poor, it matters not by what name the relation between them may be called; the latter, in fact and in truth, will be the servile dependants and subjects of the former. But if education be equably diffused, it will draw property after it, by the strongest of all attractions; for such a thing never did happen, and never can happen, as that an intelligent and practical body of men should be permanently poor. . . .

Education, then, beyond all other devices of human origin, is the great equalizer of the conditions of men—the balance-wheel of the social machinery. . . . The spread of education, by enlarging the cultivated class or caste, will open a wider area over which the social feelings will expand; and, if this education should be universal and complete, it would do more than all things else to obliterate factitious distinctions in society.[6]

Democratic education was to enlarge "the cultivated class" until it embraced the whole people. It was not to replace the ideal of intellectual cultivation by something else, on the specious ground that intellectual cultivation belongs only to an aristocracy.

Likewise absent from the thought of the great educational reformers was the heresy that intellectual training is valuable only for entrance into the learned professions, as they are called. Said Horace Mann in another passage of the same report:

For the creation of wealth, then,—for the existence of a wealthy people and a wealthy nation,—intelligence is the grand condition. The number of improvers will increase, as the intellectual constituency, if I may so call it, increases. In former times, and in most parts of the world even at the present day, not one man in a million has ever had such a development of mind, as made it possible for him to become a contributor to art or science. Let this development precede, and contributions, numberless, and of inestimable value, will be sure to follow. . . . And the greater the proportion of minds in any community, which are educated, and the more thorough and complete the education which is given them, the more rapidly, through these sublime stages of progress, will that community advance in all the means of enjoyment and elevation; and the more will it outstrip and outshine its less educated neighbors.[7]

In the third place, the founders of our school system realized that self-government requires of its citizens wide knowledge and accurate thinking, which only serious intellectual training can provide. Mann continued:

That the affairs of a great nation or state are exceedingly complicated and momentous, no one will dispute. Nor will it be questioned that the degree of intelligence that superintends, should be proportioned to the magnitude of the interests superintended.·. . . Now, as a republican government represents almost all interests, whether social, civil, or military, the necessity of a degree of intelligence adequate to the due administration of them all, is so self-evident, that a bare statement is the best argument. . . . And hence it is, that the establishment of a republican government, without well-appointed and efficient means for the universal education of the people, is the most rash and foolhardy experiment ever tried by man.[8]

These three quotations are more than a statement of democratic philosophy. They constitute also a definition of education, as understood by the men responsible for bringing our public school system into effective existence. Let us note carefully the words and phrases which are used as synonyms of education and which give specific meaning to that concept. Education is concerned with "intelligence," with the "development of mind." It aims to increase "the intellectual constituency," to make every man "a contributor to art or science." In all his efforts for American public education, Horace Mann revealed his fundamental belief in "the inherent superiority of any association or community, whether small or great, where *mind* is a member of the partnership." In every realm of human activity, he asserted, "improvement has advanced in proportion to the number and culture of the minds excited to activity and applied to the work. . . . Succeeding generations have outstripped their predecessors, just in proportion to the superiority of their mental cultivation." [9]

The ideal of Horace Mann, I believe, is as valid today as it was when he set it forth in his great series of reports in the 1830's and 1840's. The need for the kind of education he described is even greater in the complex twentieth-century world than in the relatively simple and relatively peaceful era in which he wrote. The wealth of the nation and the physical facilities of the American school system are far more adequate to the work than there was any hope of their becoming during his lifetime. If we devote ourselves wholeheartedly to the task, I see no reason why the American educational system cannot raise the intellectual and cultural level of the entire nation to as great a height as any people have been able to reach. To do so we must recapture the belief both in democracy and in education that animated the founders of our public schools.

We must remember, at all times, that education is concerned with *improvement*. It undertakes to change a man or a woman from what he or she *is* to what he or she might be and ought to be. Educational policy in a democracy is directed toward *raising* the intellectual standards of the people, just as economic policy is directed toward raising their standard of living. Poverty and ignorance were the lot of the common man in the past. The elimination, not the perpetuation, of poverty and ignorance is the mission of democracy.

To say this is not to cast a slur upon democracy. If the common man has been ignorant in the past, it is because he has never been offered an opportunity to learn. If he has been indifferent to intellectual effort, it is because he has never been shown its value. These shortcomings have not been his fault, but they are nonetheless shortcomings. They are not attitudes and qualities to be accepted and respected. They are characteristics which an educational system is designed to destroy.

Educators may not take popular indifference to intellectual training as a mandate to guide them in the discharge of their public duties. Their mandate is the opposite. They are professionally obligated to oppose anti-intellectualism, no matter how powerful a majority it may command. Democracy does not require of its servants the abdication of professional responsibility. Every professional man has the duty—the democratic duty—of seeking to guide public opinion not of succumbing to it. A public health officer may not pronounce polluted water safe when he discovers that his community is unwilling to pay for a proper filtration plant. His duty is to take a bacterial count, not a public-opinion poll, and to explain clearly what it signifies, whether the community likes the conclusion or not. So it is with the educator. If the community prefers trivia to sound learning in its schools, the educator cannot compel it to choose otherwise. But he has the solemn duty of pointing out with absolute clarity that training in trivia is not education and cannot produce the results that the community expects to derive from its educational investment.

Democratic education differs from aristocratic education in

terms of the persons it deals with, not in terms of the values it seeks to impart. One of the most dangerous fallacies propagated today by certain groups of professional educationists is the assertion that intellectual training, while "functional" in an aristocratic society, is not "functional" for the citizen of a democratic state. This argument overlooks the fundamental fact that when a government of the few is transformed into a government of the many, the functions of an aristocracy become the functions of citizens at large. What the few once needed, the many now need. The constituency of the school changes, but not its basic purposes. The men who govern a nation must be informed and intelligent, whether the governors be the few or the many. Science is a source of power, whatever be the organization of the state. Literature, philosophy, and the arts are measures of the greatness of a civilization, be it aristocratic or democratic. The question in any society is how to produce these universally valued qualities of mind in the group of young people—whether they comprise a small number or a large—which it chooses to educate. Intellectual training itself is "functional" to any civilized and organized society, not just to an aristocratic one.

A variant of this fallacy asserts that intellectual training is "functional" in the life of an individual member of an aristocracy but not in the life of an individual citizen in a democracy. This involves a most curious assumption about the life of an aristocrat. Are we to suppose that a country gentleman needs to know Greek in order to collect his rents? Does a nobleman owe his social position to his learning rather than his birth? Does a young man, because he is well born, rush to grammar and mathematics as a lover to the arms of his mistress? Is the life of an aristocratic society so austere that it offers no dissipations that might distract a wealthy young blade from his books?

If we think about the matter, how absurd this argument turns out to be! Intellectual and cultural pursuits are of no more "practical" value to a nobleman than to a commoner. *Every* member of the race has the same great *humane* reason for wishing to cultivate his highest powers. And if "practical" reasons are needed, it is actually the democratic society, rather than the aristocratic one, which furnishes them. Recollect that it is not the aristocrat, but the man without inherited advantages whose social position and income depend upon his education. The latter has the truer need for intellectual training and potentially the stronger motive for intellectual exertion.

If certain aristocratic societies have been distinguished for literature, art, and philosophy, it is because those societies have deliberately cultivated a regard for such values, in and for themselves. It is a mistake to assume that the intellectual and cultural tradition of an aristocracy was created without effort. Education is a serious business in any society, and it requires serious and sustained effort on the part of any man, whatever his birth. The ruling classes of the past began as quasi-barbaric military chieftains. They were slowly and painfully disciplined, through centuries of time, before they acquired that respect for cultural and intellectual values which we sometimes assume was inborn in them. They perpetuated that tradition by rigorous self-discipline, and by steadily directed effort in the education of each new generation. Any society can do this. And the ruling classes of the present—the people as a whole—must adopt similar means if they are to preserve their own civilization against decay and destruction.

I am not seeking to minimize the difficulty of giving to the children of all the people the intellectual and cultural background that belonged in the past only to those brought up in surroundings of opulence, leisure, and privilege. I am merely asserting that to do this was precisely the task which a democratic educational system assumed. And I am insisting that the school must devote its resources wholeheartedly to this end, for to do otherwise would be to betray the very ideal which created it.

We must, in particular, guard against the danger of confusing lack of cultural background with lack of intellectual ability. These are distinctly different matters. Much is made of the fact that the students in an aristocratic school system were a selected group, while those in the American public schools of today are not. But much of the force of this argument vanishes once one recognizes the fact that the aristocratic few were selected for reasons totally unconnected with intellectual capacity. Inherited wealth and social position are no guarantees of mental ability. The schoolmaster in an aristocratic society has the problem of individual differences thrust upon him just as truly as the teacher of a country school.

There is no reason whatever for assuming that the schools of today have a smaller proportion of students of high innate ability merely because they are drawing more students from families low on the income scale. To assert that intellectual capacity decreases as one reaches down into lower economic levels of the population is to deny, point-blank, the basic assumptions of democratic equalitarianism.

Within any given class of the population, there are *individual* differences. But as democratic educators we have no right and no reason to assume that there are *class* differences in intellectual ability as well. The student from a wealthy home does differ from the student whose family lives on the edge of poverty. But this is not a matter of innate intellectual ability; it is a difference of background, pure and simple. One child will probably have read many books, the other few or none. One will have caught glimpses of the larger world of thought and art—through discussion, through travel, through intelligent parental guidance. The other may have been deprived of all these advantages. Environment, not inherited capacity, is responsible for the difference. And the effects of environment are effects we can do something to cure— in the long run by altering the environment, in the short run by remedying the deficiencies which the environment has produced.

What is the duty of the school in this situation? The answer ought to be clear. It must make up, so far as it is able, the deficiencies of background which it finds in its students. Both in the short run and in the long, the democratic school must concentrate, as never before, upon the task of intellectual training. Intellectual effort must be made the central, inspiring ideal of the school's life. The intellectual seriousness missing in the home must be deliberately cultivated in the schoolroom. The important books must be read there. Fundamental problems must be *studied*, not merely talked about. The basic scientific and scholarly disciplines must be presented, not as mere repositories of information, but as systematic ways of thinking, each with an organized structure and methodology of its own. The student who has been deprived of intellectual and cultural background at home must receive full restitution in the school.

The public schools of today possess many resources that can be effectively devoted to this end. They make use of buildings, equipment, books, and teaching aids far more costly, varied, and efficient than those available to the wealthiest schools of the aristocratic past. They bring the average child under academic discipline for a longer span of time than that usually devoted to formal education by the privileged youths of former ages. Knowledge of the psychology of learning has greatly increased. If properly and intelligently applied in teaching, it is capable of arousing an interest in intellectual and cultural matters among persons who were beyond the reach of the cruder pedagogy of earlier days.

What seems to be lacking is a faith in the value of intellectual endeavor among those who are making American educational policy. Restore that faith, and I believe that American schools can provide the overwhelming majority of our children with the kind of disciplined education which this book describes. To those of lower mental ability, special treatment must be accorded. Most of them, I believe, can be brought at a slower pace along the same route. As before, what is necessary is faith in the value and importance of the end in view, even if incompletely attained. For those completely beyond intellectual salvation, I grant that the school must offer something completely different. But the question of what that training should be is, in my judgment, a matter to be deferred until such time as the public schools shall have made a far more determined effort than any they are currently making to guide and direct the masses of American children along the path of genuine liberal education. I suspect that fewer will fall by the wayside than most educationists assume.

To accomplish these high ends, the school must transmit to the public at large, not merely to its own students, a respect for knowledge and cultural achievement. If we are to have an intellectual life that is both democratic and worthy of democracy, the school must uphold for all men the ideal of disciplined intellectual effort. In a manifesto published some years ago, an eminent American educator asked the question "Dare the school build a new social order?" [10] I would answer in the affirmative, but in a somewhat different sense from the author. The American public school was created to build a new social order, a social order in which intellectual training would be offered without discrimination to every citizen, in which respect for the highest cultural values would be universal, in which every man would be expected to bring trained intelligence to bear on personal and public problems, and in which scientific and scholarly effort would be so valued that assaults upon intellectual freedom would be impossible. Only the school can build this kind of social order. This is its great task in a democracy.

The American people, to their eternal credit, accepted this ideal, which the founders of our public school system held up to them. As a people they labored to carry the implications of the democratic philosophy from politics into ever wider areas of national life. In their ideal of equal opportunity, the life of the mind was included. Americans valued democracy too highly to believe for a moment that a democratic society had to be inferior in any respect to societies otherwise constituted. To them democracy was not a sacrifice but an enlargement of values. Equality of opportunity did not mean its diminution. The *opponents* of the American experiment were the ones who said that men would have to choose between democracy and literary cultivation, between democracy and scientific eminence, between democracy and intelligently conducted government. To the American people, however, democracy was perfectly compatible with the highest scientific, scholarly, and artistic achievement.

When Americans, a century or so ago, committed themselves to the ideal of universal democratic education, they were not thinking in terms of the trivia that fascinate many present-day educationists. They did not intend, by making education universal, to debase and destroy it. They were not seeking to water down the great tradition of disciplined and liberal study. They were undertaking the heroic task of raising an entire nation to the highest attainable level of intellectual competence.

Liberal education, they believed, was not and should not be the exclusive prerogative of the aristocratic few. Even the humblest man, whatever his trade, was capable of a liberal education. In a democracy he was entitled to it. His intellectual horizon should not be limited, as it had been for the lower classes in times gone by, to his occupation and to the routine details of his everyday life. He should receive training for his occupation, true. But far more important than that, he should be given the opportunity to develop his mind to the fullest extent possible. He should be given command of the intellectual resources that had once been the badge—and one of the principal bulwarks—of aristocracy. His mind furnished with the knowledge and disciplined to the strength that had made the old ruling classes great and powerful, the American freeman would be in a position to rule himself. And the civilization he built would be a humane and magnificent civilization because it would offer to every man not only equality before the law, not only the right to vote and to work, but, most precious of all, the opportunity to develop through liberal education his own highest qualities of manhood.

Let us never be satisfied with less.

# 4

## Progressive Education and Regressive Education

What kind of training should the schools offer if they are to endow future citizens with the disciplined intellectual powers that we have been discussing? This question is at once the most important and the most difficult that can be asked in the realm of educational theory. It is far wider in scope and far more profound that the question, What methods of instruction should be used? Persons who are trained to deal with the latter question, the question of pedagogy, do not necessarily possess any particular qualifications for dealing with the former, the question of the curriculum. No single group of specialists, in fact, can claim special competence in the matter. The idea that there can be a "curriculum expert" is as absurd as the idea that there can be an expert on the meaning of life.

To devise a balanced and adequate curriculum for any system of schools is pre-eminently a work in which the wisdom of many men must be enlisted. It presupposes a clear recognition of the role which each of the various intellectual skills must play in preserving the intellectual, the civic, and the practical life of the nation. It calls for an insight into the ways of thinking in more fields than a single individual can hope to encompass. It is, in short, a task which belongs to the learned world as a whole, not to any particular segment of it.

Now pedagogy is a segment, and only a small segment, of education. Experts in pedagogy have no qualifications that entitle their views on the public school curriculum to greater consideration than the views of any other group of specialists. Let me not be misunderstood. I am not criticizing in any way the efforts that educationists have made to determine the most effective methods of giving instruction in the recognized fields of knowledge. Important work has been done, and it must continue to be done, in investigating the psychology of learning, in developing effective textbooks and teaching aids, in experimenting with classroom procedures, in adapting instruction to students of differing intellectual capacity. As a teacher of history, I am directly interested in every improvement that increases the effectiveness with which history is being taught—provided that what is taught is still history. This is a most important proviso, as the sequel will make clear.

Pedagogy itself—that is to say, the careful investigation of the processes of teaching and learning—is a legitimate field of study. But its exact nature and its limitations need to be fully understood. Like the various branches of engineering, pedagogy is an applied science. It answers practical questions, not ultimate and philosophical ones. It tells *how* something can be taught most effectively, but it provides no basis whatever for deciding *what* should be taught. In this it is like civil engineering, which tells how a dam can be constructed across a given river, but not whether it ought to be built. A specialist in pedagogy is entitled to respect when he talks about the most effective methods of teaching a given subject in the elementary or secondary school. The question of *what* subjects should be taught is a totally different one. It cannot be answered on the basis of pedagogical considerations alone, for it involves the ultimate purposes of education.

In point of fact, however, the content of public school instruction is today being decided almost exclusively by specialists in pedagogy. And the process has been facilitated by a misuse and misapplication of the word *education*. In modern American universities there are numerous experts in pedagogy. They make use of the title Professor of Education, and theirs is denominated a College or School or Department of Education. This terminology is misleading. The college or university as whole is devoted to education, and every department in it is a department of education in the legitimate sense of that word. My own department is actually a department of education in historical thinking. The term Department of History is merely a convenient abbreviation. The division that calls itself a Department of Education is in reality a department of education in pedagogical methods, that is, a Department of Pedagogy. It has no right to imply, by its name, that it has a greater concern with education than any other department.

This is not a mere matter of words. Faulty language leads to faulty thinking and to faulty action. This is precisely what has happened in the field of education. Professors of pedagogy, considering themselves the only authentic professors of education, contemptuously dismiss as impertinent and incompetent the educational views of their colleagues in all other departments.[1] Taking advantage of the unfortunate laxness of academic terminology, professors of education represent themselves to the general public as the only members of university faculties who need to be consulted with respect to the ultimate aims and purposes of education. Misrepresentation is often carried a step farther. Because a professor of education belongs to a university faculty, he is commonly supposed to be presenting the accepted opinions of the university and the academic community as a whole. The professor of education is tempted to conceal from those who consult him the fact that the program he offers has never even been discussed with university scholars in the field it purports to cover. He may even allow his hearers to assume that since his proposal deals with high school history or high school mathematics he himself is an historian or a mathematician. School surveys are subject to the same abuse. The arrangements for such a survey are nominally made with the university, but actually with its department or college of education. The average citizen doubtless imagines that the final recommendations embody the

considered views of the learned world as a whole. In all probability, however, none but professional educationists have participated, and no independent scholar or scientist in any of the
disciplines represented in the school curriculum has been so much
as consulted.

Local school boards are not to blame. They have acted wisely
in allowing room for change and experiment in the school curriculum. The difficulty has been that they have rarely had access
to independent responsible advice such as would enable them
to judge of the wisdom and soundness of particular changes proposed. The school superintendent can see to it that no professional
advice save that of the educationists is brought to the attention
of the board. If a new program in the social studies is under discussion, for example, the favorable opinion of a professor of education is supposed to be accepted as the last word on the subject.
A school board is rarely if ever encouraged to seek the views of
professional historians or professional economists concerning the
scholarly soundness of a proposed program.

By accepting the unfounded pretensions of so-called professors
of education, we have permitted the content of public school
instruction to be determined by a narrow group of specialists in
pedagogy, well-intentioned men and women, no doubt, but
utterly devoid of the qualifications necessary for the task they
have undertaken. These pedagogical experts are making decisions
that involve considerations far outside the realm of pedagogy.
They are deciding not merely *how* subjects should be taught in
the public schools, but also *what* subjects should be taught. Under
the guise of improving the *methods* of instruction, they have
undertaken to determine its *content* as well. They are usurping
a function that belongs to the learned world as a whole. It is the
entire body of scholars, scientists, and professional men, not one
particular group among them, who possess collectively the expert
knowledge that should be applied to curriculum-making. They
are the men and women who know the kinds of intellectual skills
that are vitally necessary to maintain the life of the nation in
flourishing condition, for they are the ones who are actively engaged in advancing knowledge and in applying it to the practical
problems of the present-day world. They are the ones who ought

to be advising the people concerning the content of the public school curriculum, in order that the people's decisions may be wise ones.

As a result of the intrusion of the pedagogues into curriculum-making, the schools are being more and more completely divorced from the basic disciplines of science and learning. Intellectual training, once the unquestioned focus of every educational effort, has been pushed out to the periphery of the public school program. Into the vacuum have rushed the "experts" from state departments and colleges of education: the curriculum doctors, the integrators, the life-adjusters—the specialists in know-how rather than knowledge. Out of their overflowing minds they offer to furnish ready-made a philosophy to guide the entire educational system. All that scientists and scholars need do is supply little facts to fill up the blanks in the great schemata which the educationists devise. The curriculum engineers will do the rest. They will be happy to draw the really vital generalizations from the data which grubbers in laboratories and libraries so obligingly but so uninspiredly amass. They will point out to the teachers (unimaginative dullards, as they see them) the relationships that exist among the great fields of knowledge. That a discipline may have order, logic, and proportion within itself is a fact that seems to have escaped their notice. Is it any wonder that the curricula of many American public schools today are so trivial, so unbalanced, so out of harmony with the thinking of trained scientists and scholars that they constitute a mere parody of education?

In the discussion thus far I have not used the term "progressive education." I have deliberately refrained from doing so, because the phrase is vague and ambiguous. It is applied to a multitude of different programs, with many of which I am in hearty sympathy. On the other hand, many tendencies in contemporary American education that are labelled progressive can be more accurately described, I believe, as "regressive education."

So long as students of pedagogy recognized the inherent limitations of what they were doing, they made important contributions to the improvement of public education. Through careful study of child psychology and through controlled experimentation in the classroom, they pointed the way to notable advances in the technique of imparting such elementary skills as reading

44

and arithmetic; they increased the effectiveness with which such high school subjects as history, chemistry, algebra, and foreign languages were taught; and they succeeded in so increasing the efficiency of instruction that students were prepared to undertake in the high school certain studies usually considered as belonging to the college program. In the early part of the present century these improved methods of instruction went by the name of progressive education. For that type of progressive education I have sincere respect. If professional educationists had concentrated their efforts upon putting these improvements into effect throughout the schools, instead of turning aside from their proper work to tamper with the curriculum itself, then educational progress over the past half century would have been an unquestionable fact.

Educational progress *was* a fact so long as progressive education meant the things I have just described. I consider myself fortunate to have received my high school training, from 1922 to 1926, in one of the most progressive schools in the country, the Lincoln School of Teachers College, Columbia University. In those years, and in that school, progressive education seems to me to have been definitely on the right track. With uninfluential exceptions the faculty of that school did not think of defining the aims of secondary education apart from the aims of liberal education generally. They believed thoroughly in the intellectual purposes that had always been central in education as a whole. They knew that the work of the secondary school must intermesh with the advanced work carried on by scientists and scholars. Adequate preparation for college was not a separate goal; it was the natural consequence of a sound secondary school program based on the great intellectual disciplines. Mathematical instruction in the Lincoln School culminated in a senior course in the calculus, a branch of mathematics ordinarily commenced only in college. A full year was devoted to each of the sciences of chemistry, physics, and biology. The classical languages, it is true, were sacrificed to modernity—a serious mistake, I believe—but the promise that they would be replaced by sound training in the living foreign languages was honestly fulfilled. Work in English included the study of contemporary authors, but with no slighting of the great literature of the past. Composition meant a study

45

of grammar and syntax, and in addition the practice of original writing of the sort published in Mr. Hughes Mearns's admirable *Creative Youth.*[2]

What progressive educationists undertook to do, in those fruitful years, was to bring the teaching of the basic disciplines to the highest perfection possible in the light of modern pedagogy. They did so by emphasizing the relevance of knowledge and intellectual skill to the problems of practical life and citizenship. They experimented with more effective methods of instruction, and they never forgot that the good faith of an experimenter is measured by his frankness in conceding failure. Above all, they sought the ablest teachers, not the ones most fanatically devoted to newness for its own sake. The success of the Lincoln School in attracting brilliant men and women to its faculty was remarkable. To several of my teachers there I owe as much as to any of my instructors in college and graduate school, and I am proud to say that I am in correspondence with at least two of them more than a quarter of a century later.

Yet the shadow of the future began to fall upon the Lincoln School even in the middle twenties. Alongside excellent instruction in history, a course in the "social studies" was introduced. Subsequent work of my own in several of the fields supposedly embraced within this course has merely confirmed the opinion which my classmates and I entertained at the time. I remember being struck at the outset by the inferiority of this hodgepodge to the straightforward treatment of great public issues that I had learned to expect from my instructors in history. The "social studies" purported to throw light on contemporary problems, but the course signally failed, for it offered no perspective on the issues it raised, no basis for careful analysis, no encouragement to ordered thinking. There was plenty of discussion, but it was hardly responsible discussion. Quick and superficial opinions, not balanced and critical judgment, were at a premium. Freedom to think was elbowed aside by freedom not to think, and undisguised indoctrination loomed ahead. I am surprised at how accurately we as students appraised the course. I cannot now improve on the nickname we gave it at the time: "social stew."

The course in the social studies, and the more destructive programs that ensued, marked a turning point in progressive education. The label remained the same, but the thing itself became appallingly different. Progressive education ceased to be an effort to accomplish more effectively the purposes which citizens, scholars, and scientists had agreed were fundamental. Progressive education began to imply the substitution of new purposes. Experts in pedagogy were feeling their oats, were abandoning their proper task of improving instruction, and were brazenly undertaking to redefine the aims of education itself. By disregarding or flatly rejecting the considered educational views of the scholarly, scientific, and professional world, these new educationists succeeded in converting the division between secondary and higher education from a mere organizational fact into a momentous intellectual schism. Progressive education became regressive education, because, instead of advancing, it began to undermine the great traditions of liberal education and to substitute for them lesser aims, confused aims, or no aims at all.

Regressive education is the direct consequence of the fact that public school educationists have severed all real connection with the great world of science and learning. The only test of a public school program today is whether it is good in the eyes of an expert in pedagogy; whether it is sound in the eyes of a scholar in the field is a question that is no longer asked. Regressive education, in fact, is simply the mind of the typical professor of pedagogy writ large. That mind has its virtues, and those virtues appeared in the genuine progressive education of a generation ago, for enlightened pedagogy was then applied to the realization of aims in which all educated men concurred. But the pedagogic mind has its grave limitations also, and these have come to the fore in proportion as scholarly and scientific influence over educational policy has weakened. Most men's intellectual defects, of course, are counterparts of their virtues. A good quality is corrupted into a vice by being carried to excess. This is largely true of the situation I am describing. The interests and preoccupations of the pedagogical expert, praiseworthy when controlled and directed, have received so abnormal an emphasis in contemporary school programs as to be destructive of the very purposes of the school.

To be specific, the unremitting attention that specialists in pedagogy pay to the problem of arousing and holding the interest of pupils is indubitably an excellent thing. When harnessed to the traditonal program of intellectual training in the schools, it contributed greatly to the advancement of education. This combination produced what I would call genuine progressive education. But when this preoccupation with the learning process grew so intense that educationists lost sight of ultimate educational purposes, it produced the monstrosity of regressive education. Let me examine, in the remainder of this chapter, the shortcomings of a system in which pedagogy has become an end in itself, instead of a means of inculcating sound and systematic learning.

Effective teaching presupposes a vivid and deeply felt interest on the part of the student. Learning involves effort, and genuine incentives are necessary if anyone is to engage in sustained and productive labor. External pressures—rewards and penalties, competitive rivalry, and the like—provide incentives of a sort, and these ought not to fall into disuse to the extent that they have in American public schools. Nevertheless, it is perfectly true that external motivations of this kind will not carry a man along very far in the development of his highest intellectual powers. If he is to use his mind effectively throughout his life, the incentives must come from within himself. The school must develop these incentives. To do so, it must find the most vivid and effective ways of attracting the student's attention at the outset, and it must keep constantly before him, throughout the process of teaching, the relevance of what he is learning to the problems and interests that he himself considers significant.

The arousing and sustaining of interest, however, is only a means to an end. It is easy enough to keep children amused, if that is all one wishes. But a school is no mere entertainment hall; it arouses interest for a purpose. The test of a school, after all, is how much the students learn. Granted that they will learn little unless they are interested and hence happy; nevertheless the fact that they are interested and happy is no proof in itself that they are learning. Hence a preoccupation with arousing interest may—indeed frequently does—lead to the introduction into the schoolroom of projects totally without educational value. The fallacy that extra-curricular activities are as important as the curriculum itself is frequently asserted by regressive educators. And programs of the utmost triviality are defended time after time on the meretricious ground that they interest the student. Motivation is important, but it may be likened to a fuse. It burns to no purpose unless at last it touches off something more powerful than itself. If its far end is embedded in nothing, it will sputter and glow through its entire length, and then die out, leaving only a trail of ashes behind. The teacher must lay the fuse, but his larger task is to arrange the charge at the end and see to it that the explosion takes place.

There is another and even more significant fact about motivation. The methods of arousing and sustaining interest differ markedly according to the age of the student and according to the level of learning he has reached. The procedures that will kindle interest in the elementary school will not do so in the high school. They may even destroy interest, for nothing is more repellent to the youthful mind than something he considers childish. Moreover, once a student has reached in his thinking a certain level of maturity, to require him to use a less mature kind of thinking is to set him back in his educational progress. Repeated shocks of this kind can induce a kind of intellectual infantilism.

Now the fact of the matter is that most modern students of pedagogy, from Pestalozzi's day to the present, have devoted the bulk of their attention to the learning process in its earliest stages. They have had little to do with, and have paid less attention to, the process by which a man already equipped with certain kinds of fundamental knowledge proceeds to the learning of more complicated forms of knowledge. Professors of pedagogy doubtless know a great deal about the way in which a child passes from the stage of counting his toes to the stage of doing arithmetical sums in a notebook. They know next to nothing of the process by which a man moves from analytic geometry to differential calculus. This is a stage of learning that occurs under the guidance of professional mathematicians, and it is one about which scholars know vastly more than professional educationists.

Experts in pedagogy, however, seem blithely unaware of their ignorance concerning the higher stages of the learning process. They mistake their special knowledge about learning in childhood, or about the first steps in the learning of an unfamiliar subject, for a comprehensive understanding of how learning goes on at every stage. They calmly extrapolate. They assume that advanced students, already trained in the processes of abstract thought, can be brought to higher stages of intellectual maturity by employing teaching procedures analogous to those that are found effective in dealing with the infantile mind. Such unwarranted reasoning is the cause of that unmistakable childishness which characterizes so many of the proposals which professors of pedagogy make with respect to the secondary school curriculum.

Students of pedagogy have repeatedly shown that young children begin to think in terms of concrete objects and situations rather than abstractions. This insight has resulted in the complete reorganization of work in the kindergarten and the earliest elementary grades. On the whole, the results have justified many of the changes. But progressive education became regressive education when it projected these methods upward into higher levels of the school system, without adequate consideration of the changes which the learning process undergoes as the mind matures. After all, the importance of abstract thought itself was never in question. The discovery that one could not begin at the abstract level did not imply in any way that one should not proceed toward it. And once a child has learned to generalize, good teaching requires that his power to do so be continually exercised and expanded.

It may be necessary for a child to start arithmetic by adding four apples and three apples to get seven apples. But the aim, soon attained, is to enable him to think of four and three and seven apart from particular objects. It is thereafter an impertinence to ask him to study arithmetic by waiting on customers in a model grocery store, for he already possesses the ability to perform the elementary processes in his mind, and he needs to go forward to more complex and abstract operations. What is true of objects is equally true of situations. The fire department is more real to a child than government in general, and the railroad is more real than the modern industrial system. Let the first-grader, then, find out all he can about the local fire department and the choo-choo. But this process is not to be repeated indefinitely. In the end, the child can learn to think clearly and effectively only by learning to analyze into their elements the problems connected with these matters, and by thereafter studying such elements systematically, according to the recognized and appropriate categories of mature thought. Studies of the local community are all very well to start with, but they are a dead-end street unless they lead on into the disciplined study of economics, political science, history, and ultimately philosophy. Moreover, once the student has been brought to the point of studying these matters systematically, it is an intellectual crime to thrust him back to the starting point time after time.

Audio-visual aids (to use the educators' jargon) are subject to the same law of diminishing returns. Pictures have their place in even the most mature forms of learning. But in general the human mind advances from pictures to words and to abstract symbols. Once it has made the advance, many kinds of visual aids become time-wasting, round-about, burdensome methods of conveying information that can be got more quickly, accurately, and systematically by means of the printed word.

The social studies program which I described on an earlier page was an example of regressive education, because it pushed back to the infantile level again students who were already trained in systematic, analytical, critical thinking. This has happened on a tremendous scale in American education in recent years. It has happened because experts in pedagogy have insisted on applying to the secondary school and even the college certain rules of thumb that worked successfully in the primary grades. Extremists among professional educators have gone so far as to argue that examination of immediate, local, contemporary situations, already known to the child, constitutes an educational end in itself, not a mere starting point from which to go forward to more comprehensive and theoretical kinds of understanding.

In doing so, the regressive educators have turned their backs upon all the great educational thinkers of past times. Not least, they have repudiated the original principles of progressive education itself. The points I have been making were stated in the following words by John Dewey in a chapter on "Progressive Organization of Subject-Matter," published in 1938:

Anything which can be called a study, whether arithmetic, history, geography, or one of the natural sciences, must be derived from materials which at the outset fall within the scope of ordinary life-experience. . . . But finding the material for learning within experience is only the first step. The next step is the progressive development of what is already experienced into a fuller and richer and also more organized form, a form that gradually approximates that in which subject-matter is presented to the skilled, mature person. . . .

It is a mistake to suppose that the principle of the leading on of experience to something different is adequately satisfied simply by giving pupils some new experiences. . . . It is also essential that the new objects and events be related intellectually to those of earlier experiences. . . . Improvisation that takes advantage of special occasions prevents teaching and learning from being stereotyped and dead. But the basic material of study cannot be picked up in a cursory manner. Occasions which are not and cannot be foreseen are bound to arise wherever there is intellectual freedom. They should be utilized. But there is a decided difference between using them in the development of a continuing line of activity and trusting to them to provide the chief material of learning. . . .

It is absurd . . . to argue that processes similar to those studied in laboratories and institutes of research are not a part of the daily life-experience of the young and hence do not come within the scope of education based upon experience. That the immature cannot study scientific facts and principles in the way in which mature experts study them goes without saying. But this fact, instead of exempting the educator from responsibility for using present experiences so that learners may gradually be led, through extraction of facts and laws, to experience of a scientific order, sets one of his main problems. . . .

No experience is educative that does not tend both to knowledge of more facts and entertaining of more ideas and to a better, a more orderly, arrangement of them. . . . This principle determines the ultimate foundation for the utilization of *activities* in school. Nothing can be more absurd educationally than to make a plea for a variety of active occupations in the school while decrying the need for progressive organization of information and ideas. Intelligent activity is distinguished from aimless activity by the fact that it involves selection of means—analysis—out of the variety of conditions that are present, and their arrangement—synthesis—to reach an intended aim or purpose.[3]

Dewey's concluding sentence leads naturally enough to another comment on the regressive education of the present day. Most of what is labelled "integration" or "synthesis" in the public schools is not that at all. Synthesis is a step in thinking that presupposes a prior step of analysis. But the so-called "integrated"

programs of the American schools—the "core curric
"common learnings program," and the like—are efforts
a synthesis of knowledge before there is any analyzed ai
knowledge to integrate.

Consider for a moment the process by which a mai
solves a complicated problem. In his earliest encounte
he experiences it (to employ the phrase of William Ja
one great blooming, buzzing confusion." [4] The first in
step is analysis. He cannot solve the problem by simply
ing in it. He must stand off from it and separate it into
ments. Having done so, he must take inventory of his
knowledge and intellectual skill to determine whether the
suffice to deal effectively with the various constituent pr
he has recognized as crucial. If the powers he already po
will not suffice, he must acquire additional ones. To a n
man, already trained in a variety of disciplines, this mi
merely a matter of a few hours' work. To a young student,
ever, it may point forward to months or years of systematic s
The stage of integration or synthesis arrives—for the mature
and for the student alike—after, but only after, he has marsh;
the array of separate intellectual powers that he knows are
quired. Integration is simply the bringing of these powers to b
in combined fashion, upon the original problem.

In mature life, the labor of synthesis may follow almost i
mediately the labor of analysis, thanks to the knowledge a
skill already acquired by education. In the educational proce
itself, however, a wide interval must usually separate the fir
step from the last, an interval filled with systematic study ir
spired and motivated by the student's own discovery of wha
he needs to know.

What is falsely called "integration" in most secondary schools
is not this process at all. It is a futile and fallacious attempt to
by-pass the stage of analysis entirely. The original problem or
situation is never broken down into its constituent parts, and
these parts are not studied separately and systematically. Instead
the original problem remains the "one great blooming, buzzing
confusion" that it was to begin with, and children wrestle futilely
with it year after year through an intellectual infancy indefinitely and artificially prolonged.

The attempt to by-pass essential stages in the process of learning to use the mind is characteristic of regressive education. Most present-day proposals with respect to the public school curriculum bristle with pious words about teaching children to think. Upon careful analysis, however, an appalling number of them depend upon finding some short-cut to intellectual discipline. Their authors seem to believe—against all reason and experience—that it is possible to train men to perform the culminating acts of thought, while skipping all the antecedent steps.

Now effective thinking, I would suggest, involves at least four things. In the first place, it requires a thorough command of the essential intellectual tools. The most important of these would certainly be the ability to read, by which I mean the power to grasp the full meaning of the printed page, no matter how difficult, and in which I would include the ability to read more than a single language. Almost equal in importance would be the ability to write, which is not just the ability to make decipherable marks on paper, but the ability to put complex ideas into intelligible prose and to handle the niceties of syntax with the assurance born of grammatical analysis. Some command of mathematical thinking, beyond the mechanical processes of arithmetic, is also requisite to thinking, certainly for this present age in which quantified data are so significant.

In the second place, effective thinking depends upon a store of reliable information, which the mind can draw upon. It is commonly said that men do not need to carry information in their minds, because they can look it up in reference books. Every man, of course, no matter how well educated, must look up many items of information in connection with every enterprise he engages in. But in order to do so, he has to possess a great deal of information to begin with. A reference book merely explains one thing in terms of another. The user can pursue a chain of cross references, of course, but eventually he must trace a connection to something he already knows, else the pursuit is an utterly meaningless one. A man must bring to any reference book a fund of ready knowledge sufficient to make it intelligible.

In the third place, effective intellectual effort presupposes long-continued practice in the systematic ways of thinking developed

within the various basic fields of scholarly and scientific investigation. To approach a new problem from the point of view of its historical origins involves much more than a knowledge of certain facts of history. One must have already thought through other problems of historical causation, and one must have become aware of the pitfalls that exist in the interpretation of historical data. A man needs to know the inner structure and logic of any system of thought if he is to use its resources to any serious purpose.

Finally, but only finally, comes the culminating act of applying this aggregate of intellectual powers to the solution of a problem. In a sense, perhaps, this is the only step which can properly be called thinking. But it is not a step that can be taken by itself; it presupposes the preceding steps. And one cannot teach men to think by training them to perform this final act alone, any more than one can build a house from the roof downwards.

A disregard of every step in thinking but the last—even a contempt for every step but the last—is characteristic of regressive education. Extremists of this school have even brought themselves to deny the importance of reading itself, the cornerstone of all intellectual effort. The following words were spoken by a school principal to a formal meeting of the National Association of Secondary-School Principals and were duly published in its official proceedings:

Through the years we've built a sort of halo around reading, writing, and arithmetic. We've said they were for everybody . . . rich and poor, brilliant and not-so-mentally endowed, ones who liked them and those who failed to go for them. Teacher has said that these were something "everyone should learn." The principal has remarked, "All educated people know how to write, spell, and read." When some child declared a dislike for a sacred subject, he was warned that, if he failed to master it, he would grow up to be a so-and-so.

The Three R's for All Children, and All Children for the Three R's! That was it.

We've made some progress in getting rid of that slogan. But every now and then some mother with a Phi Beta Kappa award or some employer who has hired a girl who can't spell stirs up a fuss about the schools . . . and ground is lost. . . .

When we come to the realization that not every child has to read, figure, write and spell . . . that many of them either cannot or will not master these chores . . . then we shall be on the road to improving the junior high curriculum.

Between this day and that a lot of selling must take place. But it's coming. We shall some day accept the thought that it is just as illogical to assume that every boy must be able to read as it is that each one must be able to perform on a violin, that it is no more reasonable to require that each girl shall spell well than it is that each one shall bake a good cherry pie. . . .

When adults finally realize that fact, everyone will be happier . . . and schools will be nicer places in which to live. . . .

If and when we are able to convince a few folks that mastery of reading, writing, and arithmetic is not the one road leading to happy, successful living, the next step is to cut down the amount of time and attention devoted to these areas in general junior high-school courses. . . .

One junior high in the East has, after long and careful study, accepted the fact that some twenty per cent of their students will not be up to standard in reading . . . and they are doing other things for these boys and girls. That's straight thinking. Contrast that with the junior high which says, "Every student must know the multiplication tables before graduation."

Such a requirement attaches more importance to those tables than I'm willing to accord them.[5]

An anti-intellectual point of view that would have furnished grounds for dismissing a first-grade teacher a half century ago is now a respectable one to address to the most influential body in the field of secondary school administration. Nor is higher education safe from such subversive attacks. Certain regressive educationists are drawing up blueprints for the college of the future. There has been at least one dress rehearsal in Michigan, described in a volume entitled *A College Curriculum Based on Functional Needs of Students.* Here is an enthusiastic report of the work in college mathematics:

Originally there was no time set aside for instruction in mathematics except a small amount for remedial work on the simple, everyday uses of addition, subtraction, division, multiplication, and other fundamental operations. With the development of other fields of instruction certain abilities became necessary: ability to interpret and make graphs, profiles, charts, and tables; ability to interpret test scores; understanding of certain statistical terms; ability to use the other skills necessary to the general curriculum. . . . This has led to the setting-aside of two hours each week throughout the Freshman year when the student can go to the mathematics laboratory to work, under the supervision of an instructor, on his own inadequacies in the field.[6]

This program was doubtless adequate to accomplish the ends of higher education as these pedagogical experts conceived them, for in their comprehensive list of the "functional needs" which a college education should serve appears the following high objective: "Ability to read long numbers and to 'round them off.'" [7]

Professional educationists are fond of talking about the complexity of modern problems. They speak oracularly of "education for the atomic age." And *this* is how they propose to train citizens to cope with the vast technical questions that are posed by science, by an intricate industrial system, and by international anarchy. After nine full years of formal schooling a student need not be expected to read his mother tongue or to know the multiplication table. And in college he is doing satisfactorily if he can read long numbers and "round them off."

Let no one be lulled into the fatal belief that the professional educationists are merely reopening the old debate concerning the relative value of different intellectual disciplines. No one doubts that it is legitimate, and has always been legitimate, to raise such questions as these: Should the modern languages be emphasized at the expense of the ancient ones? Should the physical sciences occupy a larger place in the curriculum, relative to the humanities? Should economics and political science and sociology receive attention alongside history in the high school? These were the issues that educational thinkers discussed in days gone by. But these debates are things of the past in pedagogical circles. The new programs of regressive education involve the indiscriminate rejection of all these different alternatives.

The classical languages have virtually disappeared from the high schools, but the modern foreign languages have been buried alive with them in a common, unmarked grave. Fifty years ago *half* of all the students in public high schools were studying Latin; today less than a *quarter* (in fact, little more than a fifth) are enrolled in courses in *all* foreign languages put together.[8]

In the past, educational theorists differed over whether grammar should be taught through the medium of Latin or directly through analysis of the student's mother tongue.[9] Latin grammar has obviously departed, but now grammar itself has become an obscene word to most professional educationists.

The older curricula were attacked because they gave insufficient attention to science. But the United States Office of Education now reports that "percentage enrollments in algebra, geometry, physics, and Latin have shown progressive decreases in all investigations [of high school enrollments] since 1915."[10]

Everything connected with the past has been scrapped, out of a pretended devotion to the contemporary, but where is the high school student who has been systematically trained in economics, sociology, political science, or recent history?

In its most recent study of *Offerings and Enrollments in High-School Subjects,* the federal Office of Education discusses, with evident approval, the alterations that have taken place. "For the most part," reads its summary, "the changes are in the direction of more functional education. They represent efforts to meet life needs of increasingly diverse bodies of pupils."[11] The summary then goes on to report: "Enrollments in both mathematics and foreign languages in the last 4 years of high school . . . were smaller percentages of the total pupil bodies in 1949 than in 1934."[12] It is a curiously ostrich-like way of meeting life needs to de-emphasize foreign languages during a period of world war and postwar global tension, and to de-emphasize mathematics at precisely the time when the nation's security has come to depend on Einstein's equation $E = mc^2$.

We must face the facts. Up-and-coming public school educationists are *not* talking about substituting one scholarly discipline for another. They stopped talking about that years ago. They are talking—as clearly as their antipathy for grammar and syntax permits them to talk—about the elimination of all the scholarly disciplines.

Can we afford to entrust to men who think and act like this the power to direct the first twelve years of American schooling? Can we build a skyscraper by commissioning architects and engineers to erect the superstructure, while leaving the foundations to be planned by village masons who have never seen a building more than three stories high? The years from six to eighteen are the years in which young men and women must learn to think clearly and accurately if they are to learn to think at all. Command of written English, foreign languages, and mathematics—to say nothing of the abstract processes of analyzing, generalizing, and criticizing—cannot be acquired in a year or two when a student or a citizen suddenly finds himself in desperate need of them. The seed must be planted at the beginning and cultivated continuously if the crop is to be ready when it is required. And these intellectual abilities *are* required, not merely as a prerequisite for advanced study, but also and especially for intelligent participation in the private and public affairs of a world where decisions must be made on the basis of informed and accurate thinking about science, about economics, about history and politics.

The disciplined mind is what education at every level should strive to produce. It is important for the individual. It is even more important for society. It is most important of all for a democratic society. In that terrifying novel of George Orwell, *1984*, the Party of Big Brother developed the ultimate in ruthless dictatorship precisely because it devised the means of enslaving men's minds. It began by undermining the discipline of history, setting all men adrift in a world where past experience became meaningless. It continued by undermining the discipline of language, debasing speech until it could no longer be the vehicle of independent thought. And the crowning triumph of its torture-chambers was the undermining of the disciplines of logic and mathematics, the forcing of its victims not only to assert, but actually to believe, that two plus two equals five.

Fortunately it is as yet only through fantasy that we can see what the destruction of the scholarly and scientific disciplines would mean to mankind. From history we can learn what their existence has meant. The sheer power of disciplined thought is revealed in practically all the great intellectual and technological advances which the human race has made. The ability of the man of disciplined mind to direct this power effectively upon problems for which he was not specifically trained is proved by instances without number. The real evidence for the value of liberal education lies, where pedagogical experimenters and questionnaire-makers refuse to seek it, in history and in the biographies of men who have met the valid criteria of greatness. These support overwhelmingly the claim of liberal education that it can equip a man or woman with fundamental powers of decision and action, applicable not merely to huckstering and housekeeping, but to all the great and varied concerns of human life—not least, those which are unforeseen.

# 5

# The School and the Practical
# Needs of Youth

Liberal education has always been conceived as a preparation for life. This means that it can properly include preparation for the making of a livelihood. But education ceases to be liberal if it is directed exclusively to that end, because then it produces not free citizens but men enslaved by their occupations. The relation between liberal education and vocational or professional training must be carefully considered, for many of the ills of modern education can be traced to confused thinking on this subject.

The most culpable confusions are those that have occurred in universities and colleges. In the realm of vocational training, if not in other matters, the sins of secondary school administrators may justly be imputed to others, for the public schools have merely followed the wretched example set by American institutions of higher learning.

The college of liberal arts and sciences has a responsibility, greater than that of any other institution whatsoever, for exemplifying and defending the proposition that disciplined intellectual training is the foundation of enlightened citizenship, of humane culture, and of successful practical endeavor. To betray these ideals in their very citadel is to commit the highest of high treasons. That crime has been committed, mainly by university and college administrators. But liberal arts faculties, by their acquiescence, have made themselves accomplices or at least accessories after the fact.

The overt act—to which there are a cloud of witnesses, not the mere two which our constitution requires—was to adopt the principle that any kind of educational program, provided only that it adds up to a prescribed number of hours in the classroom, is the equal of any other as a means of liberal education. This preposterous scheme of academic bookkeeping is one of the evil legacies of the free-elective system into which the college curriculum disintegrated at the end of the nineteenth century. The arrangement did indeed provide a convenient way for the university to grant recognition to newer fields of science and scholarship that had long and fully deserved it. But the free-elective system also opened the door to courses in subjects that had no conceivable claim to scholarly or scientific standing. The university quickly became a bustling educational cafeteria, where every dish is plainly marked with its price in semester hours, and where a full-course dinner is defined (so far as the management is concerned) as any assortment costing 120 such credits, whether it consists of roast beef and vegetables or a trayful of candied ginger.

The pseudo-subjects that wormed their way into the curriculum under these circumstances were not offered for the purpose of advancing fundamental knowledge. They were frankly proposed as a means of preparing groups of students for certain specified jobs. Some of the offerings, viewed simply as isolated, optional courses, could be defended on utilitarian grounds. A student, alongside his serious academic work, might profitably pick up some practical training in accounting, or pedagogy, or public speaking, or home economics, or library cataloguing. The difficulty was that teachers of these supplementary, vocational courses began to aspire to higher things. With fatuous disregard of intellectual realities, university administrators permitted the development of departments and even colleges devoted to these academic byways, and eventually students were allowed to take degrees in them.

One perfectly good reason for refusing to devote an extensive amount of time to instruction of this kind is its relative ineffectiveness. The popular sneers at book-learning are not really directed at learning in the liberal sense. They arise because of the bumbling inefficiency shown in real life by students who have learned so-called "practical" subjects from a book, under an instructor who perhaps never practiced the trade he purports to teach. It is not the liberally educated man who becomes a laughing stock. It is the journalism major whose sentences no editor would print, the speech major whom no one would hear with patience in a public hall, the home economics major who is unable to run her own house, the education major who knows less about the subject she teaches than the parents of her own pupils, the commerce major who cannot carry on a business as successfully as the man who never took a business course in his life. The school makes itself ridiculous whenever it undertakes to deal *directly* with "real-life" problems, instead of *indirectly* through the development of generalized intellectual powers.

Besides being ineffective, formal instruction in trivial problems of vocational or personal life is dangerously *mis*educative in its effect. It generates in the student the belief that he cannot deal with any matter until he has taken a course in it. Timidity, self-distrust, and conformity are pathetically evident among the graduates of American teacher-training colleges (the most blatantly vocational and anti-intellectual of our institutions), for many of these poor souls seem to doubt their ability even to open a schoolroom window until they have been told in a textbook or by a professor of education how high it should be raised. But the decline of resourcefulness, imagination, and independence of mind is alarmingly apparent in the entire mass of present-day students. Alma mater has become a typically overprotective mother, and her children have been spoonfed so long that they dare not begin to live until they have received detailed instructions from her on all their most personal affairs.

Liberal education is designed to produce self-reliance. It expects a man or woman to use his general intelligence to solve particular problems. Vocational and "life-adjustment" programs, on the other hand, breed servile dependence. Originality, reason, and common sense are at a discount; maxims, formulas, and rules (the most degraded kinds of book-learning) are at a premium. The nation should view with grave alarm the undermining of that self-reliance upon which our greatness was based. One can search history and biography in vain for evidence that men or women have ever accomplished anything original, creative, or significant by virtue of narrowly conceived vocational training or of educational programs that aimed merely at "life adjustment." The West was not settled by men and women who had taken courses in "How to be a pioneer." The mechanical ingenuity which is a proverbial characteristic of the American people owes nothing whatever to schoolroom manipulation of gadgets. I for one do not believe that the American people have lost all common sense and native wit so that now they have to be taught in school to blow their noses and button their pants.

A citizen today needs an *education,* not a headful of helpful hints. The problems of modern life are so complicated that a vast fund of knowledge and a developed skill in the use of intellectual processes are required to handle them. Engineering and medicine, for example, rest upon formal education—not, however, the kind that purports to satisfy immediate "real-life" needs, but the kind that consists in prolonged and systematic study of the basic disciplines of mathematics, chemistry, and biology. Statesmanship, which we need even more desperately, calls for education, and for something more substantial than high-school civics. The men who drafted our Constitution were not trained for the task by "field trips" to the mayor's office and the county jail. They were endowed with the wisdom requisite for founding a new nation by *liberal* education, that is to say, by an education that was general rather than specific, intellectual rather than "practical," indirect rather than (in the vocational sense) direct. Through study of the classics they came to the study of history and political philosophy and jurisprudence. And through these great disciplines they reached an understanding of the general problems of government. This understanding they applied, with attention both to ultimate principles and local peculiarities, in the creation of the greatest single constitutional document in the history of mankind.

To deny that liberal education in the basic disciplines is a preparation for life is to deny the testimony of those who have accomplished most in life, practical as well as intellectual. The principles derived from experience can be applied to educational programs that are directed toward the eventual making of a livelihood. In preparing a man for his future profession or occupation, liberal education has always made a fundamental distinction. With one aspect of vocational training it has had as little as possible to do. To practice any profession successfully one must know something about how the profession operates, about the everyday situations that are likely to arise, about the shortcuts that are legitimate and necessary, about the human relations involved. These are the tricks of the trade, and they are learned most rapidly and effectively in actual practice. Apprenticeship, combined perhaps with a brief period of down-to-earth counselling, can be relied upon to provide an intelligent man with all that he needs in advance. To dilute the basic program of training in disciplined thought with courses in matters of this kind, devoid as they are of intellectual content, should have forever remained unthinkable.

Liberal education is based upon something very different from trivial and ineffectual training in the tricks of a given trade. It is based on the conviction that a good teacher needs to know a great deal more than methods of teaching, a good librarian a great deal more than cataloguing and routine book-selection, a good newspaperman a great deal more than the quirks of journalistic writing. And liberal education concentrates upon the great deal more. It believes that a man's real value in his profession is measured by what he brings to it over and above the knack that any assiduous clerk can acquire. This is not a gratuitous assumption, it is a conclusion derived from our knowledge of what has made men useful and humane and great in the past. It is a conclusion supported by rational considerations as well, for scholarship and science are nothing else than tremendously powerful intellectual tools, applicable to the solving of the widest variety of problems, including those that face a man in his public and professional life.

The debasement of higher education began when persons who repudiated this concept of liberal study began to infiltrate the faculties of colleges and graduate schools. An example in point

can be drawn from the field of pedagogy, now generally mis-
labelled education. Pedagogy came into existence as a subject
for formal instruction largely as a result of the founding of normal schools. The latter were purely vocational institutions, designed to provide a basic minimum of training to future teachers
in the elementary schools, at a time when genuine standards of
liberal education could not possibly be upheld for that particular
vocation.[1] The normal school drilled its students in the rudimentary branches of learning, and gave them instruction in pedagogical technique in order to equip them in the quickest possible
time with a certain degree of classroom proficiency. Rote-learning
was better than no learning at all, and a set of pedagogical rules
of thumb was at least a usable substitute for the kind of mature
reflection upon learning and its relationship to life which a liberally educated teacher might be expected to bring to his task.
Resources were limited, and so was the time of students. Shortcuts were necessary. Under the circumstances, the original normal
schools performed their tasks capably, honorably, and without
exaggerated pretensions.

Liberal education came into conflict with the narrow vocationalism of the pedagogues only when normal schools began
to imagine themselves colleges, and only when men with the
pedagogical mentality began to erect miniature normal schools
within the universities themselves. Then the shortcomings of a
purely vocational approach to education became evident. In any
vocational school, including a school that provides training in
pedagogy, students are rarely called upon to think of knowledge
as the fruit of original inquiry. Knowledge is simply fact, "subject matter," a body of established data, stubborn, inert, and unquestioned. It is raw material fed in from the outside, to be
worked up and packaged for the ultimate consumer. The important thing, in a vocational school, is to learn the techniques
of processing and packaging, while taking for granted that the
raw material will always be forthcoming. A college of liberal arts
and sciences, however, is concerned with precisely those operations of the mind which the vocationalist takes for granted,
namely the methods of inquiry by which knowledge is attained.
The vocationally minded instructor, whether concerned with
pedagogy or with some other technique or skill, always finds

in an institution devoted to liberal education a spirit and point of view completely alien to his own. It is apt to baffle and anger him, and conflict frequently ensues.

Unfortunately the vocationalist often occupies the stronger position, so far as power politics is concerned, for he can appeal to unthinking support from without. And in American universities, in recent years, the professors of pedagogy and the other vocationalists have usually been successful when they have demanded that they be allowed to train their students in their own fashion and that the degrees of the university be awarded for purely vocational proficiency, instead of being reserved for graduates who have seriously attempted to learn to think.

A century ago the nation was forced to tolerate shortcuts in the training of teachers. Now, however, it is in a position to require a really adequate period of preparation. Society today has a right to expect its teachers to bring to their profession a broad intellectual and cultural background. Its need is for liberally educated men and women, exemplifying in their own lives the value of that knowledge and disciplined intellectual power which it is their high calling to impart to others. In effect, however, both society and the teachers themselves are being defrauded. Though longer years of training are now required, the pedagogical locusts have devoured the harvest. The educational bureaucracy has juggled requirements so that much of the newly allotted time has to be wasted in intellectually sterile courses in methods of teaching. In place of solid work in the sciences, departments of education offer their students "advanced" courses in "Science in the Elementary School," the description of which, in at least one university catalogue, says frankly: "No science background is assumed and no attempt is made to cover content." [2]

The final degradation has been the bestowing of advanced degrees in education, so called. Printed in university catalogues, the offerings of colleges and departments of education may be dressed up to look like genuine graduate work. But pretentious terminology hardly disguises the fact that most of the offerings have nothing to do with the advancement of basic knowledge. At the very highest level of graduate instruction in a single university we find the following *separate* courses: "Elementary School

Organization and Administration," "Supervision of the Elementary School," "Administration and Supervision of Junior and Senior High Schools," "Supervision in Home Economics Education," "Educational Administration," "School Finance," "Public School Business Management," "Current Problems in School Administration," "Public School Finance and Business Administration," "Administrative Leadership," "Public Relations of the Schools," "Legal Basis of School Administration," and "Administration and Supervision of Industrial Education." [3] This is vocationalism run riot. A department which can seriously offer for the doctorate, courses so endlessly repetitious and so devoid of intellectual content as these is already far gone in anti-intellectualism. It no longer even pretends to deepen a student's understanding of the great areas of human knowledge or to start him off on a disciplined quest for new solutions to fundamental intellectual problems. It obviously does not believe in preparing him for professional activity by enlarging the store of information and insight which he can bring to bear upon the matters that come up for discussion in the classroom. It is doing the work of a low-level trade school, while professing to be a legitimate part of an institution of higher learning.

When doctorates began to be offered under such conditions as this, other professions and trades were encouraged to develop narrow vocational programs of their own. Librarians who were also scholars were in demand, and a Ph.D. in history or English literature or economics or biology was a valuable added asset. Library schools, however, soon found ways of expanding their courses in the techniques of librarianship until they were in a position to send out graduates with a doctorate in library science. But this new-fangled degree no longer signified that a man was *both* a librarian and a scholar. It merely indicated that he had spent more time than his undoctored colleague in learning the tricks of the trade. The law of diminishing returns was treated as repealed, and three years of this sort of thing were considered twelve times as valuable as three months.

One occupation after another sought this dubious academic recognition—journalism (now beginning to be rechristened "mass communications"), business, physical education, hotel management, and the rest. For years responsible administrators and boards had been seeking men with disciplined intellectual training over and above their professional skill, and had learned to accept the Ph.D. as a symbol of this. A fraud—the term is not too harsh—was perpetrated upon them by these new doctorates, which signified no tested grasp of a recognized field of knowledge, no special command of the tools of intellectual investigation, no proven ability to advance science or scholarship.

Genuine professional training—as given, for example, in engineering, law, and medicine—is something completely different from this. It does not replace liberal education but builds upon it. Educational standards in these genuinely learned professions have risen steadily over the years. This has meant a constantly lengthened period of training. But how has the added time been spent? Primarily in two ways. An education in the liberal arts and sciences—the four years required for a bachelor's degree— has been made the prerequisite for admission to professional training in one after another of the leading professional schools. And more and more thorough work has been required in the basic disciplines—physiology, bacteriology, mathematics, chemistry, history, as the case might be—which the profession undertakes to apply in practice. The specialized scientific training has sometimes unduly crowded the liberal arts, but leaders of the various professions have ordinarily taken a strong stand against the sacrifice of either. And they have certainly never been tempted to ape the pedagogues by frittering away precious time upon endless courses in bedside manner, in how to set up a law office in a small town, in the psychology of engineer-client relationships.

The contempt which the new vocationalists feel for science and scholarship is nowhere more clearly revealed than in their disregard of the varying educational requirements of different professions and occupations. If the profession of medicine requires graduate training leading to the doctorate, if fundamental research in physics requires the kind of intensive study represented by the Ph.D., then the job of writing advertisements for the radio should have its program of graduate training culminating in a doctorate too. One is reminded of Gilbert and Sullivan's "Gondoliers," where equality is achieved by granting exalted titles to everyone. To paraphrase a bit:

> The Ph.D. who rules the state—
> The Ph.D. who cleans the plate—
> The Ph.D. who scrubs the grate—
>    They all shall equal be!

Since American intellectual life itself is endangered by such nonsense, scholars must remember the words that Emerson addressed to them and must not hesitate to proclaim their belief "that a popgun is a popgun, though the ancient and honorable of the earth affirm it to be the crack of doom." [4]

Let me not be misunderstood. I am not asserting that a lawyer is a better man than a truck driver. I am not asserting that lawsuits are more important to the nation than truck transportation. I am not asserting that a man who is a lawyer is entitled to a better education than a man who drives a truck. I am simply asserting that specialized training for the law requires more time than specialized training for truck-driving. I believe that, as citizens, both are in need of, and both are entitled to, the broadest and most liberal education that can be provided. As a matter of fact, if both can spend the same amount of time at study, the truck-driver is actually the better off, educationally speaking, for he needs to divert less time from the studies that are of most general worth.

Society needs thoughtful citizens and cultivated men, whether by profession they be butchers or television announcers or civil engineers. They ought to receive sound and extensive education, regardless of their profession. The point is that the schooling which will make them intelligent men is liberal education, not courses in meat handling or script writing or strength-of-materials. There ought to be no limit on the education offered to every man. But the segment of this education that is devoted to mere vocational training should be strictly limited by the actual requirements of the occupation itself. To spend more time in specialized training than is absolutely essential for the practice of the trade or profession means the diversion of time from liberal education. What counts in making an intelligent and reflective man is the effort he expends upon the generalized intellectual and cultural disciplines. A rough measure is the total time he has spent in study, *minus* the time that has had to be diverted to vocational training and the time that has been wasted on sheer trivialities.

This invaluable residue in many educational programs of the present day is pitiably small.

In the university and the public school alike, vocational training is to be thought of as a final stage in education. It is a superstructure to be built on the broadest and firmest foundation of liberal education that a student is in a position to acquire. If that foundation is narrow, the student can be trained as a mechanic. Extend it, make it broad enough to include mathematics and physics and English composition, and he can be trained as an engineer. The point at which liberal education is cut off determines the vocational or professional height which a young man can be expected to attain. This rule is not absolute, for certain men have the native ability and the perseverance to gain a liberal education through their own exertions even amidst the distractions of practical life. By and large, however, the point at which concentrated vocational or professional training commences is the point at which systematic study of the generalized disciplines of intellectual life must be laid aside. This point should be set as late in a student's educational career as it is possible to set it.

It should be set late for another important reason. No training is more worthless than specialized training for an occupation which a man finally decides not to pursue. By beginning vocational training too early a student runs the grave risk that he may change his mind and thus find all his effort wasted. Liberal education is training in intellectual disciplines of general applicability. The man who possesses it has an automobile that can travel freely over every public highway, not a switch-engine that can run only on a standard-gauge track owned and controlled by somebody else.

A few basic principles emerge from what has just been said, principles according to which vocational training can be integrated with liberal education without destroying the values of either.

To begin with, specialized training required for any given profession or vocation should be determined by those who know at first hand its real requirements. The courses of a purely vocational sort (as distinguished from the general intellectual training that is likewise requisite) should be formulated as a specialized vocational program, designed to be completed in a few

71

months, a year, or a period of years, as the case may be—the rule being, of course, that no more time is allotted than is absolutely required to assure the necessary technical proficiency. Once such programs have been agreed upon, students should be fully informed of their character and especially of their duration, and should not be permitted to embark upon them at an earlier stage of their education than their situations and their academic prospects warrant.

The prerequisites, as well as the content, of such specialized programs should be clearly set forth. By prerequisites I mean simply the basic intellectual disciplines that ought to be mastered before the professional or vocational training begins. We need to specify what mathematics and physics a future engineer should have before he begins to specialize in engineering, what history a future attorney should know before he enters law school, what languages a future research worker should master before he enters graduate school, or (to take an instance of different sort) what proficiency in reading and spelling and what acquaintance with literature a future printer should possess before he commences to learn the trade. These prerequisites should be known to the student so that he may wisely choose among the options which are open to him in a flexible program of liberal education. But the prerequisites should be met as a *part* of his liberal education; they should not be offered as special pre-vocational courses, taught from the vocational point of view.

Such arrangements as these can give reality to the concept of a "single educational ladder," which educators so frequently (and so properly) eulogize. Schools are not making this concept a reality merely by housing all sorts of classrooms in the same building. A single educational ladder is one which all children climb together, pursuing the same basic studies until they reach the point, near the very end of each one's educational career, when each must commence highly specialized, and hence divergent, technical training.

Besides vocational training in the specialized sense, there are many kinds of practical training, non-intellectual in character, which a school or college may nevertheless properly offer as complements to its central program of liberal education. Home economics, shop work, typewriting, and bookkeeping represent skills of such general value that no student is likely to find them inapplicable to the life he eventually leads. They remain technical skills, not intellectual disciplines, but if they are clearly recognized as such and are not permitted to become substitutes for training in the ability to think, no valid reason can be given why the school or college should not offer supplementary instruction in them.

As a matter of fact, to define the school as an agency of intellectual training does not preclude the carrying out by the school of many ancillary tasks, important to the child and to society. The school does bring together almost all the children of the community. Consequently many health and welfare services can reach children and their families most conveniently through the school. Instructions concerning health and safety precautions, including emergency and civil defense arrangements, can be disseminated most efficiently through the school. The school ordinarily conducts a program of social activities, and some of the niceties of social intercourse can receive unobtrusive attention in connection therewith. A pupil is better known to his teachers than to anyone else save his parents, hence the school can engage in certain kinds of counselling and can refer problems to agencies that might otherwise never learn of them.

So far as the school is able to do so without interfering with its essential programs of study, it should make its facilities available for these services. The list I have just given, however, indicates the variety of demands that can be made upon its time. It is all too easy for a school administrator to give in to the pressures that are brought upon him by well-meaning groups of various kinds, and to allow the school's own program to be engulfed by activities only distantly related to its central purpose. This has actually happened to an almost unbelievable extent in many American public schools. Only a firm conviction of the importance of fundamental intellectual training, and a stern insistence upon subordinating all other activities to this one, can enable teachers and administrators to preserve the educational system from utter chaos.

It is this fact which renders so objectionable the effort of many modern educationists to redefine the purposes of the school explicitly in terms of the needs of youth. Let me quote one of the most influential statements of this point of view:

Youth have specific needs they recognize; society makes certain requirements of all youth; together these form a pattern of common educational needs, which may be expressed as follows:

1. All youth need to develop salable skills.
2. All youth need to develop and maintain good health and physical fitness.
3. All youth need to understand the rights and duties of the citizen of a democratic society.
4. All youth need to understand the significance of the family for the individual and society.
5. All youth need to know how to purchase and use goods and services intelligently.
6. All youth need to understand the influence of science on human life.
7. All youth need an appreciation of literature, art, music, and nature.
8. All youth need to be able to use their leisure time well and to budget it wisely.
9. All youth need to develop respect for other persons.
10. All youth need to grow in their ability to think rationally.

It Is the Job of the School to Meet the Common and the Specific Individual Needs of Youth.[5]

No one can take serious exception to these ten items in themselves. Young men and women do have these needs. One must, however, point out that the needs of the nation, not the needs of young people alone, are at stake. The pupils in a schoolroom are children, of course, and the school must make its first appeal to the interests which they have as children. The purpose of the school, however, is not primarily to teach children to solve children's problems, but to prepare them to solve the problems of the men and women which they are to become.

This is a fundamental defect of the statement, but there are many shortcomings of a more specific sort. Why should not students understand science itself, rather than merely "the influence of science on human life"? What exactly is meant by the "appreciation" of nature? Why is nothing said about understanding the past in order to grasp the problems of the present? Why is it not considered important for young men and women to be able to express themselves clearly and accurately in their mother tongue? Why is there not even an indirect reference to arithmetic or to the more advanced forms of quantitative thinking? Is provincialism so desirable that students have no need to understand the world outside the boundaries of their own country and time by studying geography, or comparative government, or foreign languages, to say nothing of history?

Weaknesses of logic are also apparent in the statement, or rather in the philosophy behind it. A fundamental ambiguity of thought is concealed within its vague inclusiveness. An attempt is being made to define education exclusively in terms of the needs of youth, without reference to the capabilities of the school. The attempt ends in a *reductio ad absurdum,* embodied in the last sentence, a sentence that is fantastically untrue. It is *not* the job—it cannot possibly be the job—of the school to meet the common and the specific individual needs of youth. If it were, then the school should undertake to meet needs even more basic than any mentioned in the list: All youth need food, clothing, and shelter.

The idea that the school must undertake to meet every need that some other agency is failing to meet, regardless of the suitability of the schoolroom to the task, is a preposterous delusion that in the end can wreck the educational system without in any way contributing to the salvation of society. Much of the cant about education for "home and family living" is a disguised way of saying that the school must take the responsibility for things that the family today is supposedly failing to do. If family life is in a parlous state, that is a national calamity. But it does not mean that we can or should reproduce its intimacies in the schoolroom. Even if it were true, for example, that parents are not giving adequate sex instruction to their children (and I suspect that they are giving it more fully and explicitly than in any earlier period) does anyone seriously expect an embarrassed school teacher to explain the physiology of human reproduction to boys and girls in public, and to use franker and more explicit terms than their parents are willing to employ in private?

The school promises too much on the one hand, and too little on the other, when it begins to think so loosely about its functions. In order to reason logically about education we require two premises: one concerning the needs of youth, the other concerning the nature and capabilities of the school. The two matters are not identical, and neither can be deduced from the other. The nature of the school—what it is designed to do, and what it is able to do—is a fundamental consideration. The school is a particular kind of institution, and, like every institution, it has a definite field of competence and definite limitations. We must know what these are before we can determine *which* needs of youth the school is in a position to satisfy. And only by considering this question can we decide which responsibilities of the school are primary and inescapable, and which are secondary and optional.

A failure to distinguish between men's needs in general and their specifically educational needs is one basic cause of the anti-intellectualism so rampant in the American public schools. Regressive education is a monstrosity in the literal sense of that word. It consists in the abnormal overdevelopment of certain features of the school program and the withering away of other and more important features. It is a vicious educational program, not because the elements in it are bad, but because they are completely out of balance. A well-intentioned but incidental concern with the personal problems of adolescents has grown so excessive as to push into the background what should be the school's central concern, the intellectual development of its students. To such an extreme have many educationists gone that they seem anxious for the school to satisfy all imaginable needs except those of the mind.

Genuine liberal education is not a course in first aid. It is a serious effort to train men to recognize symptoms, to trace them to fundamental causes, and to deal intelligently with the latter. When education becomes completely enmeshed in the petty, surface details of a student's everyday life, it loses the opportunity of equipping him with the intellectual powers that he will need to solve the deeper problems that lie beneath the surface. By frittering time away upon the "felt needs" of adolescents, the school runs the risk of leaving its students helpless in the presence of the real "real-life" needs that will come later and that will put to the test all the resources of a mature and disciplined intelligence.

In a vast number of American schools, the greatest of all the contributions which the school can make to society—the production of well-informed and intelligent citizens—is being sacrificed in favor of a multitude of minor social services which, even in the aggregate, are of far less ultimate consequence than the things that are being irretrievably lost. One thoughtful and succinct interpretation of the present situation is embodied in a private letter to me from a distinguished member of my own profession, an historian who has devoted as much time and effort to co-operation with professional educators as any scholar in the field. Though I differ with him (as I shall indicate in a moment) concerning the course of action we ought to adopt, I quote his letter in full, omitting only the signature and the purely personal concluding paragraph:

I read with great interest your article on "Aimlessness in Education," [6] and assure you that I share your feelings quite fully. Perhaps in times past I have been more closely associated with the problem than most of my colleagues in history, and it seems to me that there are one or two facts that must be taken into account.

First, I think we should recognize the fact that the public school system in this country has ceased to be concerned primarily with education. It has become an agency of society to offset both juvenile delinquency and the possible competition of teen-age youth for jobs. How successfully these objectives have been [met] is a matter of opinion, I presume.

Some school administrators admit this very frankly. It means that they must try to keep the youngsters in school satisfied or entertained sufficiently to make them want to continue in school. Academic standards of a necessity have been abolished; promotion is chronological; the subjects to which there is no royal road have been more or less eliminated from the curriculum. That would include such items as foreign languages, even history (though public pressure requires the teaching of American history) and specialized mathematics. Some school administrators view this with regret; others approve of it and are enthusiastic about helping to equalize all by preventing bright students from being able to do any extra work outside of school hours.

It seems to me that the development has gone so far that it is idle to become angered about it. I think it is best for us to direct our attention to seeing how, in view of this situation, we can make it possible for students with ability and interest to acquire an education during the school years. Private schools, of course, are able to maintain educational standards, ideals, and practices. I think it would be a mistake from the point of view of the conservation of our national mental resources to prevent able pupils from getting an education if their only avenue is the public school. That is the problem and the danger.

I sympathize with our colleagues at Illinois who seem to have become aroused over the problem, but I think our best efforts should be directed to finding a formula whereby education, at least for those who have ability, can be preserved in the midst of this overwhelming social demand upon the schools. It is, of course, unfortunate that there have been some among the so-called leaders of education who have tried to rationalize the situation and talk in terms of real education, when they know that it no longer is the main aim. Some of them, I am sure, are self deceived, but there are others who have more intelligence and whose public utterances must be regarded as hypocritical. But let's try to save education as you and I understand it. . . .

If the policy-makers of our public schools are inspired by purposes like these—and ample evidence supports the view that many of them are—then two ways are open for those of us who believe in preserving the modicum of intellectual training without which the nation cannot possibly survive in the modern world. One is the way suggested in this letter. We can accept the situation as it is and attempt to discover a means of providing intellectual training for a select few somewhere in the interstices of the system. That, I believe, would be to fight a losing battle. Too few students can be trained in that way; too many of the ablest young men and women of the nation will be condemned by such an arrangement to intellectual starvation.

But there is a deeper reason. A school creates an environment. If that environment is friendly to intellectual effort, intellectual effort can flourish in it. If it is indifferent, intellectual effort will be discouraged and destroyed wherever that school makes its influence felt. A non-intellectual school is a positively anti-intellectual force in society. To expect that intellectual training can be nurtured in the bosom of an institution which openly denies intellectual values is like expecting the cat to nurture a nest of young robins.

There is, however, a different path we can follow. We can

reaffirm, before it is too late, our own and our nation's belief in the value of intellectual training to all men, whatever their occupation, whatever their background, whatever their income or their position in society. This is to retrace our steps, I grant. It is to retrace them back to that period when professional educationists really believed in education and when public school leaders really believed in democracy. Instead of denying our faith in either education or democracy, let us proclaim our faith in both. Let us say, as did the friends of public schools in New Jersey in 1838:

We utterly repudiate as unworthy, not of freemen only, but of men, the narrow notion that there is to be an education for the poor as such. Has God provided for the poor a coarser earth, a thinner air, a paler sky? . . . Have not the cotter's children as keen a sense of all the freshness, verdure, fragrance, melody, and beauty of luxuriant nature as the pale sons of kings? Or is it on the mind that God has stamped the imprint of a baser birth, so that the poor man's child knows with an inborn certainty that his lot is to crawl, not climb? It is not so. God has not done it. Man cannot do it. Mind is immortal. Mind is imperial. It bears no mark of high or low, of rich or poor. It asks but freedom. It requires but light.[7]

The founders of the American public school system believed in the importance of knowledge, of cultural standards, and of the power to think. They believed in the capacity of the common man to acquire those resources, those standards, and those powers. They recognized, moreover, that intellectual training is a serious business, demanding sustained effort and genuine devotion. "It may be an easy thing to make a Republic," wrote Horace Mann, "but it is a very laborious thing to make Republicans. . . . But if . . . a Republic be devoid of intelligence, it will only the more closely resemble an obscene giant . . . whose brain has been developed only in the region of the appetites and passions, and not in the organs of reason and conscience. . . . Such a republic, with all its noble capacities for beneficence, will rush with the speed of a whirlwind to an ignominious end." [8]

Our Republic need not rush—I pray that it will not rush—to such an end. But is it not ominous, in these middle years of the twentieth century, that men who profess themselves to be both educators and democrats should consent to define democratic education in precisely the terms that have always been used by its bitterest enemies? In the writings of many professional educationists, democratic schooling is equated with intellectual mediocrity. Disciplined training in the arts and sciences is regarded as wasted if extended to the common people, who are supposed to require no training above and beyond that which is required for their own petty concerns. And a democratic populace is assumed to lack both the desire and the will to engage in serious and sustained intellectual effort.

In every other realm of activity, the American people have refuted by their achievements the charge that democracy is incompatible with greatness. Let us not allow the control of our public schools to fall irrevocably into the untrustworthy hands of those who believe that democracy is incompatible with *intellectual* greatness.

# 6

## "Life-Adjustment" Training: A Parody of Education

Liberal education and vocational training may exist side by side in a sound school system, provided the role of each is understood and respected. The school should pay attention to certain non-educational needs of youth, provided the effort does not interfere with its fundamental task of intellectual training. This was the thesis of the preceding chapter.

An educational program becomes regressive, however, when it loses its sense of comparative values and refuses to subordinate incidental activities to essential ones. In its extreme form, regressive education threatens the destruction of liberal and of vocational education alike. Among the most extreme programs is a currently popular one labelled "life-adjustment" education. In the present chapter I should like to examine this program in its entirety, so that no one may be misled into supposing that its absurdities are confined to certain incidental details. The separate proposals, in actual fact, are more appalling when read in context than when examined in isolation.

"Life-adjustment" education took its rise from a resolution—

now hailed as "historic"—which was adopted at a conference of educators in 1945:

It is the belief of this conference that, with the aid of this report in final form, the vocational school of a community will be able better to prepare 20 percent of the youth of secondary-school age for entrance upon desirable skilled occupations; and that the high school will continue to prepare another 20 percent for entrance to college. We do not believe that the remaining 60 percent of our youth of secondary school age will receive the life-adjustment training they need and to which they are entitled as American citizens—unless and until the administrators of public education with the assistance of the vocational education leaders formulate a similar program for this group.[1]

Consider for a moment the extraordinary implications of this statement. Sixty percent—three-fifths—of the future citizens of the United States, it asserts without qualification, are incapable of being benefited by intellectual training or even training for skilled and desirable occupations. If this is true, it is a fact of the most shattering significance, for it declares invalid most of the assumptions that have underlain American democracy. It enthrones once again the ancient doctrine that a clear majority of the people are destined from birth to be hewers of wood and drawers of water for a select and superior few. The "mud-sill" theory of society has come back with a vengeance, and likewise the good old argument that schooling for the ordinary man must teach him to know his place, to keep it, and to be content with it.

So eager were these educational leaders to proclaim their distrust of the abilities of the American people that they seem to have drawn their actual figures out of a hat. At any rate, their percentages differ markedly from the conclusions of another educational commission which found, almost contemporaneously, that "at least 49 percent of our population has the mental ability to complete 14 years of schooling" and "at least 32 percent . . . the mental ability to complete an advanced liberal or specialized professional education." [2] The discrepancy is not of particular moment, for "life-adjustment" training is not a matter of statistics, it is a philosophy of education. It is the philosophy which asserts that the public schools must "adjust" a majority of our children—

three-fifths or some other proportion—to the bitter fact that they are good for nothing but undesirable, unskilled occupations, and that intellectual effort is far beyond their feeble grasp.

On the curious assumption that this represents a democratic American view of education, the United States Commissioner of Education in 1947 appointed a Commission on Life Adjustment Education for Youth. In the same year an Illinois Secondary School Curriculum Program was launched under the auspices of the State Superintendent of Public Instruction. The points of view of both programs—phrased in such terms as "life-adjustment" and "basic needs of high-school youth"—were so similar that the state project eventually affiliated with the national one, and the controlling body adopted the name "Steering Committee of the Illinois Secondary School Curriculum Program and the Illinois Life Adjustment Education Program." [3]

The "life-adjustment" ideology was widely held in professional educational circles throughout the country. It was embodied, for example, in a volume entitled *Developing a Curriculum for Modern Living*, which was published, also in 1947, by Teachers College, Columbia University. "Fundamentally," the authors announced, "this concept of curriculum development is one in which the basic problems and situations of everyday living in our democracy, which are central in life itself, also become central in the education of learners." The idea was neatly summed up in one of the section titles, "Life Situations Are the Curriculum; Organized Bodies of Subject Matter Are Resource Areas." [4]

The National Commission on Life Adjustment Education for Youth sized up with considerable realism the difficulties it would have to overcome in eliminating intellectual training from the schools. "Traditional subjects are logically organized," it had to admit, and the contrast with what it was proposing was all too obvious. "Effective teachers are enthusiastic about the subjects they teach," the Commission lamented, and such enthusiasm was going to be hard to stamp out. The public, too, presented a problem, for the Commission regretfully observed that "there are enormous continuing pressures for teachers and principals to continue doing the things they do well"—a hopelessly old-fashioned attitude that would require a good deal of propaganda to eradicate. "The Commission," according to its own modest statement, "recognizes these difficulties and it has no panacea for overcoming them." [5] Refreshing as it is to encounter a group of educationists without a panacea, one cannot escape the feeling that under such circumstances the Commission desperately needed one.

It is well that the Commission refused to recognize as an additional difficulty what others might regard as such. The curriculum, it asserted, should be planned "to meet the imperative needs of all youth," but the Commission did not believe it should give first consideration to the needs of pupils now in school. "Even more, it is concerned with the types of education needed by the adolescent youth who drop out of school because their needs are not being met realistically." [6] Apparently the Commission felt justified in sacrificing the interests of the students who were already attending school with the intention of studying, if it could thereby lure back into the classroom those who never wanted to be there in the first place.

Refusing to be daunted by difficulties like these, the sponsors of "life-adjustment" education have made heroic efforts to put into effect the program which, it would seem, neither teachers, parents, citizens, nor pupils particularly want. The most valiant (and probably the most expensive) effort has been made in the state of Illinois. Here the Illinois Secondary School Curriculum Program has been at work for five years. At least sixteen printed bulletins have appeared, to say nothing of mimeographed documents of many kinds. Questionnaires have gone out, IBM machines have clicked off the results, and sponsors of the program have carried the glad tidings at public expense to all parts of the state.

The Illinois Curriculum Program (to use the shortened name that is now accepted) comprises some seven "local studies basic to curriculum development." [7] The last three of these reveal most clearly the anti-intellectualism implicit in the thinking of this group of professional educators. But before examining them we need to look at the four preceding studies in order to grasp the full context.

The first three studies are unexceptionable in purpose and principle. The first, called the "Holding Power Study," aims to discover how many potential students fail to attend high school or to continue in it until graduation, and what characteristics are typical of the pupils who drop out. The next two studies are based on the legitimate premise "that the vast majority of the youth who drop out of school come from families low in the income scale." Accordingly a "Participation in Extra-Class Activities Study" looks into the question of whether such students are being " 'included out' of the fun-yielding, prestige-bearing extra-class activities of the high school." And a "Hidden Tuition Costs Study" undertakes to bring to light the various incidental fees, subscriptions, and expenses which a pupil must pay in order to be a self-respecting participant in the complete high school program, and which consequently bar the way to poorer students even in a nominally tuition-free public school.[8] Such information, when gathered accurately and efficiently, is obviously desirable if undemocratic discrimination is to be eliminated, as it must be, from the American educational system. Note, however, that the data provided by the two last-mentioned studies can afford no justification for tampering with the curriculum itself, for nonattendance is treated as the consequence of economic factors entirely independent of the school's offerings of subject matter.

The fourth, "The Guidance Study," is designed to discover (with the idea of remedying) defects in the "pattern of organized personnel services for students," that is, services "concerned with the educational, occupational, social, and personal adjustments of young people."[9] The principal danger here is the tendency to overemphasize the auxiliary services of the school at the expense of its central purpose of intellectual training.

The "Guidance Study" is only a step in the direction of substituting vaguely conceived and heterogeneous educational objectives for clear and attainable ones. The "Follow-Up Study," the fifth in the series, is a leap into the very center of the bog. Its starting point is a document entitled "Problems of High School Youth,"[10] which is described as "the list of real-life problems of youth around which the entire study centers."[11] Five separate questionnaires are based upon this list, and the answers are supposed to reveal what parents, citizens, teachers, and pupils "think is the job of the secondary school."[12] The problems are divided into eight groups, each of which consists of from three to twelve separate items. The study is to be a statistical one, and the managers of the project consistently assert that the list contains "56 real-life problems." [13] Simple arithmetic reveals that there are only 55. But simple arithmetic is not listed as a real-life problem, hence such errors are probably unavoidable in the studies that make up the new "science" of education.

The first thing that strikes one on reading the list is the grotesque disproportion between the different problems presented. Trivia are elaborated beyond all reason, and substantial matters are lumped together in a very small number of separate items, thus reducing them to relative insignificance in the whole. Among the fifty-five points are such ones as these: "the problem of improving one's personal appearance," "the problem of selecting a 'family dentist' and acquiring the habit of visiting him systematically," "the problem of developing one or more 'making things,' 'making it go,' or 'tinkering' hobbies," and "the problem of developing and maintaining wholesome boy-girl relationships." Scattered about in the list are a few items like the following, each of which constitutes but a single point among the fifty-five: "the problem of acquiring the ability to distinguish right from wrong and to guide one's actions accordingly," "the problem of acquiring the ability to study and help solve economic, social, and political problems," and "the problem of making one's self a well-informed and sensitive 'citizen of the world.' " [14] There is not the slightest suggestion anywhere in the entire study that these problems are any more important or any more difficult to solve than the others, or that the school should spend more than a small fraction of its time upon them.

Needless to say, the scholarly and scientific disciplines have no place among these "real-life problems." Arithmetic has sometimes been considered of practical importance, but though "athletic games," "camping," "collecting art objects," and "doing parlor stunts" are mentioned by name, each in a separate item of the list of fifty-five, not one of the branches of mathematics is even hinted at. The word "science" occurs nowhere in the list, nor any term synonymous with it or descriptive of its various branches. That history and foreign languages are absent, even by remotest implication, goes without saying. The final item on the list is "the problem of securing adequate preparation for successful college work. . . ." [15] One can imagine that this will prove the most difficult problem of all.

The authors apparently think that it is enough to say—in another pamphlet, not circulated with the list or questionnaires themselves—that "neither the order in which needs are given nor the amount of space devoted to each need is indicative of the relative significance of the different needs." [16] This is an insult to the citizen's intelligence. No incidental disclaimer could save me from the charge of disordered thinking if I offered the following as an inventory of my possessions: (1) library, (2) sauce pans, (3) umbrella, (4) furniture, (5) fountain pen, (6) house and lot, (7) doormat, (8) automobile, (9) clothing, (10) lawn-mower.

The list of "Problems of High School Youth" is not a hasty private memorandum. It is a formal statement of educational principles, drawn up by those who purport to be specialists in the matter, and circulated to large numbers of citizens under the auspices of the highest public educational authorities of the state. It is professedly designed to stimulate serious thinking about "the job of the secondary school." As such it is nothing less than a proclamation of utter educational irresponsibility.

The intermingling of the trivial and the important in these lists and questionnaires is not an accident but a symptom. The arrangement of items in a list, and the attention devoted to each, do have a meaning and a very profound meaning. The order and emphasis of a man's writing are just as truly a part of what he says to his reader as any of his particular assertions. And what the list of "Problems of High School Youth" says to the reader is that order, balance, discrimination, and a sense of values are matters of no consequence whatever to the pedagogues who are remaking the curricula of our public schools.

The questionnaires not only fail to encourage serious thinking about educational problems. They do their best to prevent it. They purport to ask parents, citizens, teachers, and pupils what they "think is the job of the secondary school." But the persons questioned are not permitted to give the slightest indication that they believe the job of the secondary school is to give intellectual training. In the entire battery of questionnaires there is not a single blank that one may check in order to express the view that the public schools should offer sound training in mathematics, in natural science, in grammar and composition, in foreign languages, or in history. The citizen may respond in the negative to every question implying the substitution of frivolous aims, but he cannot indicate in any manner whatsoever the kind of positive program he would favor. He is not even permitted to indicate the weight he would give to the various items that are actually presented to him. Concerning each listed problem the respondent is asked to indicate whether he thinks the secondary school should help to solve it. If he answers "no," he puts himself down as a calloused enemy of social welfare. If he answers "yes," he is permitted to indicate further whether he considers it "very important," "important," or "not particularly important" for the school to give this help.[17] That is all. A parent, citizen, teacher, or pupil may think two problems "important" yet may also believe that one is a hundred times as important as the other and ought to receive a hundred times the emphasis. The questionnaires offer no means whatever of indicating this simple yet profoundly important judgment concerning relative values.

It may possibly be that American citizens do not want their children to know how to read, write, spell, and calculate. It may possibly be that they do not care whether their children know anything about history or science or foreign languages. I doubt this very much. It is quite certain, in any case, that these questionnaires do not furnish, and cannot furnish, one iota of evidence in the matter. They allow no more free expression of opinion than a Hitler plebiscite. The questionnaires are so rigged that the results are predetermined from the beginning. However overwhelming the public sentiment in favor of disciplined intellectual training may be, the professor of education who constructed the questionnaires has taken care that this sentiment shall not appear anywhere in the answers.

The "Follow-Up Study" is not an attempt to ascertain public opinion but a deliberate effort to manipulate public opinion. It is obviously designed to manufacture the appearance of public support for curricular changes that the professional educators have determined upon in advance. This purpose comes out stark and clear in the official statements explaining the questionnaires:

"Given the American tradition of the local lay-control of public education, it is both necessary and desirable that a community (patrons, pupils, teachers) consensus be engineered in *understanding support* of the necessary changes before they are made." [18] I find difficulty in following some of the involved syntax of this sentence, but I have no difficulty whatever in grasping the significance of a "consensus" that is to be "engineered." We approach here the real meaning of what educationists euphemistically describe as "democracy in education." It is the democracy of the "engineered" consensus.

Men who cannot compile a simple list without losing their sense of proportion and cannot ask questions without revealing a pervasive bias, hardly inspire one with confidence that they will know how to accomplish even the saner of their objectives, or that they will bother to try. Take, for example, "the problem of acquiring the ability to study and help solve economic, social, and political problems." All thoughtful men would agree that the school should assist the student to grapple with these questions. The great disciplines of history, economics, sociology, and political science have come into existence as the result of hundreds—indeed thousands—of years of serious effort by able men to do precisely this in an orderly, systematic, cogent way. To dismiss these organized disciplines with the contemptuous epithet "subject-matter fields," to label them as mere academic exercises or college-preparatory work, is to reject out of hand whatever experience mankind has been able to gain in the reasoned solution of the great problems of social existence.

Responsible scholars in these fields do not offer quick and easy solutions. But they do believe, on the basis of experience and sound reason, that serious, sustained, objective, critical inquiry into these matters will equip a man with the knowledge, and develop in him the maturity of judgment, that are essential to intelligent and effective action. Only a quack will promise more than this. Responsible scholars and educators consider it their duty to do more than proclaim their ultimate objective. They feel a solemn obligation to specify clearly and publicly the means they intend to employ to reach that objective. And they are prepared to explain why they consider those means effective and appropriate. They recognize that perspective is essential, hence they advocate the disciplined study of history. They recognize that analysis and comparison are necessary, hence they propose systematic courses in political science and economics. To the "life-adjustment" educators, however, all this is sheer pedantry, just as bacteriology is so much learned nonsense to a group of happy faith-healers.

Political, economic, and social problems that have taxed the intelligence of the best educated men from antiquity to the present are to be solved, so the new educationists assure us, through a "common learnings course" in the high school wherein "materials from science, literature, history, mathematics, industrial education, homemaking, business education, art, music, and all other areas of the curriculum would be included." [19] This is the short-cut to wisdom which the educationists propose as a substitute for disciplined, analytical, critical thinking. Having tied the world's problems up in this curious bundle, they consider themselves ready to pass on to other problems that seem to be of equal importance in their eyes—"the problem of acquiring the ability to select and enjoy good motion pictures," or "the problem of acquiring the social skills of dancing, playing party games, doing parlor stunts, etc." [20]

A document like this represents a complete abdication of educational responsibility. The question for the professional educator is not *whether* the school should train future citizens to deal intelligently with political, economic, and social problems—who, in heaven's name, doubts that it should? The professional educator is supposed to deal with the question of *how*. He presents himself as an expert in *methods* of teaching. He pretends to know how the school should go about doing the job that is assigned to it. Hence when he makes grandiose promises, at the same time proposing means that are obviously inadequate to the ends in view, he lives up to the very definition of a charlatan: "one who pretends to more knowledge or skill than he possesses." High-sounding objectives—such as teaching children to "help solve economic, social, and political problems"—are being offered today as the preambles to educational proposals of the utmost vagueness. Their vagueness is one of the principal dangers, for all the established guideposts vanish into the mist. The public is forced to take everything on trust. And the professional educationists deny, in the name of holy pedagogy, the right of scholars and scientists, representing the established fields of learning, to examine the soundness or adequacy of the programs that are proposed.

In defense of the "Follow-Up Study," the author of the list of "Problems of High School Youth" and of the questionnaires based upon it has made the following statement to me:

> From studies previously conducted . . . it was believed that the principal reason that youngsters dropped out of high school was that they saw little or no relationship between the subjects they were studying and the life problems of which they were more or less acutely aware. Once the legal school-leaving age had been reached by these youngsters, it seemed apparent that they could be kept in school only if the courses they were taking were in some way or ways more convincingly related to their life problems—that if this were not done the values potential in the high school courses in literature, science, history, foreign languages, etc., would probably be lost to them by virtue of their departure from the institution. . . .
>
> When a community which has seen fit . . . to utilize the *Follow-Up Study* as a starting point for its discussions has worked out a reasonably satisfactory agreement as to what life problems (whether these problems be those included in the printed materials of the study, or others not suggested therein, or some combination of both, is not material) are to be utilized to make the courses taught in the local high school make more sense to more pupils . . . , the next obvious step is that of incorporating these problems in the courses and/or extra-class activities to which they sensibly relate. There is no thought . . . that these problems are to constitute the whole of the curriculum or to replace any of the existing courses in the curriculum. Instead, the purpose in spotting the life problems which the community believes to be important, and in treating these problems in the courses to which they sensibly relate, is to make the courses make more sense to more pupils and patrons, and thus to keep more  pupils in high school in order that they may be more fully benefited by the secondary school. It is recognized, of course, that any school that might see fit to design some new offering around some sensible cluster of various of these problems might with propriety do so.[21]

This puts the matter in the best possible light, but there are many difficulties in the way of accepting it as a valid description of the purposes and probable consequences of the study.

To begin with, two of the "studies previously conducted"

91

came up with conclusions quite different from those stated in the opening sentence of this letter. The "Participation in Extra-Class Activities Study" showed "that the vast majority of the youth who drop out of school come from families low in the income scale." [22] And this, and its companion "Hidden Tuition Costs Study," attributed the fact to obvious financial barriers. The "Follow-Up Study" shifts ground, without explanation or justification, to the totally different contention "that the principal reason that youngsters dropped out of high school was that they saw little or no relationship between the subjects they were studying and the life problems of which they were more or less acutely aware."

I find it hard to believe, moreover, that a student who is indifferent to school will recognize as a personal, compelling, "real-life" need the "problem of making one's self a well-informed and sensitive 'citizen of the world.'" If he can see no practical point in history, geography, arithmetic, and grammar, is he going to rush back to school filled with a burning desire for sensitivity and world citizenship?

In reality the problem of relating the subject matter of a course to the life problems of the students enrolled in it is primarily a matter of intelligent and imaginative teaching methods. The important thing is for the teacher to know his subject and his students' problems well enough to make the connection. This elaborate polling of entire communities is not going to help him in any appreciable way. Especially is this true when the sponsors of the program abdicate all responsibility for indicating how their goals—sublime and foolish alike—are actually to be realized in the classroom.

An even graver doubt rises to my mind. If the object of the study were simply to demonstrate to the public and the student the immense practical value of the recognized scientific and scholarly disciplines, why is this clear and admirable purpose never stated in straightforward fashion in any part of the voluminous literature of the Illinois Curriculum Program? Why are references to the basic academic subjects so carefully and completely avoided in the documents distributed to the public? No sentence suggests that intellectual training can answer "real-life" problems. Pupils are asked to say "what we should teach you," [23] but are not permitted to mention any of the recognized fields of knowledge. Parents are informed that the schools "desire to teach all the children of all the people whatever they need to know," [24] and are asked to indicate what these things are. But they, too, may not specify intellectual training in the basic academic subjects. If the sponsors genuinely desired to safeguard the fundamental intellectual disciplines and to enhance public esteem for them, they showed the most wretched incompetence in planning their study. Every document placed in the hands of citizens or pupils teaches the recipient to think of the schools in utterly non-intellectual terms.

In point of fact, the published literature of the Illinois Curriculum Program flatly contradicts the assertion of the private letter that "there is no thought . . . that these problems are to constitute the whole of the curriculum or to replace any of the existing courses in the curriculum." Even the introduction to the bulletin containing the questionnaires explains: "The Follow-Up Study furnishes the data which can be used to arrive at broad policies (consensus) which must be obtained before a faculty or administrator may safely embark on material changes in the scope and content of the secondary school curriculum." [25] In its very first publication the Illinois Curriculum Program announced that its goal for the curriculum was "common learnings organized in comparatively large units on [the] basis of youth and societal needs," [26] and it relegated to the status of electives the "regular courses . . . in English, mathematics, science, foreign language, . . . and the like." [27]

By the time of its ninth bulletin the Steering Committee of the Program had grown bolder. This publication, entitled *New College Admission Requirements Recommended,* contained the following complaint:

The specification by the colleges of certain high school courses to be taken by all students seeking college entrance, sets definite limitations to curriculum revision. If a considerable block of courses must be retained in the high school to provide for the preparation of students who hope to go to college, the opportunity to re-examine the total high school curriculum and to replan the program in terms of the needs of all high school youth is thereby curtailed. For example, school administrators and teachers frequently mention the restrictive effect on their revision of the curriculum of the specification by some of the colleges that only high school majors and minors in English, foreign language, mathematics, science, and social studies will be counted for admission. The effect of such college entrance specifications is particularly limiting for smaller schools which comprise the great majority of Illinois high schools. The smaller schools cannot afford to provide a large number of courses; hence, when courses are specifically required for college entrance, most of them must also be the courses taken by students not going to college. . . .[28]

This statement makes the sharpest kind of distinction between "life-adjustment" education and education in the established intellectual disciplines. It makes it on the basis of "either . . . or." If a smaller high school wishes to offer "life-adjustment" education, it cannot afford also to offer programs in "English, foreign language, mathematics, science, and social studies." The latter are treated as nothing more than college-preparatory subjects, of value only in meeting "the specialized needs of parts of the student body." I see no possible way in which this statement can be reconciled with the assertion that the sponsors of the Illinois Curriculum Program do not intend "to replace any of the existing courses in the curriculum."

In the larger high schools, admittedly, training in the recognized intellectual disciplines would presumably continue for segments of the student body. The bulletin uses as an example the group of students planning to go into engineering. These ought to have an opportunity to acquire some competence in mathematics, if convenient for the school to offer it. But "the Committee recognizes that smaller high schools will not always be able to provide a sufficient variety of specialized courses to meet the needs for special programs of all its graduates. In such cases, the colleges are urged to make provisions for the basic specialized work with as little handicap to the student as possible." [29] This is the end result toward which the Illinois Curriculum Program is tending. Fundamental intellectual training will continue to be offered to an élite group in a few of the larger and wealthier schools, but the graduate of the typical high school must acquire it when and how he can. And the colleges are urged to deal gently with those who come to them intellectually handicapped through no fault of their own.

There is not a page in the publications of the Illinois Curriculum Program that supports the view that it is designed to preserve "the values potential in the high school courses in literature, science, history, foreign languages, etc." They are not mentioned by name in the questionnaires of the "Follow-Up Study." They are to be tossed pell-mell into a common learnings course where they can be dealt with or disregarded at will. In a few schools they may continue to be offered in a systematic way, with respect for their particular methods and structures, but only as electives. And colleges are to give up expecting their students to have received disciplined training in them.

The purpose of the entire Program is clearly stated in its jaunty prospectus, which contained the following exhortation: "There are many ways of getting underway in a program of curriculum revision. The important thing is that we need to pry ourselves loose from the present situation. Maybe one lever will do the prying loose; perhaps, it may require several. . . . Pick your lever(s) and let's get started." [30] The metaphor is apt. The kind of lever that one uses for prying things loose is sold in hardware stores under the name of wrecking-bar.

Pry loose from what? The answer is implicit in the entire program. The secondary school curriculum must be pried loose from the established disciplines of science and scholarship. It is to do so by ignoring and belittling them. The public school must be pried loose from its relationship to institutions of higher learning. The lever for doing this is to be found in the new guiding principle which the Curriculum Program advances: "Since the high school carries the responsibility for educating all youth, it, and not the college or university, has the responsibility of specifying the content of the high school curriculum." [31] And who is to do the specifying? The superintendent and principal, the members of the state educational bureaucracy, and their allies among professors of education. Who else? They run the machinery and engineer the consensuses.

The "Follow-Up Study," which we have examined at length, is itself followed up by others, and these, it is sometimes alleged, will cure any defects in the preceding ones. Particularly emphasized, in this connection, is the sixth, a series of "Local Area Consensus Studies." The documents and procedures to be used are still being "pre-tested and otherwise readied for the field," [32] but the plan is outlined in already published bulletins of the Currriculum Program.

In this study the starting point at last is the school program itself. This is considered to be composed of at least nineteen "subject or service areas." The recognized academic subjects of English, foreign languages, mathematics, science, and social studies are specifically named among these "areas," and a separate study is to be conducted for each of the nineteen. Mathematics is used as an example. To begin with, "some recognized leader in this curriculum area will be asked to draw up a concise statement of the principles which would probably govern, and of the chief purposes which would probably be striven for, in the mathematics program of a really up-to-date high school." This statement will be submitted to what is called a "jury," which is to include at least one university specialist in "mathematics education," along with public school teachers, administrators, and other professional educationists. The statement, revised by the jury and cast into question form, will be used as the basis of questionnaires and then of local discussions by teachers, pupils, and citizens. Ultimately each local participant will receive a second questionnaire and will be asked "to indicate which, if any, of the principles or purposes of its mathematics program he believes his school should attempt better to implement or achieve." Once a consensus has been reached locally, "the central leader-and-jury group will . . . supply the school in question with an instrument designed to enable the local school to work out *its own plan* of concrete and specific ways of making each of the desired improvements in its mathematics program." [33]

The most charitable thing to be said about the nineteen enormously complex and costly studies here projected is that they do not intensify the anti-intellectualism implicit in the "Follow-Up Study." But they certainly have little chance of reversing or even checking that disastrous tendency. Even assuming that the specialist in mathematics education on the "jury" turns out to be a mathematician and not another professor of education, he has no chance whatever of calling in question any of the basic assumptions of the Curriculum Program or of counteracting its anti-intellectualist characteristics, which have been fortified by the preceding studies. The scholarly validity of such an enterprise as this cannot be attested at so late a stage by the mere participation of one or two scholars, capable of being outvoted on every question. The only review of the final recommendations that could carry weight in this direction would be review by a committee representing the national learned society in the field and empowered to reject the entire program if its structure seemed unsound from the scholarly point of view. Anything less is mere academic window-dressing.

Actually this curious procedure of passing each proposal from group to group is not as pointless as it seems. It is one of the standard devices by which professional educators filter out every germ of an idea different from theirs and make sure that any final proposal is completely their own, even though they have maintained the pretense of consulting the opinions of citizens and scholars.

The utility of this device is beautifully illustrated by the seventh and last of the studies of the Illinois Curriculum Program, embodied in a volume entitled *The Schools and National Security*. This was done in the grand manner. "More than twenty-five hundred professional educators and laymen" were involved, the foreword proudly announces.[34] There were three great panels. The first consisted of twelve distinguished discussants, representative, beyond all cavil, of important areas of American public and professional life. Their names give prestige and standing to the report, and seemingly guarantee that the conclusions are something more than a rehash of the professional educationists' peculiar notions. But what were these discussants permitted to do? The panel was brought together under the chairmanship of a professional educationist, and its members were asked to discuss "the nature, dimensions, and requirements of the national security situation" and the impact upon society of the measures that are likely to be adopted.[35] But the discussants were distinctly forbidden to consider the implications for education. The sponsors of the study made this absolutely clear: "It should be noted that the purpose of this meeting was *not* to talk about education; this was to come later." [36] This statement from the introduction is most revealing. Men in public and professional life might be expected to have ideas about education, but for them to have

expressed their views on the matter would have been an impertinent intrusion into the field reserved exclusively for professional
educationists. To make sure that such extraneous ideas did not
creep into the record, no less than six educationists sat with the
panel as "recorders," and they wrote the summary of its discussions. After the members of the panel approved this text, they
were honorably discharged from all further service.

Then began the great filtering process. Panel II, made up of
eighteen school administrators and professors of education, took
the report of the first set of discussions (now cast into six chapters
of the projected volume), and drew up, in four additional chapters, their own statement of the "Major Educational Implications
of the National Security Situation." The document was now safe
enough to be distributed more widely; laymen's ideas of education, if any had crept in, had by this time been authoritatively
counteracted. The filtering, however, continued. The ten chapters
produced thus far were passed on to Panel III, whose 130 members consisted of professional educationists and "Parent-Teacher
Association and school board leaders generally regarded as outstanding." [37] The twenty-three "subgroups" of this panel produced
twenty-three more chapters describing "what they thought the
national security program of the schools ought to be in regard to
each of the subject areas of the school, its guidance program, . . .
and so on." [38] Trial copies of the entire report went to 2,000 more
educators and Parent-Teacher Association leaders for discussion.
Three educationists undertook to revise all parts of the report
on the basis of the suggestions received. And the final document
was "sieved"—the word is from the introduction [39]—by the august
Steering Committee of the Illinois Secondary School Curriculum
Program. The final conclusions are simon-pure educationalism,
warranted free from polution by the common sense of ordinary
citizens.

Chapter 30, dealing with the "Social Studies," is worth looking
at more closely. The "subgroup" of eight that was responsible for
its drafting contained four professors of education and one school
superintendent, so that the professional educationists were in a
position to vote down any unorthodox, academic ideas that might
conceivably have come from the two high school teachers and

the college professor of social science who constituted the minority group.[40]

No such heterodoxies have crept in. Because the theme is "national security," some of the old ideas are dressed in new costumes, just as the chorus of a Broadway revue sometimes does a number with muskets and a flag to remind the audience that a war is on. But the chapter as a whole gives the reader the comfortable impression that the world crisis amounts to nothing more than a slight shifting about of the old familiar "real-life" needs. The first task of the social studies, the report begins, is to "reduce the tensions and meet the *needs* of children and youth." Absent is any idea that the nation is in danger and that it may require of its future citizens some very hard thinking, not about their personal problems first of all, but about the means of national survival. Someone else can train young men and women for that job. The social studies cannot waste their time on the nation's problems when the tensions of young people are there to be reduced. "If we neglect the tensions," says the report, "we neglect also drives, motivations, and interests. We neglect the many personal life problems of youth. We run the risk of being academic." God forbid!

"Reducing the tensions of young people," says the summary, "illuminating the social realities, and developing an understanding and practice of democratic values—these are our basic tasks in peacetime. *They are also our basic tasks in a period of defense or national emergency or total war.* The tasks do not differ from period to period." [41]

The vagueness and ambiguities of the program do not differ from period to period either. Back again are the grandiose old promises, unsupported by any statement of the means to be employed: "develop a constructively critical attitude toward foreign policy," and "develop an understanding of the ways of living, attitudes, and ideologies of different nationalities throughout the world." [42] Back again is the dear old muddle-headedness that poses such questions as "Why do nations like India waver in their loyalty to the United States when the United States is friendly to India?" [43] without bothering to consider whether loyalty is something that one sovereign nation is ever supposed to owe to another.

99

Back again, too, are the marvelous trivia into which the educationists throw themselves heart and soul. Ask the students, the report recommends, to "make studies of how the last war affected the dating pattern in our culture." [44]

Here we have "life-adjustment" education in a nutshell.

# 7

## Interlocking Directorate of Professional Educationists

The anti-intellectualism of programs like "life-adjustment" education is so extreme that it refutes itself. The good sense of the American people can be trusted to repudiate it, once they grasp what it is about. In the long run, anti-intellectualism is bound to be self-defeating. But if powerful interests promote and sustain it, the run can be long and dangerous indeed. To destroy anti-intellectualism we need to do more than combat its arguments. We need to identify and expose the groups that are promoting it, so that we may check their disastrous influence upon policy-making.

Where, then, did these preposterous educational notions come from? Who originated them and who is propagating them? They are obviously not the ideas of scientists, scholars, and professional men. The evidence that the public supports them is manufactured evidence. Under compulsion from their administrative superiors some public school teachers docilely indicate their approval, but

101

the ablest and most courageous of the classroom teachers are beginning to express a sense of outrage that is undoubtedly shared by vast numbers of their intimidated colleagues. None of these groups can be held responsible for the anti-intellectualism that is sapping public education.

There is no mystery about the source of the proposals that I have been examining. By checking the list of authors and studying the roster of sponsoring committees one can fix responsibility clearly and unequivocally. The writers of these books and pamphlets, the members of these committees and commissions, the men and women actively engaged in questionnaire-making, curriculum-outlining, and propagandizing are drawn almost exclusively from three interrelated professional groups. First of all, there are professors of education in universities, colleges, and normal schools. Second, there are superintendents, principals, and other local public school administrators and supervisors. Third, there are officials, "experts," and other bureaucrats in the state departments of public instruction and the federal Office of Education. These three groups, collectively known as professional educationists, have drawn together in recent years into what now amounts to an interlocking public school directorate. To make this clear we need to examine the composition of certain recent educational committees.

The personnel of the Illinois Curriculum Program (discussed in the preceding chapter) is typical and illustrative. First of all, the list of "Problems of High School Youth," central to the "Follow-Up Study," was formulated by a single professor of education, a member of the faculty of the College of Education of the state university. He, in turn, acknowledged that his problems were derived from a list of "Basic Needs of High School Youth," which was "prepared by the Committee on the Reorientation of the Secondary School Curriculum, a sub-committee of the Curriculum Committee of the Illinois Secondary School Principals' Association." [1] This committee (or sub-committee) of eight comprised three professors of education, two high school principals, two representatives of the State Department of Public Instruction, and the executive director of the Illinois Association of School Boards. [2] The fundamental philosophy of the entire program, in other words, was determined by professional educationists, who occupied seven of the eight positions on the committee. The one other place was assigned to a citizen who was not a professional educationist, it is true, but who was closely associated with the administration of the school system. No scholar or scientist representing a basic intellectual discipline participated in the work of the committee, though its avowed purpose was "the reorientation of the secondary school curriculum."

The minority position assigned to citizens, scholars, and scientists is just as conspicuous in the large "steering committee" of approximately sixty which exercises general supervision over the Curriculum Program. Its membership has changed slightly over the years, but its basic composition has remained the same. Out of a membership (in 1952) of fifty-eight, all but thirteen were professional educationists or persons directly connected with or employed by the public school system: twenty-seven superintendents, principals, professors of education, and representatives of the State Department of Public Instruction; fifteen high school teachers of various subjects; two other members of high school faculties (a dean of girls and a librarian); and the director of teachers' welfare in the Illinois Education Association. Upon the minority of thirteen devolved the responsibility of representing both the public at large and the entire learned world outside the secondary schools. This minority comprised seven representatives of non-educational organizations, two college presidents, one head of a parochial school unit, and three college teachers.[3]

These figures reveal how inadequately the great intellectual disciplines have been represented in the process of curricular study and revision. A maximum of twenty members, out of fifty-eight, can be said to have stood in any way for the recognized fields of scholarship and science—the three college professors, the two college presidents, and the fifteen high school teachers. Actually the number was considerably smaller, for many of the high school teachers represented vocational and other non-academic fields, and the college presidents were doubtless concerned primarily with administrative questions. The three college teachers came from geography, music, and speech—hardly the central intellectual or scientific disciplines of modern life.[4] That a "steering committee" so constituted would chart its course by any of the recognized beacons of science and scholarship is hardly to be expected. Absurdities like "life-adjustment" education could never have gained a foothold in the secondary schools if scholars and scientists had played any real and continuing part in the making of American public school policy.

How has it happened that scholars and scientists have lost all effective voice in public school curriculum-making? And what is responsible for the creation of an educational directorate powerful enough to cut the schools loose from their natural ties with the recognized world of learning?

The present situation is clearly the product of historical forces. This does not mean that the development was inevitable. It certainly does not mean that the trend was desirable. Least of all does it mean that the present situation cannot be altered. In this matter, indeed, we need to understand the course of past events because we need to recognize, as a step toward rectifying, the mistakes that have been made.

Quantitatively speaking the American educational system of today is an enormous enterprise. In creating it we have necessarily brought into existence a vast administrative bureaucracy. Public school superintendents and principals direct the education of more than twenty-five million young Americans in the public schools. They control the expenditure of close to six billion dollars of public funds a year. They employ more than nine hundred thousand teachers.[5] Theirs is a complex and responsible task, and on the material and managerial side they have conducted it honestly, efficiently, and well. The buildings and equipment of our schools, and the orderliness of their operation, are monuments to the skill and devotion of the educational bureaucracy.

But the acumen that is necessary to manage the organizational details of such an enterprise successfully is not precisely the same as the knowledge and discernment that are necessary to determine the intellectual content of programs that are conducted within these well-ordered school buildings. The public school administrator of today is practically never an active scholar or scientist—how could he possibly find the time to be? Despite the "Dr." which often precedes his name, he has rarely been educated as a scholar. He has been trained as an educational technician, and his degree is often an Ed.D., not a Ph.D. Neither by training nor by occupation is he prepared to judge the kinds of intellectual skills that are necessary to maintain the scientific, technological, and professional progress of the nation. The problems of the children under his care so engross his attention that he often comes to believe that schools exist primarily to meet the personal needs which these children feel, completely forgetting that the nation supports the schools in order to provide for many needs of society which children are quite incapable of comprehending.

The school administrator requires, and has always required, guidance in curriculum-making from those who are in a better position than he to judge of the intellectual skills that are needed by mature men in a complex society and that must therefore be developed in the lower schools. Until forty or fifty years ago that guidance was furnished by the men professionally engaged in the higher branches of science and scholarship. Much of this guidance was taken for granted. School administrators received their training in the recognized academic disciplines and accepted the postulates common to all the learned professions. The aims of education could be considered settled by common consent. Training in the basic intellectual skills and disciplines formed the unquestioned foundation. The arrangement and grading of subjects was more or less fixed by tradition. And at the top the known entrance requirements of the colleges provided a kind of ultimate directive. Under such circumstances the school administrator had clear standards to guide him in exercising his responsibility with respect to the curriculum.

With the rise of the new American university in the last quarter of the nineteenth century, this guidance was placed on a more formal basis. University scholars served on commissions which, in co-operation with educational administrators, labored thoughtfully and effectively to work out, for each school subject, a course of study that would meet the criteria both of scholarly soundness and of pedagogical fitness. In 1894 appeared the *Report* of the Committee of Ten on Secondary School Studies, appointed by the National Education Association. Its chairman was President Charles W. Eliot of Harvard, and its membership included five college presidents, one college professor, one high school principal, the heads of two private preparatory schools, and the United States Commissioner of Education. Its recommendations on history, civil government, and political economy were drawn up by a group which comprised six college professors, one college president, two high school principals, and one private school headmaster.[6] The same responsible scholarly participation characterized a long series of subsequent studies in the field, up to and including the report on *The Study of History in Secondary Schools,* published in 1911 by the Committee of Five of the American Historical Association.

This promising form of co-operation petered out in the second decade of the twentieth century. In 1916 appeared a report of the Committee on Social Studies of the Commission on the Reorganization of Secondary Education of the National Education Association. The composition of this committee of twenty-one stood in the sharpest possible contrast with that of the Committee of Ten two decades earlier. Only four university professors were among its members, plus one teacher from Hampton Institute, and there were no representatives of preparatory schools. But there were ten high school teachers and principals, two superintendents of schools, one state high school inspector, two officials from the United States Bureau of Education, and one member of the faculty of a School of Pedagogy.[7] This established a completely new pattern in curriculum making, and a pattern which has persisted.[8] The old pattern of co-operation, indeed, has been emphatically repudiated by most present-day educationists. "Until about 1910," says a recent textbook, with obvious condescension to the backward past, "curriculum-making was largely in the hands of subject-matter specialists who were dominated by a philosophy of formal discipline, the sacredness of subject matter, and a worship of the past and the status quo." [9]

For this rejection of academic co-operation, scholars themselves were partly to blame. Their responsibilities within their own fields—in graduate instruction, in research, and in public service—grew heavier, and the content of each field grew increasingly more complex. University professors tended to turn their backs upon elementary and secondary education. They are reaping today the whirlwind which their indifference helped to sow.

In the long run, however, the negligence of scholars was less significant than another development, which promised to make co-operation even more effective but which actually impeded and destroyed it. This was the rise of pedagogy as an independent subject in the university curriculum, with offerings even on the graduate level. At the outset, this was a promising development. Research in pedagogical methods was to be conducted under university auspices by scientists and scholars educated in the recognized disciplines applicable to the problems involved. Many thoroughly trained psychologists, philosophers, historians, statisticians, linguists, and others accepted the title of professor of education, and shouldered the new responsibilities that went with it. These responsibilities were clear. Professors of education were to be mediators between the more advanced and the more elementary sectors of the educational world. As members of a university community they were supposed to grasp the growing complexity of intellectual life and to see its implications for secondary education. As teachers of teachers they were expected to translate these developments in science and scholarship into the language of the classroom. They were expected to make clear to school administrators the increasingly heavy intellectual requirements of modern life, and thus to encourage the development of public school curricula more thorough and rigorous than those of the slipshod past. The great responsibility of professors of education was to stimulate and encourage rising standards of disciplined intellectual training throughout the school system, using the prestige of their university position to advance the ideals of liberal education to which the university is dedicated.

The men who undertook to deal with pedagogical problems at the university level in the late nineteenth and early twentieth centuries took these responsibilities seriously and acquitted themselves well. They have their true successors at the present day—men bred in the liberal arts, trained at the advanced level in one of the basic disciplines, and imbued with faith in the value of intellectual endeavor. These men I honor, and I am gratified that many of them have written me approving both the positive affirmations and the negative criticisms set forth in preceding chapters of this book. Such men, however, form but a small minority among professors of education at the present day. The pedagogical departments at most universities have developed in quite a different direction during the past half century. The change was the result of certain factors which were neither recognized nor foreseen at the outset.

University and graduate departments of education began as agencies of genuine interdisciplinary investigation and teaching. When, however, they began to recruit their faculties from young men trained by themselves, they gradually lost their original character. Several academic generations have now passed, and the overwhelming majority of present-day professors of education have received virtually all their advanced training in departments of education. Their knowledge of the disciplines that are required to solve pedagogical problems is for the most part elementary and secondhand. And this knowledge is being passed on, increasingly diluted and increasingly out-of-date, to new generations of professional educationists. John Dewey was himself a philosopher, and he brought philosophy to bear upon educational problems. Today, however, the so-called "philosophy of education" offered in most departments of pedagogy has lost touch with living philosophical thought, for it is taught mainly by men trained not in philosophy itself but merely in their predecessors' courses in the philosophy of education. What began as the free and creative speculation of philosophic minds upon educational questions has congealed into educational dogma passed on from generation to generation by men who no longer speculate but merely expound.

This has happened to each of the great disciplines that ought to be contributing to vital educational thinking. Educational psychologists maintain closer connections with the parent discipline than other educationists, perhaps, but the gap is wide and growing wider. The history of education and educational sociology are rarely taught by men trained as historians or sociologists. Professors of educational administration have practically nothing to do with the experts who study and teach public administration in general in departments of political science. Even the courses in the teaching of specific subjects—mathematics, history, English, and the like—are mainly in the hands of educationists, not mathematicians or historians or scholars in the field of English language and literature.

Cross-fertilization, the original purpose of departments of education, has ceased, and we are up against the fact that the products of cross-fertilization—the hybrids—are frequently sterile.

The quality of purpose has declined with the decline in the quality of staff. University and graduate departments of education

were founded with the idea of raising school-teaching from a vocation to a profession. This was to be accomplished—it could only
be accomplished—by requiring a thorough training in the liberal
arts before permitting a student to embark upon specialized
training in pedagogy. But the founders of advanced departments
of education failed to reckon with the fact that a large number of
institutions and instructors had a vested interest in a lower and
narrower type of pedagogical training. Normal schools were re-
luctant to give up what they had been doing. They expanded into
colleges, but rarely sloughed off completely their narrow vocational approach to the problem of training teachers. The old-time
specialists in normal-school pedagogy were insistent that they be
recognized as full-fledged professors of education, and they began
to migrate to the new university departments. As a result there
occurred a rapid debasement of the original ideal. Instead of a
new and genuinely professional approach to education there
was a mere upgrading in the numbering of the old courses in
pedagogical method. For most students these courses were apt
to be piled, layers thick, upon an undergraduate major in pedagogy, not upon a major in one of the liberal arts. In the end,
so-called graduate work in education tended to become merely a
prolonged and attenuated program of vocational training.

Another unforeseen factor leading to the deterioration of university departments of education was the tremendous influence
that came to be exerted upon them by the administrative bureaucracy of the public schools. It was peculiarly necessary for professors of education to maintain their independence from such
pressures, since one of their major responsibilities was to examine,
criticize, and judge with scholarly impartiality the programs that
school administrators were carrying out. Their duty was to transmit to superintendents, principals, and teachers in the field the
considered judgment on educational matters of the academic
world. Such a pattern, however, never came into being. Instead,
public school administrators and university departments of education drew together in a community of interest that was far
stronger than any which developed between the department of
education and the other faculties of the university. The direct
consequence was that professors of education abandoned any
pretence of being independent, academic critics of public school

development, and became hard-and-fast partners of the administrative bureaucracy in the making of public school policy. Their role thereafter could only be that of apologists, and rather indiscriminate apologists, for every new program introduced into the public schools.

To the scholar from an established discipline, one of the most shocking facts about the field of education is the almost complete absence of rigorous criticism from within. Among scientists and scholars, criticism of one another's findings is regarded as a normal and necessary part of the process of advancing knowledge. But full and frank criticism of new educational proposals rarely comes from other professional educationists. The educational journals are almost devoid of critical reviews, which form an essential part of similar publications in other fields.[10] The paean of praise that greets every novel program, the closing of ranks that occurs whenever a word of criticism is spoken from outside, is a symptom of the fact that independence of thought has ceased to be a virtue among professional educationists. This monolithic resistance to criticism reveals the existence and influence of what can only be described as an educational party-line—a party-line that protects the vested interests of both school administrators and professors of education. Even in Parent-Teacher Associations—admirable bodies in many respects—free discussion of the basic educational philosophy of the public schools is tightly controlled through frequent invocation and strict interpretation of a national by-law which provides that the organization "shall not seek to direct the administrative activities of the schools or to control their policies."[11] Communication thus becomes a one-way affair. The theories of professional educationists may be freely expounded in P.T.A. meetings. But program committees are often given to understand that they may not schedule speakers of opposite views, for this would constitute an attempt to interfere with the policies of the schools.

The extreme unwillingness of professional educationists to submit their proposals to free public discussion and honest criticism frequently assumes the even uglier form of showering critics, no matter how upright and well-informed, with vituperation and personal abuse. A scientist or scholar who publishes a criticism of educational trends, even in a scientific journal, is liable to be denounced by professional educationists in responsible positions who do not think it beneath their dignity to hurl at him such epithets as these: "a peripatetic hatchet man," "a demagogue rather than a scholar," and "a master of the pointed phrase rather than the finished thought." [12] Other educationists shamelessly employ the doctrine of "guilt by association" and try to show that because certain criticisms made by responsible scholars have been utilized in the propaganda of reactionary opponents of public education, all alike are to be regarded as "enemies" of the public schools.

Implicit in this kind of statement is the idea that no person can have an informed opinion on school matters save one who has been trained in pedagogy. A lifetime of teaching apparently cannot make a scholar or scientist anything but a meddlesome amateur when public educational policy is up for discussion. Such notions tend to inspire among the lesser lights of the educationist world an arrogance such as one meets in no other profession and which occasionally erupts in an attempt even to suppress freedom of discussion on public educational questions.[13]

This hushing up of criticism is an attitude that belongs, not to a company of independent scholars, but to a bureaucracy, a party, a body united in defense of a vested interest. Professors of education are too deeply involved in the current public school situation to be reliable and fearless critics of it. They have aided the educational administrators in freeing the schools from their rightful responsibility to science and scholarship. In return, the educational bureaucracy has aided the professors of education in gaining within the universities a position of power which has enabled them to defy the academic standards of other departments of the institution. The structure of power within the educationist profession has much more to do with the present state of the public schools and the teaching profession in America than citizens are apt to realize.

The existence of what amounts to an interlocking directorate involving professors of education and school administrators is most clearly revealed in the policies governing the training of teachers. State educational officials exert control over such programs by the requirements they lay down for the certification of teachers, and these universally include substantial course work

111

in pedagogy.[14] Public school superintendents and principals re-
inforce this emphasis by the criteria they use in employing and
promoting teachers. The beneficiaries are the professors of education, who are thus assured of a steady flow of students through
their courses. This elaborate and rigorous prescription of pedagogical courses is rather curiously at variance with the principles
which educationists profess in other matters. They wish as little
as possible of the secondary school curriculum to be prescribed
by outside authorities, and they vehemently assert that the colleges need not and should not insist upon any particular set of
courses as a prerequisite for admission.[15] But educationists are
quite ready to invoke the coercive power of the state to compel
every prospective teacher to take a specified number of courses
in pedagogy.

Another inconsistency is involved. If an historian asserts that
a knowledge of history can contribute to intelligent citizenship,
the educationist is apt to condemn him for believing in "transfer
of training" and to insist that history must prove its right to a
place in the curriculum by incontrovertible experimental evidence that its study does produce better citizens. But the educationist demands a state-imposed requirement in pedagogy without presenting any experimental evidence whatsoever that such
course work produces better teachers. A professor of education
informs me that nowhere in the literature of the "science" of education "can be found a single study, or controlled experiment, that
establishes that a person is any better teacher by virtue of professional courses in Education. Surely this is a primary question
into which their research organizations ought to inquire, and the
worth of courses in Education could be established easily by the
use of control and experimental groups equated as to initial
ability, if there is any worth there. Is it not a little curious that
such elemental research has been avoided by them?" I have called
the statement to the attention of a number of educationists, and
none has been able to point out to me a single study that would
invalidate the generalization.[16]

Justifiable or not, the state-enforced requirement in pedagogy
is the taproot of the great educationist upas tree. The one inescapable prerequisite to a career in public school teaching and
administration is course work in a department of education. Con-

sequently this is the one department in which every student must enroll who wishes to teach or to be eligible to teach. The typical department of education knows very well how to extort every possible advantage from this strategic position. In most institutions it has managed to seize effective control over the placement of teachers. It frequently undertakes to plan all teachers' programs for them, regardless of their academic interests. It institutes programs of its own leading to a major or even a separate degree in education. It encourages its students to pile up course work in pedagogy far beyond the legal minimum. It frequently creates among its students the impression that they will be suitably rewarded for strict adherence in class to the educationist party line, and that too-vocal dissent will hurt their chances of future employment.

Protected behind state requirements which no department but itself can satisfy, the department is able to defy, or even to wage aggressive warfare against, the academic standards of the university. It exerts almost continuous pressure to break down admissions requirements, particularly those that might affect the work of the high schools. It frequently works to eliminate general graduation requirements that specify work in foreign languages and mathematics. The department of education typically refuses to look upon the university as a community of scholars working to a common end, and attempts to arrogate to itself control over all course offerings relating to educational problems. It sets up courses of its own in the teaching of the various school subjects, and gradually withdraws all future teachers from courses of this kind offered by the subject-matter departments. It generally refuses to entrust the teaching of educational psychology to independent departments of psychology, or the philosophy of education to departments of philosophy. In its relationship with the university of which it is a part, the typical department of education shows no real interest in interdisciplinary co-operation and no sense of academic partnership. Instead its faculty manifest a desire to insulate the schools and their teachers from every possible contact with recognized academic disciplines.

The abuse is even more appalling at the graduate level. The argument that pedagogical courses are necessary to prepare a novice for an unfamiliar vocation no longer has the slightest relevance, for graduate students in education are, as a rule, teachers with considerable experience. But administrators and teachers have been so thoroughly indoctrinated with the view that course work in pedagogy is the one thing of supreme importance, that experienced teachers return year after year, or summer session after summer session, to thresh old straw in departments of education, completely overlooking the glaring inadequacies of their training in the disciplines they profess to teach. Such inadequacies are unavoidable in a beginning teacher, for he cannot well know in advance what courses he may be assigned to handle outside the field of his major interest. If teacher certification requirements were designed for the benefit of the schools, however, instead of the benefit of professors of education, they would be phrased in such a way as to compel a teacher to bring his training in every subject he teaches up to a respectable minimum before embarking on additional courses in mere pedagogy.

Certification standards and the various other requirements imposed upon teachers have far more to do with the power politics of the educational bureaucracy than with the welfare of the schools. The academic empires which can be built by such methods are observable in almost every large state university. The University of Illinois may serve as an example. The certification requirement of the state has been kept down to sixteen semester hours in education, yet the College of Education of the university offers no less than sixty-one distinct courses open to undergraduates, and it comprises a faculty of one hundred and twenty-four members with the rank of instructor or above, including thirty-three full professors.[17] The inflation at the graduate level is even more preposterous, for seventy-four courses *at the very highest graduate level* are listed. In the same institution the Department of Chemistry and Chemical Engineering has won recognition as one of the most distinguished in the country, but it carries on its complex and important work through only forty-two courses at the highest graduate level,[18] and with a faculty totalling forty-two, of whom nineteen are full professors.[19]

The enslavement of the classroom teacher, not his advancement to a position of professional independence, is the consequence of this system of teacher training. Any profession is degraded in proportion as its members fall under the domination, in professional matters, of the kind of administrator who thinks of them as mere employees. This is the situation in the public schools. As far back as 1895 a school superintendent, addressing the National Education Association, summed up the *Führerprinzip* that characterizes public school administration: "The whole law in a nutshell should be: Every teacher responsible to the superintendent alone; the superintendent, and he alone, responsible for the schools." [20] Such a conception of a well-run school can mean only one thing: Teachers are hired to do their jobs as their superiors tell them to. When curriculum revision is under way the teachers may be called in to work out the details, but it is not for them to question the general principles laid down by professors of education and by the public school directorate. Occasionally a professor of education on the defensive will assert that "every teacher, either as an individual or as a member of curriculum committees, is a curriculum maker." [21] This is sheer mythology, true only in the sense that the laborer who spikes down the track is a railroad builder.

Educational policy in institutions of higher learning is formulated according to theories of academic responsibility utterly at variance with those of the public schools. Even the practice, despite certain encroachments by college administrators, is markedly different. In colleges and universities administrative officers derive direct authority from the board of trustees only in supposedly non-academic spheres. In matters of educational policy they are theoretically responsible to the faculty. This is true in actual practice, as well as in theory, so far as course offerings are concerned, for departments and colleges are rarely subject to administrative pressure in these matters. Faculty committees, on paper at least, determine the policy of the university with respect to larger questions like admissions and requirements for degrees. It would be unrealistic to deny that administrators exercise considerable influence in these matters, but even so, no president or dean in a college of reputable standing could hope to succeed in imposing new and far-reaching academic policies upon his institution without the consultation and approval of his faculty.

In opposing the encroachments of administrative authority upon the field of educational policy, the faculty of a college or

university derives its strength from many sources. College administrators are drawn ordinarily from the ranks of the faculty.
Heads of departments are always regular faculty members, still
active in teaching and research, and in most instances their tour
of duty as an administrative functionary is for a limited time only.
Deans likewise are customarily appointed from among regular
members of the faculty, and frequently continue to carry a partial
teaching load. In the top levels of the academic hierarchy, it is
true, there are many administrators whose previous participation
in the intellectual life of a university has been exceedingly limited. There is likewise an alarming tendency for college administration to be viewed in certain quarters as a career in itself, distinct from college teaching and scholarly research. But at their
very worst, these deleterious tendencies are not likely to produce
in the near future a self-conscious caste of professional administrators comparable to those who domineer over the public
schools.

College faculties derive strength also from the active participation of individual professors in the learned societies pertaining
to their respective fields. A scholar's true standing in his profession depends far more upon the judgment of his colleagues in
the same discipline, as represented in such associations, than upon
the recognition he may gain, deservedly or undeservedly, from a
local college administrator. Consequently the existence of strong
ties among scholars through their learned societies is an important bulwark against the lowering of college standards through
administrative influence and encroachment. In the affairs of the
learned societies themselves, it should be noted, university administrators as such play a completely negligible role.

Finally, the support which the faculty of one university can
secure from outside in a legitimate battle over educational policy
is a genuine source of strength. In part this results from an *esprit
de corps* and a public opinion which recognize that the standing of the university itself is jeopardized if the faculty fails to
maintain its authority over educational policy. To support their
position, scholars and scientists as a group have their own organization devoted to the protection of academic standards, the
American Association of University Professors. One of its functions is to investigate, and if necessary censure, the administra-

tive officers and the governing board of an institution which fails to observe "the generally recognized principles of academic freedom and tenure." Furthermore, unlike the organizations in the field of secondary education, the Association relegates to associate membership any active member "whose work becomes primarily administrative." [22]

The professional independence and responsibility of the scholar or scientist on a university faculty are the greatest of all guarantees of the integrity and standards of higher education. The lack of such professional independence and responsibility among high school teachers has done as much as anything else to lay our schools open to the virulent anti-intellectualism which we find in them today. Much of the blame rests upon the interlocking directorate of professional educationists, for they have done little to encourage and much to prevent the development of such intellectual independence among public school teachers.

The greatest source of independence to any teacher, whether in school or college, is his sense of being a full-fledged member of a recognized profession that includes all those working in his field, the most eminent as well as the most obscure, and of belonging to an organization which is run by the active members of the profession, not by those who may happen to be their employers. No educational association or teachers' organization of the usual sort meets these vital tests. In the meetings of societies like these, the high school teacher does not associate with the college professor in the same field, though both, after all, are teachers of one discipline. In other words, he does not make the acquaintance of those who are dealing with the same problems on a different level and in a different context. He gains none of the intellectual stimulus and none of the sense of belonging to a mature profession which would come to him through participation in the work of a genuine learned society. Instead he finds himself, in a teachers' association, classified merely as a member of an occupational group facing common vocational problems, not as a member of a profession united by common intellectual interests. He discovers, finally, that his administrative superiors, far from being relegated to a back seat, are parading their authority as on every other day of the year.

The natural allies of a serious and competent teacher in the high school are his colleagues in the same discipline on university and college faculties. The educational directorate has worked with vast ingenuity and almost complete success to prevent such an alliance from coming into being. A chemist or an historian, for example, who teaches in the public schools, is discouraged from thinking of himself in the terms I have just used. He must be careful to describe himself as a science teacher or a social studies teacher—better still, as a high school teacher, pure and simple—lest he be considered lukewarm in his devotion to "education." His administrative superiors give him to understand that his proper affiliation is with the National Education Association not the American Chemical Society or the American Historical Association. He is expected to improve his mind by devising new pedagogical procedures, not by performing experiments or investigating historical problems. If he is found too often in the company of professional chemists or historians, or if he seeks publication in the pages of scientific or historical journals, he is liable to the charge of being that pedagogical pariah, a "subject-matter specialist."

So completely has the field of education, so called, abandoned the ideals and standards of recognized scholarship, that extremists among professional educationists view an interest in intellectual, scientific, or scholarly matters as a positive liability in a public school teacher. Illuminating is the recent experience of a graduate student in English at a middle western state university. Having met all the requirements for teacher certification, she consulted the professor of education in charge of teacher placement about the possibilities of a teaching position in the public schools of the state. Here is her report of the interview:

When he saw my scholastic record, he told me that I probably would not be a satisfactory teacher, because my grade average in English was too high. When I questioned this, he told me that prospective teachers of English who had straight-A averages or A-averages were very apt to become scholars rather than good teachers, concerned only with academic research. Although I told him that I wanted very much to be a teacher and had met all requirements, he informed me that I probably would be unhappy and unsuccessful in the teaching profession. He stressed over-enthusiasm for subject matter, saying that good students seldom have the ability to understand people, because they prefer to bury themselves in their books and become introverts. Emphasis on subject matter and knowledge of it, he implied, were out-dated, because "we don't teach subject matter, we teach children." He advised me to get a master's degree in Education to remedy this shortcoming. He also stressed "democracy in the classroom," saying that because I had an extremely good record in my English courses, I was apt to be impatient and undemocratic with slow learners.[23]

The function of a master's degree in education—to destroy intellectual interest and to expunge knowledge—has never been so clearly and frankly put.

Low salaries are a handicap in attracting the ablest students into public school teaching, of course. But the scandalous fact is that many professional educationists seem not to want able, thoughtful, well-trained teachers. They apparently prefer docile ones, devoid of intellectual curiosity and independence, perhaps because these alone can be counted upon to give fanatical loyalty to the party-line that professors of education lay down. A teacher with intellectual interests is an ever-present menace to a curriculum that enthrones anti-intellectualism.

In the past, fortunately, the stranglehold of the educational directorate upon the training of teachers has been less complete than it is now becoming. Thousands of exceedingly competent teachers, well-trained in the various branches of learning, and alive to the values that underlie sound education, have found their way into the public schools. Hundreds of superintendents and principals and professors of education are honored and respected in their communities because they uphold and exemplify the ancient ideals of accurate learning and disciplined intelligence. These teachers and administrators are the ones who, according to the complaint of the new professional educationists, are "enthusiastic about the subjects they teach." They are the ones who second the embarrassing demand of the public that the schools "continue doing the things they do well." [24] They are the ones who have preserved American public schools from utter devastation at the hands of rampaging educational theorists and power-hungry educational politicians.

We need more and more such teachers. We are going to get fewer and fewer, as the educational directorate tightens its system of control. Much of the work offered in departments of education has already become so stultifying that able students do not willingly submit themselves to it. Even the then dean of one prominent College of Education has publicly conceded that "there is little value in most present courses and texts in education." [25] College students are well aware of this fact. Good students, it is true, are dragooned into pedagogical courses by the operation of teacher certification laws. But among those who actually enroll as majors in education the level of ability is appallingly low. Of 97,800 college freshmen who took the draft-deferment tests recently, 53 per cent secured a passing grade. Taken by fields, 68 per cent of those in engineering passed the tests, 64 per cent of those in physical science and mathematics, 59 per cent of those in biological science, and 57 per cent of those in the social sciences—all above the average. Freshmen in the humanities fell just below the average, 52 per cent of them passing. But among students majoring in education only 27 per cent passed, the poorest showing of any category of students. This far-below-average standing characterized upperclass students in education as well as freshmen.[26] Every professor is aware of students who, after struggling unsuccessfully with academic subjects, have re-enrolled as candidates for degrees in education. These statistics show that such happenings are not isolated events but symptoms of a trend.

On every hand there is evidence of the debasement which the teaching profession is undergoing at the hands of the interlocking directorate of professional educationists. Forced to undergo the humiliation of piling up credits in sterile courses in pedagogy, virtually forbidden to align himself with scholars and scientists in his chosen field, ceaselessly indoctrinated in an "official" educational philosophy, subjected to minute control and supervision by a professional educational hierarchy, the public school teacher cannot hope to resist administrative dictation or to secure a real voice in the formulation of educational policy. Though large numbers of able teachers oppose the anti-intellectual trend in education that is so obvious today, they are powerless to do anything about it. The educational directorate has seen to that. It does the hiring and firing, and it knows how to check thereby the expression of critical opinions.[27] The organs by which teachers might bring their views to public attention—the educational associations and the journals—are under the throttling control of the direc-torate. The public has been led to believe that the educational philosophy now guiding the public schools is a philosophy to which the teachers and the scholars of the nation willingly sub-scribe. Actually, however, the voice which the citizen hears in favor of programs like "life-adjustment" education is the voice neither of the classroom teacher nor of the scholar. It is the voice of the professor of education or one of his allies in the public school directorate.

Across the educational world today stretches an iron curtain which the professional educationists are busily fashioning. Be-hind it, in slave-labor camps, are the classroom teachers, whose only hope of rescue is from without. On the hither side lies the free world of science and learning, menaced but not yet con-quered. A division into two educational worlds is the great danger that faces us today. American intellectual life is threatened be-cause the first twelve years of formal schooling in the United States are falling more and more completely under the policy-making control of a new breed of educator who has no real place in—who does not respect and who is not respected by—the world of scientists, scholars, and professional men.

# 8

## First Steps in Educational Reform

Unity of purpose is necessary for the success of any great undertaking. It is peculiarly essential for the success of a great national undertaking like American public education. Literally hundreds of thousands of different institutions—from kindergartens to graduate schools—are involved in the enterprise. Somehow their work must fit together into a reasonable pattern if the intellectual training of any given student is to be continuous and cumulative from the beginning of his schooling to the end.

In simplest terms this means that there must be some measure of common agreement among those concerned with education—that is to say, among college professors, school teachers, administrators, and citizens—with respect both to the main objectives of education and to the kinds of training by which these can be attained. Teachers at every level, from the most elementary to the most advanced, must feel themselves bound together in a common endeavor. Unless they make substantially the same assumptions there cannot be an educational *system* at all, but only a hodgepodge of schools. If teachers work at cross purposes to one another, they are bound to produce intellectual confusion instead of intellectual order. The world is deranged enough as it is, without allowing education, too, to become subject to the reign of Chaos and old Night.

By and large, unity of purpose did characterize the less complex and less extensive educational systems of earlier times. School teachers and professional scholars believed in and were guided by the same basic conceptions of education. The public —at least such persons as concerned themselves with the matter—understood and supported the objectives set forth unitedly by the learned world and the teaching profession. Needless to say, there were plentiful differences of opinion, of method, and of emphasis, but these differences were stimulating and healthful because subordinated to a common aim.

Within the lifetime of the present adult generation this fundamental unity of educational purpose has been shattered. Elementary and secondary education have parted company with higher education and research. The resulting situation is dangerous in the extreme. Elementary and secondary schools are only part of our educational system. What goes on in them, however, affects every aspect of the intellectual life of the nation—its scientific and technological progress, the professional skills that serve and protect it, the cultural activities that give dignity and meaning to its existence. All these rest upon foundations that must be laid in the public schools. The aims of secondary education can be properly and safely defined only if all aspects of the life of the nation are taken into account. The yawning gap that exists today between those who are actually using intellectual training—in the sciences and professions, in business and public life— and those who are supposed to be laying its foundations in the public schools is, in my judgment, the fundamental cause of the unsatisfactory state of American public education today.

Scholars and scientists must bear much of the blame for permitting this situation to develop. They should have exercised constant vigilance over developments in secondary education. They should have brought their views on public school policy forcefully to the attention of the public and the legislatures. They should have resisted the debasement of college entrance requirements and the seizure by departments of education of control over the training of teachers. They should have provided, through their learned societies, continuous, organized leadership in the process of developing and strengthening the secondary school curriculum. The people expect intellectual guidance from the scientific and scholarly world in matters pertaining to education at every level. It has not been furnished in the recent past. It must be furnished in the future.

The first step, as I see it, must be for the learned world to create an agency entirely its own, through which it can state its views on public school policy independently and unitedly. It must be ready at all times to express a considered judgment concerning the intellectual soundness of the programs that are offered in the elementary and secondary schools. It must address the public directly, for they make the final decisions on educational policy. And it must speak with a voice unmistakably its own, not allowing its words to be smothered or twisted or censored by others. If scholars will create for themselves an organ through which they can expound their educational principles with clarity and force, I am confident that they will be listened to with respect.

The basis for such unity indubitably exists. Within the learned world there are differences of opinion, of course, but they are minor differences. Mathematicians and anthropologists may approach their problems in quite different ways; biologists and linguists may not completely understand each other's objectives; historians and sociologists may quarrel over questions of methodology. There will always be—there *must* always be—such differences, for they are the signs of intellectual vigor and of freedom. But scholars and scientists must never lose sight of the overarching fact that they are partners in a single great enterprise—the greatest that engages the attention of mankind. They share a common purpose: the advancement of understanding and the augmentation of that intellectual power upon which mankind depends for its very existence. They share a common respect for knowledge, for the disciplined mind, for independent, objective, disinterested inquiry. Each of them, whatever his specialized interest, must recognize at all times that these common aims and values are far more significant than any points of difference. Each must remember that it is these common aims and values which anti-intellectualism is seeking to undermine. Should it triumph, no field of science or learning will be exempt from disaster.

This sense of common purpose must be embodied in an organization capable of effective action. It is idle to think that scholars and scientists, divided a hundred ways by professional ties within their specialized fields, can exert a real influence upon public educational policy until they present a united front on the matter. They have learned to do so in meeting other problems that confront them. They look to a single great organization, the American Association of University Professors, to safeguard the standards of the profession. They bring the collective wisdom of the learned world to bear upon the broad problems of research through the great federations of learned societies: the National Research Council, the American Council of Learned Societies, and the Social Science Research Council. Such agencies take account of the fact that scholars and scientists can spare little time from their own exacting tasks to undertake responsibilities of a general nature. These societies and councils are organized to function continuously with a permanent staff, and they require of each individual professional man only a limited amount and period of service on working committees. An organization of this kind, I believe, should be created to represent scholarly opinion on public school questions. In the appendix to this volume I reprint the text of a proposal which I have made for a Permanent Scientific and Scholarly Commission on Secondary Education to perform this function.

The commission should be established by the learned societies of the nation, and by them alone. The reason for keeping the commission independent of all political and economic pressure groups, and hence of all nonprofessional associations, is obvious. The exclusion of educational associations is more controversial. This exclusion, while deliberate, is not intended as a gesture of hostility. It is merely a recognition of two facts: that the professional educationists are already thoroughly organized and vocal, and that scholars clearly differ with them on many vital issues of public educational policy. I propose a separate organization of scholars and scientists, not as a repudiation of the ultimate ideal of co-operation between educationists and the learned world in public school matters, but as a means to that end. No true co-operation is likely to take place between two groups, one of which is well organized and the other not. If there is to be genuine agreement, each side must feel that its point of view has been clearly stated and consistently maintained throughout all discussions and negotiations. The professional educationists already have associations to present and defend their position. If scholars are to exert influence in favor of the things they believe in, they must be responsibly represented by men in whose judgment they have full confidence and they must back these men up in an organized way. Then a real meeting of minds with respect to public education can take place, with assurance that the decisions will be concurred in and supported on all sides. Collaboration, to be effective, must rest upon some such firm foundation as this.

An agency of the kind proposed must make clear to the public the reasons why scholarly and scientific opinion ought to be taken into account in the making of public school policy. Educationists have so persistently emphasized the problems of childhood when defining the function of education that they have caused the public almost to forget that the schools have an obligation not merely to the children actually enrolled in them, but to the nation as a whole and to all its mature citizens. Scholars must emphasize the latter obligation, and must point out the unsoundness of public school policies that jeopardize the rest of the nation's educational, intellectual, and scientific activities.

Once the importance of scholarly and scientific participation in curriculum-planning is made clear, the proposed commission must labor to make such participation a reality. During the past thirty or forty years, scientific and scholarly opinion has not been adequately represented on the bodies that have controlled public school policy—that is to say, on local, state, and federal departments or boards of education, on publicly and privately sponsored advisory commissions, on the committees that have studied the curriculum and made recommendations concerning it, and on school surveys of various kinds. If scholars have been invited to take part at all, they have been given the role of "consultants" or have constituted a mere minority group, as in the various curriculum and "steering" committees analyzed in the preceding chapter. Educationists have insisted that every branch of their

profession be represented—professors of education, school superintendents and principals, state and federal educational officials,
classroom teachers, and specialists in such fields as guidance.
They have then asked representatives of the learned world to sit
with them, assigning to such representatives a role no greater
than that granted to any one of the four or five sub-groups of
educationists. This lopsided representation makes a mockery of
all pretensions to co-operation.

On matters affecting the curriculum and the general purposes
of education there are basically three different points of view
that must be taken into account if public school policy is to be
soundly planned. The educationists have one point of view, the
learned world another, and the public at large a third. The first
group, comprising classroom teachers, administrators, and professors of education, are particularly concerned with the problems of giving instruction at the elementary and secondary level;
they are best equipped to judge the pedagogical feasibility of a
proposed program. The second group, actively engaged in studying, advancing, and applying the fundamental intellectual disciplines, are best equipped to judge the scholarly and scientific
soundness of the curriculum. The third group, comprising not
merely parents, but also men and women in business, government, and the professions, have direct knowledge of the practical
intellectual needs of modern life. They are the group best
equipped to reconcile the divergent points of view of the other
two groups, and to insist upon a program carefully balanced and
in the national interest.

These three groups ought to be represented, and equally represented, in all the agencies concerned with broad public educational policy, especially policy with respect to the content of the
school curriculum. To give a specific example, a commission of
fifteen members, appointed, let us assume, to study curricular
problems ought to be composed somewhat as follows: (1) five
educationists, say a professor of education, a school superintendent, a state educational official, and classroom teachers of two
different subjects; (2) five representatives of the learned world,
say a mathematician, an historian, a scientist, a professor of
English, and a university specialist in one of the foreign languages; (3) five representatives of the general public, say a busi-

nessman, a housewife and mother, an engineer, a newspaper editor, and a government career man. Where bureaus, departments, boards, and committees cannot actually include in their personnel such balanced representation as this, they ought to be furnished with expert advisory committees so constituted. The proposed Scientific and Scholarly Commission might well take the lead by urging Congress to set up such a balanced advisory board to oversee the work of the federal Office of Education.

Once the point of view of the learned world on public educational policy is made clear to citizens at large, I am confident that they will give it general and effective support. The time will then have to come to effect a general revision of state legislation and state administrative procedures with respect to public school matters.

One of the first tasks is to rectify the omission from many school codes of any clear statement concerning the basic content of the public school curriculum. Most school laws were drafted at a time when it was taken for granted that the fundamental intellectual disciplines would be the central core of all school instruction. It seemed unnecessary to enact the obvious, hence the clauses of the law pertaining to the curriculum were usually brief and general. One amendment after another, often pushed through by an organized pressure group, has required the schools to teach many absurdly specific things, while their central functions have remained vaguely defined. As a consequence, educationists have been able to subordinate the essentials of the curriculum to trivialities without actually violating the letter of the law.

In the School Code of Illinois, for example, article 27 deals with "Courses of Study." With its amendments (through 1947) it consists of twenty-four sections. The last twenty-three of these constitute a mosaic of special courses and requirements that the legislature has from time to time seen fit to prescribe. Only the first section of article 27 deals with the course of study as a whole, and this in the most general terms:

*Branches of education to be taught.* Every school established under this Act shall be for instruction in the branches of education prescribed in the qualifications for teachers and in such other branches, including vocal music and drawing, as the school board or the votes of the district at the annual election of school board members may prescribe.[1]

The legislature obviously cannot, and should not, work out in detail the course of study of the public schools. But it does have the responsibility of setting forth in the name of the people the aims and the general character of the schools which the people have established and are supporting. As in other matters, it ought to state clearly the guiding principles that are to be followed by the administrative authorities charged with working out the course of study in detail.

At a public hearing on March 6, 1952, I suggested to the Commission to Study School Problems of the State of Illinois that it draft, and recommend to the Legislature, a revised form of article 27, section 1, prescribing that

Every school established under this Act shall provide instruction, at the appropriate levels, in reading, writing, spelling, grammar, and English composition; in arithmetic, algebra, geometry, trigonometry, and such higher branches of mathematics as shall be feasible; in English and American literature, classical and modern; in at least two foreign languages (with at least two years of work to be offered in each); in the natural sciences of physics, chemistry, and biology; in the history of the United States, of Europe from antiquity to the present, and of the modern world; in the principles of representative, constitutional government; in the fine arts, including music; in physical education and training; in manual training or agriculture; and in such other branches as the school board or the voters of the district at the annual election of school board members may prescribe; provided that such additional subjects shall not be introduced unless the instruction in the branches prescribed in this section shall be deemed adequate; and provided, further, that such additional subjects shall not replace those prescribed in this section.[2]

Such a clear-cut mandate would be difficult to evade, and something equivalent to it should form part of the school law of every state. The legislature would doubtless need to grant authority to smaller schools to omit temporarily certain of these branches, but it should strictly prohibit any new curricular ventures on their part until the fundamental subjects are first restored. And if a school wished to experiment with "integrated" courses or "core curricula," the burden of proof should be upon the school authorities to demonstrate that these courses were in fact providing (as in theory they are alleged to provide) instruction equivalent to that afforded by courses in the separate subjects.

Citizens must also join with scholars in urging state legislatures to review carefully and realistically the statutory requirements governing teacher training and certification. Many of these requirements were embodied in law at the behest of professional educationists, and it is to be expected that the powerful educational lobby will bitterly oppose any alteration in them. Nevertheless, a thoroughly informed citizenry should be able to force the repeal of special interest legislation and to secure the enactment of requirements that will protect the schools against incompetent teachers rather than the professors of pedagogy against losses in enrollment.

The matter is a complicated one, and a somewhat extended discussion is necessary to indicate the reforms that are called for.

The kind of preparation which a teacher must have is determined by the combined effect of requirements laid down in various ways and by various agencies. Above all, a teacher must possess a certificate from the state in which he or she intends to teach, and accordingly must satisfy requirements that are partly fixed by statute and partly spelled out by a board, commission, or designated officer. Many of these requirements are specific and mandatory, hence they cannot possibly be ignored in planning any program for the training of teachers. In addition, the schools themselves are under the constant scrutiny of regional accrediting agencies, which examine, among other things, the qualifications of the teachers employed. The power to withhold accreditation or recognition is a very real one, for the standing of a school and even its legal position is affected. Consequently the criteria used by regional accrediting agencies exercise an influence upon teacher training almost as direct and positive as though they were embodied in law. Since a bachelor's degree, at least, is ordinarily expected, the graduation requirements of universities, colleges, and normal schools also play a part in determining the things a future teacher studies. Finally, teachers are actually selected for given positions by local school authorities, whose views on the proper preparation of teachers thus have a cumulative, if rather indirect, influence upon the programs of study which teachers pursue.

On paper this appears to be a harmonious system of shared responsibility, which ought to result in well-balanced programs for the training of prospective teachers. In point of fact it is not. It is a system that results in distorted emphases of the most extreme sort. In particular it is a system that grossly exaggerates the importance of listening to classroom lectures in pedagogy, and that gives totally inadequate attention to the teacher's knowledge of the subject he professes to teach. This, of course, represents the false emphasis of the educationists, which has been discussed in preceding chapters. The point here is that this false emphasis has been institutionalized. We need to change not only the attitude of mind but also the system that imposes and perpetuates it.

As a prospective teacher looks out over his future career, one hard, inescapable fact stares him in the face. He must acquire a certain number of hours in "education." State certification requirements demand it. Regional accrediting agencies check up on the matter. Local school authorities cannot waive the requirement in his case (save, possibly, in a temporary emergency). In the university itself the department of education will constantly remind him of the fact that there is no way to get a teaching certificate except by entering the classroom of a professor of education, taking down what he says, and handing it back to him on an examination.

The question that is asked is not whether a man or woman is a good teacher, but whether he or she has course credits in pedagogy. Experience in teaching—gained, let us say, in a private school—will not satisfy the requirement. Though practice teaching may be one among the credits demanded, a certificate is never granted for brilliant performance in practice teaching alone. The credits earned in someone's course in pedagogy must be down on the record. A local school board may know a candidate well and be certain of his capabilities as a teacher, but its hands are tied. A bureaucrat in the state capital must shuffle the papers and certify that the prescribed education courses have been taken. No one is permitted to demonstrate a knack for teaching and thus slip through the pedagogical dragnet. Pestalozzi himself, after a lifetime of teaching, could not be regularly and permanently employed by the school board of the smallest hamlet in the nation, because, forsooth, the official standards would prove him ignorant of and incompetent in pedagogy.

The state zealously enforces the requirement in pedagogy. Does it show equal zeal in seeing to it that the teacher knows something about the subject he is actually assigned to teach? It does not. Requirements in pedagogy are explicit and mandatory for a teaching certificate in every one of the forty-eight states. On the other hand, the certification requirements of several states say nothing whatever about qualifications in subject matter—the euphemism to describe this situation is that such states have "general certification" rather than "subject certification." Other states specify teaching majors and minors in various subjects, but they permit the holder of a certificate to teach any course to which he is assigned, whether or not it is one of the subjects endorsed on his credentials. Various indirect controls may be exerted in the matter by certain states, but to the best of my knowledge no state forthrightly prohibits the local school authorities from assigning a teacher to a course in a subject which he has never studied.[3] I am not advocating such drastic regulations; a great deal has to be left to discretion. One must point out, however, that state authorities do prohibit outright the employment of a teacher without course work in pedagogy. They allow wide discretion in one matter and none whatever in the other. Can there be any doubt as to which is thereby made the more important?

In point of fact, the present arrangement is completely topsy-turvy. Authority is divided according to principles that are the precise opposite of those which logic and common sense would suggest. Local school authorities, who can interview teachers individually as well as examine their credentials, are in a far better position to judge a candidate's personal pedagogical competence than a bureaucrat who works solely from records of courses taken. Conversely, an agency of the state is far better equipped than a local school board to determine a student's competence in his chosen subject, for it can compare his academic record with hundreds of others, it can administer standardized examinations, and it can call upon specialists in all the fields of knowledge for advice and assistance. Under the existing system, however, the responsibilities are completely reversed. The matters which local authorities are competent to determine for themselves are precisely the ones that the state educational bureaucracy insists on controlling from above; and the kinds of minimum requirements which the state is in the best position to enforce are precisely the ones that are left largely to local discretion.

The first step to reform in the matter is to clear the statute books of those provisions which specify a fixed number of hours in education (that is, in pedagogy) as a requirement for certification. This means simply dethroning those requirements from their privileged position and putting them on the same basis as requirements in subject matter. A careful study of the whole problem should next be made by a commission representing educationists, scholars, and citizens—in other words, by a commission constituted on the principles stated earlier in this chapter. Its recommendations should ultimately be enacted into law.

Such a commission, I believe, would find it desirable to deal separately with the different elements in a teacher's professional preparation. Some guiding principles should be laid down concerning the general, liberal education of the teacher, but these I shall pass over as belonging essentially to the discussion in a later chapter. Our present question is how to fix requirements which will give assurance that a certified teacher is both proficient in teaching and well prepared in the subjects he or she is to teach.

Different certificates should deal with these different matters. One would testify to the individual's proficiency in teaching. There ought to be several ways of earning this certificate. An experienced teacher ought to be granted it simply upon presentation of satisfactory evidence of a successful teaching career of a specified length of time. For a candidate without previous experience, successful completion of a period of practice teaching would be the principal requirement. The institution that supervises practice teaching usually specifies certain pedagogical courses as prerequisites, hence the state has no need to lay down pedagogical course requirements of its own in granting certificates of teaching proficiency. Provision should be made for students without either experience or practice teaching to obtain temporary certificates enabling them to offer instruction in specially designated schools, which would guarantee to give on-the-job training and special guidance and supervision to those without experience. Such programs might well be financed by the state, to aid in the recruitment of teachers, or they might be conducted by the extension departments of universities. After completing a specified period of teaching under such conditions, an instructor should be entitled to a permanent certificate of teaching proficiency. An arrangement of this kind would enable the schools to draw upon a large and brilliant group of liberal arts graduates who are at present excluded from public school employment by unjustifiably arbitrary pedagogical requirements. Once the basic certificate in teaching proficiency has been earned, further course work in pedagogy should be entirely optional with the individual teacher.

Another certificate would cover each of the fundamental subjects of public school instruction. Ideally these certificates should be granted on the basis of state-administered comprehensive examinations in the various subjects, periodically offered to all persons who believe themselves qualified. There should be at least two levels of such examinations, one leading to limited, the second to advanced certification in the subject or discipline. Pending the development of such examinations, limited certification might be granted on the basis of fifteen or twenty semester hours of college work in the subject, advanced certification for thirty or forty hours. The certification should be in specific subjects rather than general areas. In other words there should be certificates in history, in political science, and in economics; a teacher of social studies would be expected to possess at least limited certification in two or three of these subjects.

A prospective teacher would be encouraged to meet certification requirements in as many subjects as possible during his undergraduate years. The teacher already in service who returned to the university for advanced work during summer sessions and regular terms would have a definite purpose in view: to bring his certification in the subjects he had been teaching from the limited to the advanced classification, or to secure certification in additional subjects. The recognition or accrediting standards applied to schools themselves could easily be geared to this system of certification. The ideal school would be one in which every course was being conducted by a teacher possessing advanced certification in the subject or subjects covered by the course. Every deviation from this would lessen the standing of the school.

Salary increments could likewise be effectively tied to this scheme. The term "professional growth" frequently appears among the criteria for the promotion and the advancement in salary of teachers. At present this is a vague phrase. It could easily be endowed with a definite meaning. Under the proposed system, a teacher would be giving tangible evidence of professional growth every time he raised his certification from limited to advanced in a given subject, and every time he acquired a limited certificate in a new field. Each such step might well entitle him to an increment in salary. Such a system would be far more effective in improving teaching than the present practice of granting such increments primarily for the acquisition of a university degree. A master's degree or a doctorate may or may not be relevant to the work the teacher is actually doing. The present artificial emphasis on a degree, irrespective of what it represents, serves no useful purpose, and is already converting the M.A. from a genuine graduate degree into a mere diploma testifying to the completion of one additional year of college busy-work.

Besides the certificate of teaching proficiency and the certificates in the various subjects, provision would have to be made for various types of special certificates. Elementary school teaching, for example, presents special problems. A certificate in Educational Psychology for Elementary School Teachers, in addition to the general certificate in teaching proficiency, might well be established. Care should be taken to make its requirements clear and specific. This certificate should not be granted for a mere potpourri of pedagogical courses, but only for a carefully designed program comprising extensive work in the regular academic department of psychology. Another certificate in Educational Administration should also be offered, to be obtained by specified work primarily in the departments of political science (or public administration), economics, and law, with only such work in the department of pedagogy as seemed clearly justifiable. The other special certificates—and several will doubtless be needed—should be set up on analogous principles.

A reorganization of teacher training and certification requirements along the lines here outlined would correct some of the gravest abuses in the present situation. It would bring to an end the aimless accumulation by experienced teachers of credits in pedagogical courses. It would restore to teacher training a realism and a clear sense of purpose that it has lost. It would, in fact, make teacher training "functional" once more. And it would end the preposterous overemphasis upon pedagogy that produces teachers who can talk glibly about how to teach, but who know too little about any given subject to teach it satisfactorily.

# 9

# Reorganization of Teacher Training

The training of teachers for the public schools is one of the most important functions of the American university. It ought always to be treated as a function of the university as a whole. In actuality it has not been so treated, thanks largely to the state requirements which the preceding chapter has discussed. With the repeal of the unwise legislation which has given to departments of education or pedagogy their stranglehold upon teacher training, the university must assume, in good faith and with a ready will, its full responsibility in the matter.

This will require a change of heart by many departments and faculty members. Their past attitude, in fact, helped to create the present iniquitous system. Most faculties of liberal arts and sciences failed to take seriously the problem of devising sound and appropriate curricula for the education of teachers, and thus left a vacuum into which the professional educationists moved. The latter set up programs and devoted time and effort to the task when others were too proud or too lazy to do so. Their programs will continue to prevail, and will diverge farther and farther from the ideals of scientists and scholars, until the latter demonstrate a real intention of committing themselves wholeheartedly to preparing teachers properly and adequately for public school instruction.

At the undergraduate level the education of the future teacher should be an education in the liberal arts and sciences. This ought to be self-evident. The ideal of liberal education is to produce men and women with disciplined minds, cultivated interests, and a wide range of fundamental knowledge. Who in our society needs these qualities more than the teacher? We increasingly recognize that the doctor, the lawyer, and the engineer, if they are to achieve true professional eminence, must receive balanced training in many intellectual disciplines which are not directly related to their professions. How much more does a teacher need such an education! For him the fundamental intellectual disciplines are not supplements to, but the very essence of, his professional stock in trade. The teacher never knows when he may be called upon to give instruction in any or all of them. The students whose work he directs have a right to expect of him a genuine and sympathetic understanding of their various intellectual interests and ambitions. The last profession in which narrow vocational considerations should be allowed to interfere with thorough and well-balanced undergraduate preparation in the liberal arts and sciences is the teaching profession. Opportunity to satisfy minimum pedagogical requirements should be provided through electives that are a normal complement of a college program of liberal education, but under no circumstances should the department of pedagogy be permitted to exercise any sort of control over the undergraduate programs of prospective teachers.

Continued training in the fundamental intellectual disciplines is the recognized and proper purpose of graduate work. American universities have failed, and failed most miserably, to apply even rudimentary common sense to the problem of devising a sound and useful graduate program for public school teachers. We force the teacher to choose between a research program that is thorough and scholarly but too highly specialized for his needs, and a pedagogical program that is superficial and blatantly anti-intellectual and that solemnly and tediously re-instructs him in vocational skills he already possesses. The university ought not to compel the teacher to choose between such inacceptable alternatives. It should offer him a program that satisfies the highest academic standards and at the same time faces realistically the actual facts of secondary and elementary school teaching.

A little imagination should enable the university to devise a program that will be of a truly advanced scholarly character and that will possess genuine relevance to the intellectual tasks which a public school teacher is called upon to perform.

We must begin by considering the actual situation of the teacher. He is usually called upon to teach two or more distinct disciplines. Even in a single course he ought to be bringing to bear upon the subject in hand appropriate information from other fields. A wide range of accurate knowledge is his most useful asset, rather than an intensive knowledge of a limited but rapidly advancing segment of learning within which he may hope to make original contributions of his own. In simplest terms, the graduate work of a school teacher ought to be a prolongation and deepening of the liberal education which he received (or should have received) as an undergraduate. The university ought to provide him an opportunity to continue that liberal education for as long as he is willing to pursue it, and it ought to reward him with a suitable degree for conscientious and thoughtful work when rationally directed to that end.

Let me illustrate by a specific example. A student, let us assume, has received a four-year liberal education, in the course of which he has met the pedagogical requirements for teaching. He has majored, perhaps, in history, and has done a considerable amount of work in English. He has taken introductory courses in the sciences, economics, and political science, and has acquired a reading knowledge of one foreign language. According to the scheme of certification which I have proposed, he has earned a certificate in Teaching Proficiency and a limited certificate in history. A few more credits in history will entitle him to advanced certification in that field, and he is not far short of limited certificates in English and a foreign language. His first teaching assignment is to a course in the social studies, to a course in

English, and to one in algebra. He is to return for several summers to the university for advanced work. What should the university encourage him to do?

The university should permit him, first of all, to take courses that will round out his knowledge of the various fields of history and enable him to earn an advanced teaching certificate in history. For this purpose many undergraduate courses may be more appropriate than the graduate courses offered to research students. These he should be free to elect. When he has completed a sound program in history, he should be allowed to go back to the point at which he dropped mathematics in college, and to study that field systematically exactly as an undergraduate major in mathematics would do, ultimately bringing his command of the subject up to the point where he can obtain a limited or advanced certificate in mathematics. So it should be with each of the fields in which he has done previous work, in which he is required to teach, or in which, perhaps, he develops an interest for the first time.

The results of such study would be an exceptionally well-prepared teacher. More than that, the results would be a liberally educated man, with a far deeper and wider range of knowledge than a four-year undergraduate program could give him. Study directed in such a way and to such ends is advanced study, no matter what parts of it may have been pursued in nominally undergraduate courses. It is the kind of education which a university should be proud to offer, and which it has a legitimate right to reward with an advanced degree. A student who pursues such a well-thought-out program for a full academic year beyond college graduation and who brings his command of two subjects up to certain pre-established standards should receive a master's degree. A student who pursues it with distinction for three years beyond college graduation and who brings his command of five subjects up to the standards set should be entitled to a doctorate.

Much careful thought must go into the establishment of these standards in each subject. In order to receive a degree, a student should be required to demonstrate, in each proffered subject, a comprehension at least equal to that which an able undergraduate might be expected to obtain through a strong major program in the discipline. Course credits might aggregate about thirty semester hours, including undergraduate work. But the number of courses should not be the principal criterion. A comprehensive written examination in each of the subjects offered for the degree would be indispensable. In addition, an oral examination for the doctorate should cover all the five fields presented. A careful reading of certain basic works—the classics of the discipline—should be specifically required and tested. No thesis would be submitted for either degree, but a student should have been required to write at least one substantial original essay in each of his fields during the course of his studies, and these should be part of the record upon which his degree is awarded.

The new programs would obviously be interdepartmental ones. A candidate for the master's degree, for example, would be working in both history and English, or in both chemistry and mathematics. The doctoral program should probably be set up so that at least three of the fields would fall within the same general division; thus the student might be a candidate for the degree in the humanities, or the physical sciences, or the social sciences. Special programs in educational psychology for elementary school teachers and in educational administration could be set up, corresponding to the state certificates in those fields, and a student might well be allowed to enroll in one of them in place of one of the subject-fields offered for a higher degree. As a matter of academic principle, one of the five fields presented by a doctoral candidate ought always to be a foreign language.

The research program and the teaching program that I have just described should be considered parallel but distinct. Both should be under the administration of the graduate school of the university, but the degrees ought to be different. Corresponding to the traditional degrees of M.A. and Ph.D., which would continue to be awarded in the research program, the university might make use of the degrees of Master and Doctor of Education (M.Ed. and Ed.D.) for the teaching program. These degrees, of course, already exist. The present proposal, however, would put them under the jurisdiction of the university as a whole, not the department of education or pedagogy, and would permit a student to earn them by work in any regular department of liberal arts or science in the university. The degrees in education would be discontinued as mere awards for the completion of narrowly specialized vocational training in pedagogy.

Once faculties of liberal arts and sciences have conscientiously undertaken to offer sound graduate programs for teachers, the time will have come to open the valves and let some of the gas out of the over-inflated educational balloon. The university, in other words, should commence an orderly process of devolution with respect to many of the activities hitherto associated with departments and colleges of education. The university as a whole must reassert that fact that *it*, and not one department within it, is responsible for education. The department concerned with "the art, practice, or profession of teaching; especially, systematized learning or instruction concerning principles and methods of teaching" must be compelled to resume its appropriate title of Department of Pedagogy, the quoted words being, in fact, the dictionary definition of pedagogy.

To administer its re-established responsibilities in this wide realm, the university might well set up a distinct Faculty of Teacher Training, with its own committees and administrative officers. To this newly created faculty would belong all the members of all the departments offering work leading to the M.Ed. and Ed.D. In many universities a professor already belongs to two or more faculties—to the Faculty of Liberal Arts and the Graduate Faculty, for example—hence such an arrangement has ample precedent. Most of the administrative and public-relations functions of the old college or department of education would be transferred to the committees of the new Faculty of Teacher Training. These would not only approve curricula, but would also supervise teacher placement. Co-operation of the university in school surveys and in educational commissions of various sorts would be handled through the new faculty. The right to authorize the use of the label "Education" in the numbering of courses would be vested in it. Most of the old courses in education would be relabeled "Pedagogy," but a few would be permitted a second listing with an "Education" number. Courses in other departments besides pedagogy would also be allowed to use such a double listing. Thus the courses which could be used to satisfy state requirements in "Education" would be under the full control of the Faculty of Teacher Training.

In line with this reassertion of responsibility, the university as a whole, through the Faculty of Teacher Training, should assume direct authority over the curriculum in the demonstration and laboratory schools which it maintains. To the general public a university high school signifies an institution of secondary education devoted to the ideals of science and scholarship for which the university stands. It must be made precisely that. Its program should be determined by scholars, scientists, and educationists together, and it should concentrate its experimental work upon the problem of effectively teaching the basic intellectual disciplines, organized as they are in the real world of science and learning.

As part of the contemplated reorganization, university courses in the teaching of the various school subjects would be placed in the departments normally concerned, where the problems would be dealt with by men who know, in the first place, what the discipline is about.[1] Courses in the teaching of mathematics, for example, would be given by the department of mathematics, with the co-operation, but not under the auspices, of the department of pedagogy. Though courses in the teaching of history would be offered in the department of history, interdepartmental courses in the teaching of the social studies might be set up by the departments of history, political science, economics, and sociology.

Sound principles of academic responsibility are at present violated by many of the offerings in departments of education. These principles must be re-established in the course of the proposed reorganization. A university is a company of scholars, each aware of his limitations, each aware of the necessity for his students to tap resources of knowledge and specialized intellectual skill which his colleagues possess in greater measure than he. A physicist needs mathematics, and the department of physics sends its students to the department of mathematics to learn it at the hands of genuine mathematicians. The typical college of education, however, has tended to set up courses of its own to deal with the other disciplines that it considers important for teachers. It believes, quite rightly, that a teacher should have philosophic insight. But it does not call upon the specialist in philosophy. It sets up a course of its own in the philosophy of education, which, cut off as it is from philosophic thinking generally, produces not breadth but narrowness of mind. The educationist who teaches the course has a vocational ax to grind. His course is apt to become, not an open-minded and critical comparison of many different philosophical systems, but propaganda for a particular view. In one large university, for example, the course entitled "Philosophy of Education" and offered by the College of Education carries a description which begins: "Based on a careful and critical reading of selected chapters from John Dewey's *Democracy and Education.*" [2] Not since the days of the mediaeval schoolmen, with their veneration of Aristotle, has any responsible college faculty been so ready to find the sum of all truth in the pages of one book, written by one man, devoted to one highly controversial philosophic point of view. Surely it is one of the great ironies of history that John Dewey, the disbeliever in absolutes and the apostle of open-mindedness, should be the central figure in these strange rites—at once the worshipped deity and the sacrificial lamb.

This warping of the great intellectual disciplines to serve the narrow purposes of indoctrination and vocationalism characterizes other offerings of present-day departments of education. Teachers admittedly should know the historical forces which have shaped school systems, which have influenced the art of teaching, and which have determined the purposes of education itself. Historical forces are the particular subject of the historian's investigations. But the college of education does not look to the historian. It sets up a course of its own in the history of education. Torn from its context of general historical change, the history of school systems becomes a chronicle almost devoid of meaning. Worse than that, it may easily become the kind of distorted history which presents the past as a mournful catalogue of errors, redeemed by some few feeble gropings toward that perfection of wisdom which the present generation (and the instructor in particular) alone possess.

The process of reorganization which I am describing must bring these isolated fragments of the basic disciplines back into the departments where they belong. The philosophy of educa-

144

tion must be taught philosophically, the history of education historically. Educational psychology must no longer be severed from the discipline whose research techniques it employs. Courses in educational psychology belong in the department of psychology, because only thus can the university be sure that the conclusions taught are being subjected to continuous critical scrutiny by psychologists in all branches of the field. Courses in the administration of public education must be placed, along with other courses in public administration, in departments of political science, where they can be seen in the perspective of governmental responsibility generally, not from the narrow point of view of a single specialized bureaucracy.

I have described this as a process of devolution. Many of the functions of present-day departments of education will devolve upon already existing departments. The end result will be a small undergraduate department of pedagogy, offering a few courses in the general principles of pedagogy, supervising practice teaching, and perhaps offering an enlarged extension program of on-the-job training for inexperienced teachers. The graduate work for teachers will be centered in the new M.Ed. and Ed.D. program, offered through the regular departments of liberal arts and sciences.

What of advanced research in educational problems? This is a field of service which the university must not abandon or neglect. At the outset of the discussion, the reader should be reminded that there are many areas in which the university sponsors important research and original investigation, but in which it does not offer a special program of instruction leading to a degree. Such a situation exists with respect to most interdisciplinary research programs. Projects of this kind may offer training to a considerable number of advanced students, but the regular work of such students is in established departments, and degrees are awarded by these departments.

Now research in educational problems is essentially interdisciplinary research. Psychologists, sociologists, and statisticians ought to collaborate in investigating various problems of teaching and learning. Historians, political scientists, and economists ought to co-operate in studying various aspects of educational administration. The university ought to provide the opportunity, the facilities, and the funds to bring these specialists together for

145

co-operative research, without detaching them permanently from the departments to which they belong. The university could do the job it is now doing in educational research, and could do it far better, by setting up an autonomous Institute of Educational Research. The department of pedagogy should have a hand in the planning and operation of such an Institute, but so should the several other departments whose research techniques are applicable to the problems under investigation. In the administrative scheme, the institute should be under the jurisdiction of the graduate school, as should all similar interdisciplinary research institutes. Besides developing projects of its own, it should offer its services in connection with public school surveys. Many graduate students in various departments might well receive part of their training through the work of the institute, but they would take the Ph.D. in their own fields. They would be psychologists with a specialty in educational psychology, or political scientists with a specialty in school administration. Such an institute would presumably have no body of graduate students of its own, and it would obviously not be the place in which to offer advanced training to public school teachers as a group or even to practical public school administrators. These would receive the M.Ed. or the Ed.D. through the channels already described.

Such a reorganization is bound to be painful, for it *is* a major surgical operation. For this reason it must be accomplished gradually. Many of the changes should await the retirement of the persons at present charged with responsibility. And in any case, the tenure of every individual concerned, and his reasonable prospects of promotion and advancement in salary, must be scrupulously respected. Professors should be transferred from the department of education to the department in which their courses are eventually to be offered only when such a move is agreeable to the person involved and to the recipient department. Otherwise, matters should be left *in statu quo,* and arrangements worked out for a future transfer of functions whenever the opportunity arises.

The university and its faculty, moreover, must give convincing evidence of sincerity. There must be a real guarantee that every department to which pedagogical functions are delegated will accept its new responsibilities seriously and wholeheartedly, treating the discharge of them as an obligation fully as binding as any other which it recognizes. During the transitional period, special authority should be vested in the university administration and the Faculty of Teacher Training to review the policies of individual departments with respect to these new functions, and, if necessary, to institute courses and make faculty appointments within any department which may prove indifferent or laggard. Such an extraordinary power of intervention, one may hope, would never be used, but it ought to exist as a pledge of the good faith of the university.

A new curriculum for the education of teachers, based firmly upon the liberal arts and sciences, rather than upon the mere vocational skills of pedagogy, will do more to restore the repute of the public schools than any other step that can be taken. Not only will teachers be adequately trained in the disciplines they undertake to teach, they will also be imbued with respect for those disciplines and will be prepared to resist the anti-intellectualism that currently threatens the schools. And when the tide begins to turn, young men and women of genuine intellectual interest and capacity will be attracted in increasing numbers into the profession of public school teaching. They will not be repelled at the outset by being asked to lay aside their intellectual interests and fritter away their time in the courses of the pedagogues. Under a well-ordered plan, the gateway to teaching will be the gateway of learning itself.

# 10

## Re-establishment of Standards
## Through Examination

Examinations are the universally recognized means of measuring the actual training and qualifications of a man or woman.
Bar examinations, civil service examinations, and examinations
in a host of different fields constitute part of the normal procedure
for verifying the credentials and ascertaining the capabilities of
individuals who lay claim to special competence. Only in the
realm of education—where examinations presumably originated
and where they have a peculiar appropriateness—has there been
a retreat from a rigorous examination system. Educational theorists had much to do with the abandonment of regular examinations throughout the educational system. The present disorgan-
ized state of public school and even college education is a practical
demonstration that their reasoning was fallacious, and that the
retreat from examinations was a disastrous mistake.

College and university faculties must take the lead in re-estab-
lishing comprehensive, essay-type examinations as the basic means
of evaluating educational preparation and measuring educational

achievement. The obvious place to start is in connection with admission to college, for an alarming decline in the standards of American higher education can be attributed to the gradual abandonment of searching and effective entrance examinations. Professional educationists seem to prefer aptitude tests to examinations which show how much a student knows and what he is capable of doing with his knowledge. But a college needs students who are not merely apt but well trained, if it is to be an institution of *higher* learning. It requires students who can write the English language clearly and effectively, not merely those with a potentiality for literary expression. It requires students who are prepared to solve mathematical problems, not merely those with a latent talent for mathematical abstraction. It requires students who can sit down and read a book in a foreign language, not merely those who would find it easy to learn a language if they had a chance. It requires students who have fundamental knowledge in history or chemistry, which can be built upon in advanced courses, not merely students who will prove apt at acquiring such knowledge when at last they are introduced to it.

Professional educationists can be expected to object violently to the re-establishment of stringent college entrance examinations. They are certain to cite the so-called "eight-year study" and to insist that it has proved that admission requirements enforced by examinations are unnecessary and ineffective. Properly interpreted, that famous study proves nothing of the sort. Arguments purporting to be based upon it, however, have been so frequently used by those opposed to the raising of academic standards in colleges and high schools, that some attention must be devoted here to the study itself and to the illegitimate inferences that have been drawn from it.

The "eight-year study," commenced in 1932 by the Commission on the Relation of School and College of the Progressive Education Association and published in 1942, involved the careful study of the college achievements of 1,475 students who entered college in the years 1936-39 from a group of thirty secondary schools which were undertaking curricular experiments.[1] By previous agreement the colleges which admitted these students freed them "from subject and credit prescription and in most cases from entrance examinations." [2] Various measurements were made of the academic and other achievements of these students in college, and the record of each was compared with the record of "another student in the same college who had taken the prescribed courses, had graduated from some school not participating in the Study, and had met the usual entrance requirements. They were matched on the basis of sex, age, race, scholastic aptitude scores, home and community background, interests, and probable future." [3] The conclusion reached was that "the Thirty Schools graduates, as a group, have done a somewhat better job than the comparison group whether success is judged by college standards, by the students' contemporaries, or by the individual students." [4] Eighteen specific points of superiority were listed, of which the following samples include those most relevant to the present discussion:

In the comparison of the 1475 matched pairs, the College Follow-up Staff found that the graduates of the Thirty Schools
1. earned a slightly higher total grade average;
2. earned higher grade averages in all subject fields except foreign language;
3. specialized in the same academic fields as did the comparison students;
4. did not differ from the comparison group in the number of times they were placed on probation;
5. received slightly more academic honors in each year;
6. were more often judged to possess a high degree of intellectual curiosity and drive;
7. were more often judged to be precise, systematic, and objective in their thinking. . . .[5]

There have been many criticisms of the techniques employed in the study,[6] but these I shall not enter into. For the sake of the present argument it is not necessary to challenge the statistical reliability of the findings quoted above. The point I wish to make is that these findings, if true, do not support many of the conclusions that purport to be drawn from them.

The grossest misuse of the eight-year study is the illegitimate application of its findings to educational experiments that are totally different from those undertaken by the thirty schools which participated in the eight-year study. "Life-adjustment" education was not even proposed until five years after the study was completed and published, and fifteen years after it began. Nevertheless the Illinois Life Adjustment Education Program blandly cites the eight-year study as evidence that students trained in "life-adjustment" programs will be fitted for college as effectively as students in traditional programs.[7] This is extrapolation of the most irresponsible kind.

Let us note carefully the kinds of educational experimentation which the eight-year study was concerned with. The study had its inception in 1930 and it was fully under way in 1933. It was, in effect, testing the programs of progressive education that had been developed in the 1920's—a period during which, as I have said in a previous chapter, progressive education seems to me to have been definitely on the right track. Some deterioration had perhaps set in, but the extremes of regressive education were certainly never reached in the schools participating in the study. At the outset of the experiment, in fact, the commission set forth its "underlying ideas," the set of principles that presumably guided the schools in their experimentation and that were part of the understanding with the colleges concerned. The seven numbered paragraphs of this statement are quite consistent with the concepts of disciplined intellectual training which I have been presenting here. The first two of the "underlying ideas"— the crucial ones, in fact,—include practically nothing which I should regard as tainted with anti-intellectualism:

A. *Greater mastery in learning:* acquisition of such techniques as reading with speed and comprehension, observing accurately, organizing and summarizing information; ability to work with many kinds of materials; capacity to see facts in their relationships; ability to state ideas clearly; techniques essential as a foundation for later advanced study.

B. *More continuity of learning:* the elimination, wherever advisable, of limited, brief assignments and courses; a more coherent development of fields of study; provision for more consecutive pursuit of a particular subject through several years; encouragement . . . of the desire to investigate; development of the power and impetus to pursue a subject beyond the school requirement, and stimulation of the desire to put ideas to use.

There should be less emphasis on subjects and more on continuous, unified sequence of subject matter. . . . Continuous courses in the sciences and social sciences would take the place of such fragments of subject matter as chemistry or modern European history. . . . Mathematics and foreign languages also, would be reorganized in a manner to enable the pupil to get a "long" view of these fields of subject matter.[8]

The least traditional paragraphs of the statement are a far cry from "life-adjustment" education and from the notion that the ability to read is no more to be expected of a high school student than the ability to play the violin.

Accordingly, the first thing which the eight-year study proves, in my judgment, is that if the schools give clear-cut recognition to the importance of intellectual training, and sincerely attempt to advance it, their rational and considered experiments with the curriculum are likely to result in improvements in teaching the fundamental disciplines. This conclusion I gladly accept. The eight-year study, however, obviously proves nothing whatsoever about the probable college success of students trained in high schools where intellectual objectives are repudiated in favor of "life-adjustment."

A student's success in college depends a great deal upon what the college expects of him. The results of the eight-year study are in reality an expose of the low standards actually maintained by American colleges and universities in the 1930's. The colleges were, on paper, requiring students to possess certain kinds of knowledge and certain intellectual skills, but in point of fact they were not requiring the use of those skills. They were not acting as institutions of higher learning at all, so far as freshmen and sophomores were concerned. An entering student could apparently get along just as well without a particular intellectual skill as with it. A foreign language might be required for admission, but the college had ceased to expect a student to use his skill to read a book in a foreign language as part of a freshman assignment. Mathematics was required, but if a student could not actually use mathematics, the college was willing to wait until he developed the necessary skill in the college preparatory courses which the college itself offered and for which it supinely permitted college credit to be given. The eight-year study proved, what most college professors knew in their hearts to be true, that the first two years of college constituted for most students not higher education but preparatory-school work.

The college was becoming a preparatory school in its first two years primarily because it had discovered that the high school courses for which college entrance credit was being given were so varied in quality and content that the college could not depend upon them to furnish a common basis of knowledge upon which advanced work could be built. The following statements in the report of the eight-year study are essentially correct: "The customary relations of school and college are unsound in that emphasis is placed upon outworn symbols—units, grades, rankings, and diplomas. . . .The college is placed in the position of saying that certain subjects, grades, and units are essential when it knows that they are not." [9] The college was, in truth, placing emphasis upon symbols that were outworn. They were outworn because they had ceased to signify a real command of the knowledge they were supposed to represent. The college was asking the student to give evidence of having passed a high school unit in mathematics, when it should have been requiring him to demonstrate a command of certain mathematical skills. And because it was not getting properly trained students, it had given up the attempt to build a freshman program involving the use of previously acquired intellectual skills. It was in the position of merely pretending to require these skills, and the eight-year study exposed the pretence.

The most significant conclusion to be drawn from the eight-year study, in other words, was that the colleges were leaning upon a broken reed to the extent that they based admission upon the accumulation of course credits in high school, instead of upon rigorous examinations that would actually test the fully developed competency of the candidate in the intellectual disciplines he was expected to use. The commission which made the eight-year study did not, in fact, draw this inference. The inference follows, nevertheless, more logically from the evidence which the study presents than the opposite conclusion which the commission chose to draw, and which in fact was a mere *obiter dictum*, reflecting the bias of those who inaugurated the study. The commission's own conclusion was this: "The assumption that preparation for the liberal arts college depends upon the study of certain prescribed subjects in the secondary school is no longer tenable." [10] This assumption was *not* proved untenable by the eight-year study. What was proved untenable was the assumption that credits and grades in high school courses were a reliable measure of the student's ability to use the intellectual skills he was supposed to have received. These school-attested credits were actually a most unreliable criterion of the student's developed mental capabilities, and the eight-year study proved this fact by showing that students who met these nominal requirements were no better prepared than those who did not.

Rigorous entrance examinations in the basic intellectual disciplines are the proper answer to the paradox which the eight-year study revealed. Even the Commission that made the study was ready to assert the following: "No one questions the right of colleges to set up requirements for admission of students. Quite properly colleges desire only those students who are equipped to do the work the college expects. They may justly require evidence of the candidate's fitness." [11] Where the commission went wrong was in insisting that "it is the school's responsibility to provide that evidence." [12] This was a mere assertion, and it flew in the face of the study's own findings, to wit, that the evidence hitherto provided by the schools had been quite unreliable, not to say worthless. The only proper conclusion is that the universtiy must itself determine a candidate's fitness. The normal and recognized means of determining such fitness is through examination. To carry on *advanced* education effectively, a college or university needs to know that its students have acquired real command of certain definite techniques—linguistic, literary, mathematical, logical, manipulatory—and have come into full possession of certain essential bodies of information—historical, scientific, cultural. It must make sure that they have done so by testing them.

Properly designed college entrance examinations are no barrier to legitimate experimentation with teaching methods (including curricular reorganizations) in the high school. They rule out only illegitimate and anti-intellectual experimentation, and this they ought to do. If the object of improved pedagogy is to enable students to learn more rapidly and thoroughly, to think more cogently, and to express themselves more effectively, then thorough examinations at the end are no handicap. They provide, in fact, the only possible evidence that the improved methods are effective. A teacher genuinely interested in experimentation should welcome them as the proper vindication and proof of his accomplishment. Without examinations which will test the respective results of old and new pedagogical methods, the new must be taken entirely on faith. This, in fact, is the present situation. Three professors of education, writing in 1950, summed up the evidence that might show the value of the experiments thus far made in altering the course of study. Though the authors were enthusiastic enough about "curriculum development" to devote an entire book to the subject, they were forced to admit the lack of validating evidence in the following bald words: "Yet the plain fact is that the curriculum worker still . . . does not have conclusive empirical evidence that a pure-form subject curriculum is inferior—or superior—to a pure-form activity curriculum, or to a pure-form core curriculum." [13]

Rigorous examinations for admission to college cannot be imposed at a single stroke without disorganizing the entire educational system. To begin with, and perhaps permanently, they should be set up rather as *matriculation* than as *entrance* examinations. The system might well be as follows. Students would be admitted as at present, but they would remain in the status of non-matriculated students until they had passed all the required examinations. Perhaps only a few students at the beginning would enter as fully matriculated students, but eventually most would do so. Many existing college courses would be reclassified as preparatory, and would carry no college credit. Non-matriculated students would be expected to elect their programs exclusively from these. Certain carefully guarded exceptions could be made to this general rule. Thus a student who had passed the matriculation examinations in mathematics might properly be permitted to take the appropriate college courses in that discipline, and the credits earned could be validated once he had passed the rest of his examinations. No non-matriculated student, however, should be permitted in a regular college course until he had passed at least some of the basic examinations, including all those in the general field to which the course itself belonged. This rule would apply to courses in subjects that are normally commenced in college as well as those that are continued from secondary school. Thus a student might not enroll in sociology until he had passed the matriculation examinations in history, the particular social science for which such examinations are most likely to be set. Without a rule of this kind, the college courses in non-high-school subjects would be flooded with unprepared students, and the standards in them would break down at the very moment when the standards in other subjects were being re-established.

Under this system all courses carrying college credit would start off with a homogeneous body of students, whose attainments would be known through examination. Unprepared students having been excluded, there would be an end to the present appalling waste of the time of the fully qualified student. As the recent report on *General Education in School and College* points out, "every hour wasted in school does double damage: the student loses time, and more important, he loses interest and momentum." [14] With this momentum restored, the work toward the degree (which would commence only with full matriculation) would constitute genuine higher education. A college diploma would represent a degree of maturity far above that now expected; or, should some acceleration seem desirable, the college program could be shortened to three years and yet permit a higher level of attainment than at present.

The effects upon secondary education would be immediate and salutary. High school students would be permitted to take the matriculation examinations as soon as they were ready, and this would exert a continuing pressure upon school administrators to do their duty toward the abler students, whose interests are the most frequently sacrificed in our public schools today. Moreover, the amount of time which non-matriculated students would spend in preparatory courses after reaching college would be a vivid demonstration to them, to their parents, and to the public, of the shortcomings in secondary education which this book has pointed out. The public reaction would be of a sort that educationists could not disregard.

Examinations at the point of college entrance or matriculation are not the only ones needed. In many universities a rather sharp break occurs between the first two years, when more general requirements are met, and the last two, when greater specialization begins. A series of examinations covering the fundamental fields of "lower division" work would be of great value in maintaining standards, particularly since this is the point at which many students transfer to the university from other institutions, including junior colleges.[15] A basic examination for admission to graduate work is also badly needed. And even the highest of all examinations, that for the doctorate of philosophy, could be immensely strengthened if there were greater co-operation among different universities, perhaps through arrangements for an examiner from another institution to sit on every doctoral examining committee and to read the thesis submitted.

The spread of a uniform examination system to the public schools would be highly desirable. I have already suggested that teachers' certificates in the various school subjects ought eventually to be based upon examinations rather than upon credits and grades in courses. Similarly, state-wide examinations in the fundamental disciplines, administered at the ends of certain crucial segments of the twelve-year public school program would have a most vitalizing effect. The Regents' Examinations of New York provide a model that ought to be followed in every state.

Competitive lowering of standards among different institutions is an ever-present danger. For this reason, and because strict comparability is to be wished for, as many of these examinations as possible should be standardized and made uniform among a large number of co-operating institutions. The College Entrance Examination Board and the Educational Testing Service are agencies with experience applicable to the problem. They, and organizations like them, should be given the resources and the support necessary to carry this work forward as rapidly as possible.

Rigorous, comprehensive examinations, which test the power to think as well as to remember, are expensive to prepare and tedious to grade. But they are not so expensive as the waste of educational and human resources that occurs without them, and they are not so tedious as is the process of pushing unprepared students through courses they are not equipped to handle. In a complex industrial process, every stage is controlled through the inspecting and testing of the materials that are undergoing trans-

157

formation. Intellectual training is a vastly more complex and delicate matter than the smelting of iron or the brewing of beer. Education is too vital an enterprise for its various stages to be monitored merely by guesswork and wishful thinking.

# 11

## The Structure of Liberal Education

The four-year liberal arts college is a distinctive feature of the American and the English educational systems, and it has made a distinctive contribution to the public life of those two democracies. The nature of the liberal arts college ought to be better understood than it is, for we are in danger of losing a uniquely precious part of our educational heritage through sheer inattention to its essential characteristics.

To compare the educational systems of different countries accurately is an exceedingly difficult task, and to offer generalizations concerning their theoretical (let alone their actual) structure is a rash proceeding. Nevertheless such a generalization must be hazarded here. The actual standards and performance of the educational systems of other countries need not be examined at this time. Our present concern is with the theoretical relationship between secondary and higher education, or, more accurately, the way in which responsibility for secondary and higher education is theoretically apportioned among institutions of different levels. And, for purposes of this discussion, we are interested only in the student who proceeds through all the levels.

Secondary education, for such a student, is conceived of in all countries (if we except some of the American heresies that I have already discussed) as rigorous training in the fundamentals of the various fields of learning—languages, sciences, mathematics, history, and the rest. Secondary school instruction differs from higher education (in the theory of most systems) in that it is carried out methodically, in a pattern of courses that are largely prescribed, with relatively little expectation that the student will engage in independent, wide-ranging investigations of his own. At the opposite pole is the educational scheme of the Continental university, and of those portions of English and American universities that are not embraced within the undergraduate college. University work, in this sense, is highly specialized. It is concerned with training for research or for one of the learned professions. Independent reading and original investigation are generally more important than course work. Students are largely on their own. The schoolmaster is gone, and in his place is the professor, interested not in what the student does day by day, but in the results he can demonstrate at the end of his academic career through examinations and the writing of a thesis.

Here are two diametrically opposed educational procedures. On the Continent of Europe the student proceeds directly from the first to the second. Secondary education (in the *Gymnasium* or *lycée*) is more prolonged than with us; university work is from the beginning more independent and more specialized. The undergraduate college of England and America is interpolated, as it were, into this scheme. It is a transitional institution, in the sense that it partakes of the qualities of both the secondary school and the university, and it covers the years that on the Continent are divided between the two.

But the liberal arts college is a great deal more than a mere transitional institution. It has a unique character of its own. And its distinctive features have had much to do, I am convinced, with producing among the educated classes of the United States (as also of England) the kind of mutual understanding that underlies our success in maintaining national unity and harmony in the midst of social and political changes as drastic as those that have rent the societies of Continental Europe apart.

What characteristics of the liberal arts college can justify such a sweeping assertion? To put the matter simply, the liberal arts college permits students to complete their fundamental intellectual training in an atmosphere of greater freedom than the secondary school can allow. And in the liberal arts college, students move gradually toward specialization, mingling the while and exchanging ideas with comrades whose intellectual paths are beginning to diverge. A sense of sharing in a common intellectual life is produced by the liberal arts college as it is not produced by any institution in the Continental educational system.

The secondary school, of course, provides a unity of background, but this is an enforced and even regimented unity. When freedom of choice is suddenly granted, in the Continental university, the sense of unity in intellectual life disappears in the pursuit of intensively specialized scholarly and professional training. Under this system, unity is associated with intellectual immaturity; mature intellectual life is compartmentalized, divided, self-consciously specialized. The English and American conception is different. As students approach intellectual maturity, the methodical preceptorial methods of the schoolroom are gradually relaxed, and a study of the fundamental intellectual disciplines is continued under conditions of freedom and individual responsibility that approximate those of the university. A free exchange of ideas among fellow students, at the level of intellectual maturity, increases and is encouraged. And as these students progress toward greater specialization, they explore among themselves the interrelations between their various fields, and they cultivate the habit of discussion and mutual understanding. They are preparing themselves for the kind of public life in which a fundamental unity of purpose and principle underlies even the most striking differences, thus permitting honest compromise. The liberal arts college exemplifies, and prepares for the realization of, the motto inscribed upon our Great Seal, *E pluribus unum.*

Theory of course is very imperfectly carried out in practice. The contrasts I have made are admittedly too sharp, and the generalizations too sweeping. Nevertheless they help to make clear, I believe, the features of liberal education which we need to safeguard and strengthen in our colleges, if these are to serve, as they have served in the past, as the bulwarks of enlightened, harmonious, democratic public life.

The ideal of the college of liberal arts and sciences is to raise up a body of men and women who understand in common the fundamentals of intellectual life in its various branches, and who are able to apply to their own problems not one, but a choice, of powerful intellectual techniques over which they have achieved some measure of disciplined control. The crucial problem is how to encourage young men and women to range freely over the various fields of knowledge and yet to maintain that unified comprehension which will enable them to understand and co-operate in one another's intellectual pursuits.

The kind of unity we require in intellectual life is the kind that comes when educated men are able to command several, not merely one, of the distinctive ways of thinking that are central in the modern world. There is no genuine unity of intellectual life if men have merely learned the same sets of facts from so-called "subject-matter" fields. There is merely a specious unity if men have been taught to think in their respective disciplines alone, and have been offered merely a smattering of information *about* other ways of thinking. And there is only a narrrow and shackled unity if one way of thinking has been exalted above all others and made the *sine qua non* of education.[1]

Men need to know a fair number of the crucial ways of thinking upon which modern intellectual life is based. This implies that the truly distinctive ways of thinking are reasonably limited in number, and that there is a recognizable hierarchy of importance among them. The implications of this must be squarely faced. Educational reform must begin with a courageous assertion that all the various subjects and disciplines in the curriculum are *not* of equal value. Some disciplines are fundamental, in the sense that they represent essential ways of thinking, which can be generalized and applied to a wide range of intellectual problems. Other disciplines, though equal in intellectual potency, are somewhat less central to the purposes of liberal education, either because they can be studied only after the fundamental disciplines are mastered, or because they represent highly specialized intellectual techniques, restricted in their range of applicability.

Other courses in the modern curriculum do not represent disciplines at all, but offer professional preparation, or training in mechanical skills, or helpful hints on vocational and personal matters. Still other courses, alas, offer nothing at all, save collections of more or less interesting facts, opinions, or fallacies.

When we have the courage to specify which disciplines belong in the first category—that is, which ones are truly fundamental—then, and only then, can we begin to restore intellectual unity to the curricula of our schools and colleges. The decision may not be as difficult as it seems, for we are talking about disciplines, or ways of thinking, not about "subject-matter" fields. The basically different ways of thinking are few compared with the number of factual areas within which they can be applied. The method of controlled experimentation, for example, is one sort of disciplined thinking, and it underlies several different physical sciences. Mathematics is another distinctive way of thinking, historical investigation is a third, philosophical criticism a fourth. One can go on, but one cannot go on far without exhausting the ways of thinking that are genuinely fundamental, that are clearly distinctive, and that are susceptible of being introduced at the elementary or high school level and carried forward systematically in college. All choices have something of the arbitrary about them, but a decision that certain disciplines are fundamental and others not can be made on reasonable and judicious grounds.

Once these premises are accepted—and not merely accepted, but believed with the kind of conviction that will lead to action—then some plan for genuinely liberal education appropriate to the mid-twentieth century becomes possible. Such a plan must provide for specialization. It must also establish standards and prerequisites that will permit an orderly progress from introductory to advanced work. It must consider the nature of the courses that are best adapted to the instruction of the non-specialist. It must develop a philosophy for guiding the student in his quest for intellectual breadth. It must concern itself with the interrelationships between the individual disciplines. And it must set up a final test for achievement in terms of knowledge and skill acquired, not of credits accumulated. These six points will be taken up in order in the remainder of this chapter.

Intellectual training is so laborious and time-consuming that it tends to become specialized education in *a* discipline rather than liberal education in *the* disciplines. Given the complexity of modern knowledge, a high degree of specialization is an inescapable thing. In point of fact genuine specialization is not in itself an evil. It is false specialization that we need to fear and avoid.

One kind of false specialization is exemplified by the man who imagines that he will be able to solve important problems by using only one set of mental tools. No intellectual activity is ever so specialized that it involves only a single way of thinking. If a specialist is to solve new problems in his own field he must be prepared to draw upon ways of thinking that have never yet been applied to the problem. The greater his achievement as a specialist, the broader must be his fund of general knowledge and the wider his acquaintance with other ways of thinking. Specialization that is false because of its narrowness is also self-defeating. Genuine specialization always involves the careful study of related fields.

A second type of false specialization in intellectual life is more insidious. It arises from the failure to discriminate between an intellectual discipline defined as a way of thinking, and a field of study defined in some other way—defined, say, as the body of practical information connected with some specified vocation. Now vocational training, as an earlier chapter has shown, is perfectly compatible with liberal education, but it is not the same thing. The *liberal* part of the training for any profession or trade is the part devoted to the scientific and scholarly disciplines that underlie the profession or trade. The *vocational* or *professional* aspect of the training is something added to liberal education. It should not be reckoned a *part* of liberal education at all.

A man's vocational or professional training is necessarily specialized. The liberal education upon which it is based need not be, but if it is, the specialization that is considered part of his liberal education can only be in one of the intellectual disciplines. There is no place in genuinely liberal education for a major in journalism, or home economics, or pedagogy, even though courses in these vocational subjects may be taken as supplements to a program in liberal education.

Because both specialization and the quest for intellectual breadth are recognized aims of the liberal arts college, a problem arises over the proper grading of courses. In his special field an upperclassman or a graduate student will be pursuing advanced courses, but at the same time he may be receiving his first introduction to some other field. American colleges customarily assign different sets of numbers to courses of different levels. This is entirely reasonable. But they usually take another step, the logic of which is utterly specious. Thinking to uphold standards, they are apt to forbid a graduate student or even an upperclassman from taking for full credit a course whose number indicates that it is on the introductory level. This is absurd. Where, may one ask, should a student be introduced to a new subject if not in an introductory course?

The consequence of this mechanical way of treating advanced credit is that the student enrolls in an advanced course without knowing anything of the fundamental processes of thought involved. An advanced student in history may need to commence the study of economics as a supporting discipline, but he is apt to find that to secure full credit he must enroll in an advanced course in the subject, though he has never mastered the introductory material. Not one student does so, but scores, and the instructor is forced to adjust his teaching to the situation. He cannot assume that his students possess a common fund of knowledge in the field or a command of certain clearly defined intellectual skills of a specialized nature. The supposedly advanced course becomes partly an introductory one. The compromise is unsatisfactory to all concerned. Thoroughly prepared students do not advance in disciplined thinking as far or as fast as they should, and new students are not initiated into disciplined thinking as systematically or as thoroughly as they ought to be.

If the introductory course is a really rigorous one, there is no reason why it should not be elected for full credit by upperclassmen and graduate students. Only in this way can advanced courses become and remain truly advanced ones, and a rational system of prerequisites be maintained. The difference between an introductory course and an advanced one has almost nothing to do with the chronological age of the student or his academic status. No one can vault lightly over the difficulties involved in learning the elements of an intellectual discipline merely because he happens to be a senior or a graduate student. He may learn a little faster, it is true, but he does not learn differently. In particular, he cannot skip essential steps in a process of thought. Knowledge, after all, *is* cumulative, and intellectual processes do advance through clearly defined stages of increasing complexity.

Once the difference between introductory and advanced courses is firmly established, we can deal more intelligently with the harder question of the kind of course that a student should be offered in a discipline outside the field of his special interest and effort. What, for example, does a student majoring in the discipline of history need to know of mathematical reasoning, of scientific investigation, of philosophical criticism, of literary expression, of aesthetic comprehension? The answer is that he needs to know the things represented by the nouns or gerunds in the phrases above—that is to say, the nature of reasoning, investigation, criticism, expression, and comprehension, as these appear in their various special forms. He does not need to know all the different lines of inquiry pursued in a given field, but he needs to know its particular way of thinking well enough to grasp its special power and applicability.

Liberal education is training in thinking. It is not the mere communication of facts. What every student—specialist or non-specialist—should gain from a course is command, even if only limited command, of the processes of thought employed in the discipline he is studying. Far less than the specialist does the student from another field need to fix in his mind a multitude of facts already discovered and verified. These facts and formulae may be necessary parts of the equipment which a specialist requires for further work in the field, hence to him they are important in themselves. To a non-specialist, however, the facts and formulae are significant as examples, as the fruits of successful inquiry, as tests of the validity of some process of reasoning. Few are so important that they must be remembered for their own sakes.

To have solved a quadratic equation is the vital thing if one wishes to grasp the nature of algebraic reasoning. Whether to memorize the general formula of solution depends entirely on one's future use for it. Similarly, to have weighed historical evidence in order to reach a conclusion and to have explored the problems of historical causality are the crucial matters. The number of specific historical facts that the student remembers is of secondary importance. Actually a student will remember a great many facts without special effort if he has really entered into the process of investigation which produced them. His score on a factual test is thus an indirect, not a direct, measure of what he has learned. It can be a fairly reliable test (if not abused by the get-rich-quick technique of factual "cramming"), because the student who has thought a lot will remember a lot, and the student who remembers nothing has probably never thought at all. Memory and disciplined thinking do go hand in hand, but we must never forget that it is the latter which really counts.

So far as "general" education is concerned, these considerations lead to a conclusion the opposite of the one ordinarily accepted. The course for the non-specialist should emphasize theoretical reasoning to an even greater extent than the course for the specialist. The latter needs to know—and hence should be drilled to remember—facts, conclusions, and formulae for which the non-specialist has little use once he has grasped the reasoning involved. In practice, colleges and universities have acted upon a contrary premise. Courses originally planned for specialists have been adapted for general students by eliminating or reducing the discussion of methodology and theory, and crowding in as much purely factual information as possible. Such courses advance neither intellectual discipline nor mutual understanding among educated men.

If this reasoning is correct, the proper introduction to each of the great areas of knowledge is a rigorous course, emphasizing intellectual processes, in one of the fundamental disciplines lying within the area. In certain fields it may be desirable to create for the non-specialist a course somewhat different in structure and emphasis from that offered to the future specialist. In the sciences, for example, it is possible that a study of crucial principles in the historical order of their discovery (as President Conant has suggested) might be more effective for the non-specialist than the study of them in the systematic order in which they need to be known by the man who is to do research in the field. Two courses, equally rigorous and equally thorough in their use of laboratory techniques, are a possibility here. Needless to say, when alternative courses are offered, there ought never to be a qualitative difference between them. Every course must discipline the mind of every student who enrolls in it. In actual fact, however, separate courses in most fields are quite unnecessary. The typical introductory course in college would serve the needs of both specialists and non-specialists more effectively if it were reorganized in such a way as to pay *more* attention than at present to methodology, to rigorous thinking, and to abstract theory. If, however, classes for non-specialists seem necessary, the instructors in charge should eschew the encyclopaedic approach, should select with care the topics that exemplify basic methodological and theoretical questions, and should concentrate upon making perfectly clear the kinds of thinking involved.[2]

Courses alone, even though properly organized for the non-specialist, will not guarantee breadth of intellectual understanding. A plan of study outside the field of specialization is needed. And American colleges are only gradually emerging from an era of complete planlessness. The free-elective system has long since proved a faulty answer to the questions raised for education by the increasing complexity of modern knowledge. It did not solve the problem of integrating the new disciplines into an ordered structure of learning; it simply dodged the problem. Under the free-elective system, two programs of study might contain no element whatever in common. Worse than that, the very mechanics of the free-elective system put all subjects on a par with one another, and tended even to treat advanced courses as if they were quantitatively equivalent to elementary ones. It fostered the belief that a man acquires a liberal education by adding so many hours in one classroom to so many hours in another until he has served his time in full.

American colleges have begun to put behind them the follies of the free-elective system. But at best they have usually done no more than apply palliatives to the evil. A college may force the student to make his choices in such a way that each of the broad areas of knowledge is represented somewhere and in some fashion among the array of courses he offers for the degree. Or the college may institute omnibus courses designed to "survey" each of these broad areas for the student, usually in his freshman or sophomore year. Or it may seek in some other mechanical way to produce unity by adding together disunities.

It must do a great deal more than this if it is really to restore among liberally educated men a sense of participating in and comprehending the varied ways of thinking that belong to modern intellectual life. To devise an adequate scheme for that part of liberal education which aims to give a student breadth of understanding is far more difficult than to devise a scheme for that part which aims at intensive, specialized knowledge. The difficulties are not insurmountable, however, provided we make clear to ourselves exactly what we are after. We have failed, I think, to do this, and we have masked our confusions under vague and undefined terms like "general education."

The last-mentioned phrase has gained widespread currency in the United States since the end of World War II, thanks largely, I suppose, to the prestige of the Harvard report on *General Education in a Free Society* (1945). In that document, as I read its arguments, "general education" was simply a synonym for "liberal education." The report dealt with education in the basic intellectual disciplines, and it proposed various means for introducing students more effectively than before to a wider range of such disciplines. There was nothing anti-intellectual in its recommendations, but the term "general education," which was unfortunately chosen to describe them, was sufficiently ambiguous to be applied elsewhere to almost any kind of pseudo-educational program. On many campuses university administrators announced that they were following in the footsteps of Harvard, and proceeded to set up rambling, catch-all courses, geared to the meagre abilities of the marginal student. In teacher training institutions the professional educationists seized upon the term with glee, and promptly introduced into the curriculum college versions of "life-adjustment" training. At one state teachers college which I visited, a faculty member asked me in all seriousness whether a course in general education was not the proper place to teach good table manners to college students. Since "general education" has come to signify, in so many institutions, complete educational inanity, we ought to abandon the term forthwith, and restore the traditional phrase "liberal education," which, despite frequent misuse, has never suffered such utter degradation as the new one.

To get back to first principles, liberal education involves three distinct kinds of intellectual training. It aims to give a student thorough, and hence creative, command of one discipline. It undertakes, in addition, to give him control over the basic and related intellectual skills that are necessary to successful work in his field of specialization. Finally, it seeks to give him breadth of intellectual understanding.

The last two of these objectives are not very clearly differentiated in most college programs. They need to be, if we are to deal effectively with the problems involved. For the sake of clarity, I should like to avail myself, in the paragraphs that follow, of a more or less arbitrary terminology. The term "major" will be given its usual meaning, the discipline in which a student specializes. The term "supporting fields" will be used to describe the work which a student needs to do in the disciplines that are closely related to his "major." And the term "minor" will be used to describe the work outside the "major" and the "supporting fields"—the work, that is, which is designed to produce breadth of comprehension. This special usage needs to be borne in mind, for at present the term "minor" is used sometimes for the work in what I call the "supporting fields," and sometimes for that which I too call the "minor."

The fields that are necessary to "support" sound specialization include both the basic intellectual disciplines of general applicability, and the specialized disciplines that fall within the same general area as the "major." An adequately trained chemist, for example, requires knowledge of mathematics (one of the disciplines of general applicability) and also of physics (one of the related specialized disciplines). Similarly a well-trained historian requires knowledge of foreign languages and also of economics. For the most part the training in the disciplines of general applicability ought to be completed in the secondary school, and rigorous college entrance examinations should take care of the matter. Once minimum standards in English grammar and composition, in mathematics, and in foreign languages (at least one, and preferably two) are assured for college matriculation, the further requirements in these disciplines should be established in terms of the actual demands of each major field. Likewise, a rational plan of study in the related "supporting" disciplines needs to be worked out for each field of specialization. These requirements, it should be noted, are in the interests of sound specialization.

They do not, by themselves, completely solve the problem of securing breadth of intellectual understanding.

The latter problem, indeed, is the most difficult of any that can arise in liberal education. Present-day attempts to solve it have proved, in my judgment, quite unsatisfactory. The existing "distribution" requirements of most colleges—that is, the requirements that specify work in a number of different areas—are at once too impatient, too mechanical, too ambitious, and yet too distrustful. They are too impatient because they do not take into account the time required to achieve a mature grasp of a subject. They are too mechanical because they do not go beyond scattering a student's effort. They are too ambitious because they expect an undergraduate to range over more fields than he is really capable of assimilating. And they are too distrustful because they assume no ability on the part of an individual to enlarge his range of intellectual powers through his own efforts.

It takes time to acquire a usable command of any intellectual discipline. This seems to me the most neglected fact in American educational thinking. Psychologists and physiologists make use of a concept that is relevant here. A stimulus must reach a certain intensity before it can produce a response. This critical point is called the *threshold*. Below the critical point, the stimulus might as well not exist so far as any observable reaction is concerned. There is, it seems to me, such a critical point or threshold in intellectual training. The study of a foreign language, for example, if pursued for only a single school year, does not bring the knowledge of the language up to the threshold where it produces the desired response in the student, namely a sense of being at home in the language. American colleges usually proceed on the theory that at least two college years of language study are necessary to reach this threshold. I believe, incidentally, that this figure is too low, but the important fact is that a threshold is tacitly recognized in the learning of a foreign language. My conviction is that such a critical point or threshold exists for every intellectual discipline, and that to disregard it is to doom any educational program to futility.

Unless we bring a student's command of a discipline beyond the threshold, we give him nothing that he can use for ordinary working purposes. We leave him bewildered and uncomprehending. Instead of opening a door for him, we may actually slam it shut. In the early stages of learning a new discipline, the student is mainly impressed with how much there is to be known and how unfamiliar and hence difficult the processes of reasoning are. Only when he reaches the threshold does he acquire pleasure and confidence as the reward of his labors. If we cut him off before he reaches the critical point, we frustrate the process of learning. The student carries his discouragement away with him, and usually convinces himself that he could never have mastered the discipline sufficiently well to make it a part of his own thinking. Thereafter he makes no effort to understand it.

As a psychological compensation he is apt to convert what is actually self-distrust into active distaste for the discipline that he feels has betrayed him. If he becomes a teacher he communicates this feeling to his students, and they go through life with blindspots for certain disciplines, most of which are simply the consequence of bad teaching. The distaste of many students for mathematics, I firmly believe (and many mathematicians with me), is a measure of the number of elementary and secondary school teachers who are frightened of the subject because they have never been required to bring their command of it up to the threshold of genuine comprehension. And the neglect of foreign languages—one of the gravest weaknesses of our educational system —seems to me the result of a vicious circle, originating in the shame which most American teachers (including a great number of university scholars) feel, but suppress, concerning their own inadequacies in the field.

This situation must be corrected in the elementary and secondary schools which are, with devastating success, killing off every budding intellectual interest by refusing to carry forward any disciplined study to the point where the student passes the threshold into confidence and enjoyment. In the college we must avoid the same mistake when we try to counter the evils of over-specialization. If we send a student into a multitude of courses without making sure that his knowledge of each discipline reaches the all-important critical point, we run the risk of producing not breadth but an almost neurotic narrowness of mind.

In my judgment, the college should approach the problem of producing intellectual breadth in a quite different way from the one it has customarily followed. I have already pointed out that the distinctively different ways of thinking are limited in number. There is another fact to be noted. For any given discipline there is another in which the processes of thought are of an almost opposite character. The discipline of chemistry, for example, is at an opposite pole from the discipline of literary criticism. The process of inductive generalization in history stands in the sharpest possible contrast with the process of deductive reasoning characteristic of mathematics. The college of liberal arts and sciences, I suggest, should recognize this fact and make it the principal basis of its efforts to encourage a wide-ranging comprehension on the part of students.

To be specific, I propose that the college should require each student to offer (besides his "major" and his work in its "supporting fields") a "minor" in some discipline that is as remote as possible, in its way of thinking, from the one to which his principal efforts are devoted. A physicist, for example, should choose his minor from one of the humanities; an economist from one of the biological sciences. Such a minor would not be a mere collection of courses, but a systematic program of study, which would bring the student well beyond the threshold of genuine understanding. Other plans, admittedly, disperse a student's efforts more widely, but dispersed effort is no virtue in an educational program. Dispersed effort is usually half-hearted effort. One virtue of such a minor as I have described would be that it would guarantee that all a student's work—outside his own field, as well as in it—would be equally serious, equally rigorous, and equally productive of demonstrable intellectual power.

Would not such a program provide the essential basis for the intellectual breadth we are really seeking, and for the mutual understanding among educated men which we so desperately need? The danger in specialization is that a man will fail to recognize that there are cogent ways of thinking markedly different from those he customarily employs. This realization can be brought home to him by giving him a thorough grasp of one such divergent way of thinking. This experience should teach him, if he is a truly thoughtful man, that every disciplined field has its rationale and its reason for existence. It should teach him that no field is beyond his grasp, if only he will devote the requisite effort to understanding it. The arrogance that arises from narrow specialization will dissolve, and real unity of intellectual life will emerge. The liberally educated man will overcome the barriers that now keep specialists from fruitful conversation and collaboration. The liberally educated teacher (and all teachers should be such) will be able to explain to students of divergent temperament the processes of thinking in his own field because he will be able to relate them to processes of thinking in fields of remote and opposite character.

If the college aims to give a student true breadth of understanding, it should abandon the hopeless task of acquainting him with every one of the disciplines. Instead it should bring the student's efforts to a focus, first of all upon his own discipline with its related fields, then upon some discipline far beyond the normal horizon of his specialty. We cannot (to change the metaphor) enable him to conquer the whole world of learning in one undergraduate career. We can, however, assist him to win a foothold on two different continents. Thereafter we ought to be content to trust him, as an educated man, to plant his banner in whatever province he wishes and win control of it by his own efforts.

Thus far we have been concerned with the separate disciplines. These are, by nature, analytical. They break down the complex issues of life into separate problems susceptible of handling by powerful specialized methods. Somehow the techniques acquired must be combined again for a co-ordinated attack upon the original problems. The omnibus "integrated" courses of the college, and the "core curricula" or "common learnings" programs of the high school, are proposed as answers to the problem of synthesis. But synthesis, without previous analysis, is a meaningless concept. One cannot take the "one great blooming, buzzing confusion" that comes to us in experience and deal with it directly, if one expects the mind to play any role in the process. Practically all "integrated" courses in the high school, and many of those in the college, have overlooked this simple fact. They confront a student with the same unanalyzed problems that life confronts him with, and they ask him to seek a solution by using his own undeveloped mental abilities. They abdicate the responsibility of the school, which is to aid a man in standing temporarily aloof

174

from a complex problem while he analyzes it and works out the strategy of dealing effectively with its different elements.

When one has sorted out the various components of experience and subjected them to intellectual control, then one is ready to bring to bear upon the original problem as a whole the various specialized powers which the intellectual disciplines offer. This is what interdisciplinary teams of scholars are doing in the cooperative projects of research that are so marked a feature of contemporary intellectual life. This is what the liberally educated man can do as an individual when his powers are developed in many different directions. And this is what the college can, to some extent, show him how to do.

How early can the college begin this work of synthesis? Ideally, perhaps, in the very first year. But the deficiencies of the American public schools are so great that it is impossible, except in a few universities, to assume that entering students possess sufficiently developed powers of intellectual analysis for any process of synthesis to be at all fruitful. For these reasons the great omnibus introductory courses—in the humanities, in the social sciences, in the physical sciences, and in the biological sciences—seem to me to have failed of their purpose in all but a few American universities. Their undeniable success in these few institutions, all of which maintain strict entrance requirements, has begotten a general misconception of the real nature and appropriateness of these courses.

Though introductory in name, the integrated course is, in reality, a very advanced one. To be effective it must build upon some real foundation of intellectual discipline acquired by the student before his admission. But the administrators of colleges with merely nominal entrance requirements have generally overlooked this fact. They have been casting about for solutions to two quite different problems: how to introduce beginning students to each of the broad areas of knowledge, and also how to offer students an opportunity to explore the interconnections between closely related disciplines. "Integrated" courses have seemed to provide an answer to both questions at once, and their vogue has been great.

Actually the problems are not the same, and cannot properly be dealt with at the same level of intellectual maturity. Really to *introduce* a student to a way of thinking is an arduous task. It takes time to master the first steps in any intellectual process. Many more years are required to learn the elements of arithmetic than to acquire the principles of differential and integral calculus. Learning is a process involving accelerated motion, not uniform velocity. Intellectual maturity is not a function of a man's age but of the intellectual discipline he has already acquired. This fact must be recognized in any effective introductory course in a new field. The pace must be such that the student really masters the processes of thought involved. Speed, comprehensiveness, and complexity must be sacrificed, if need be, to this primary end.

Now an "integrated" course, which explores the interconnections between several related disciplines, sets the student a difficult and complicated task. It asks him to find the common element in ways of thinking that on the surface seem quite different. It asks him to explain the essential, rather than the superficial, differences between these ways of thinking. It asks him to examine the appropriateness of each method to the peculiar questions it is designed to answer. And it asks him to transfer concepts from one field to another in order to enrich the technique of thinking itself. To accomplish this task successfully requires great intellectual maturity. It presupposes on the part of the student a real grasp of at least one of the ways of thinking involved. It presupposes an insight and a power of generalization already well developed. In its very nature, the "integrated" course is an advanced course. And, contrary to a general academic assumption, it is primarily a course for students already specializing in the general area of knowledge dealt with. An "integrated" course in the social sciences, to take one example, is of utmost value to students in economics, political science, and sociology, for in such a course they are exploring the broad foundations of their own particular way of thinking. But it is usually a poor sort of course by which to introduce physicists or students of English literature to the field of social science.

When presented as an introductory college offering—and *a fortiori* when developed in the high school as a "core curriculum" —the omnibus "integrated" course almost inevitably degenerates. It tends to become a mere survey of accumulated facts rather than an inquiry into the processes by which these were discovered. If taught by several instructors it tends to break down into several courses, each too slight and brief to accomplish any serious intellectual purpose. And in proportion as it fails in its ambitious attempt to train its students in disciplined thinking over so wide a range of matters, its discussions tend to deteriorate into mere expressions of uninformed opinion. The bull-session is an important extracurricular activity in any academic institution that is intellectually alive. But it is a complement to, not a substitute for, the ordered quest for knowledge which the classroom should exemplify.

The "integrated" course, maintained at a high level of theoretical rigor for advanced students, can contribute greatly to unity of intellectual life. In the last analysis, however, the synthesis of knowledge must go on within the student. Only the things that he can bring together in his own mind has he really learned. Only the intellectual skills that he can co-ordinate for his own purposes has he really mastered. It is the responsibility of the college not only to offer the courses that might produce such intellectual powers, but also to satisfy itself that the student has in fact acquired them. The degree should be awarded only when the college is so satisfied. Indispensable to a sound college program of liberal arts is a comprehensive examination at the end. This should test the student's command not only of his own discipline, but also, if possible, of the "supporting" fields that are a necessary part of fruitful specialization. Many colleges require such examinations; every college worthy of recognition should require them.

A way should also be found to examine the student's command of the field remote from his own that he has elected to study, lest the work there be considered by him a mere accumulation of credit hours. A comprehensive examination in this minor field of concentration, administered perhaps at the end of the sophomore or junior year, should form part of the pattern of the college which strives for genuine breadth and balance in its program. And if the work in the minor field is validated by an examination, then the field itself could be safely set up, if desirable, on an interdisciplinary basis.

Liberal education—in both its specialized and its generalized aspects—can be placed on a sound basis only if we restore to the college curriculum as a whole the intellectual vitality that has so largely departed from it in recent years. We are not producing men and women with a general and liberal education by requiring students to elect specified fragments of a curriculum that has been pulverized into unrelated three-semester-hour courses, and in which the distinction between elementary and advanced work has been forgotten. We are not producing them by adding more "survey" courses. We shall not produce them until we go back to first principles and create a college curriculum which, as a whole and in its interrelated parts, provides ordered and progressive training in the various forms of disciplined thought. When we do this we shall at last train up specialists who are scholars and scientists in the highest sense, and citizens who are truly educated men. Liberal education will then become a reality, because it will introduce all men alike into that world of disciplined thought where scholars and reflective citizens meet on common ground.

# 12

## Freedom of Teaching

Liberal education is the education appropriate to free men. There is thus a reciprocal relation between liberal education and freedom. Men cannot be truly free if they are deprived of knowledge. And men cannot be liberally educated if they are deprived of freedom, particularly the freedom to think for themselves.

Liberal education, as we have seen, trains a man to weigh evidence, to reason logically, and to reach conclusions that will stand up to the severest criticism that other well-informed men can bring to bear upon them. No man, however, can be trained to think for himself, rigorously and independently, if he is told in advance what conclusions he will be permitted to reach. Only a caricature of liberal education can exist where freedom is replaced by thought-control, where education is perverted into indoctrination, and where independence of mind is sacrificed to intellectual conformity.

Of all the forms which anti-intellectualism is taking in contemporary America, none is more menacing than the attempt to restrict freedom of inquiry and freedom of teaching. The professional educationists, whose views on many matters I have criticized on preceding pages, are completely in the right when they insist that the schools must have freedom to investigate critically every field of human knowledge and to discuss in responsible fashion the great issues that arise in public affairs.

Freedom, however, implies obligation. And freedom of teaching cannot be understood or defended without understanding and accepting the obligations that go with it. These obligations are all too frequently neglected in current discussions of the subject. And those men and women who would restrict freedom of teaching can honestly argue that freedom without responsibility is a dangerous thing. The cure, as I shall attempt to show, is not to restrict freedom but to make sure that those who exercise the right to teach freely shall demonstrate their ability and their willingness to teach responsibly also.

Freedom of teaching is related to freedom of speech, but it is not the same thing. The two rights are exercised in two quite different situations. To put the matter in baldest terms, the teacher is not a mere private citizen but a public functionary, and those whom he addresses constitute, in a sense, a "captive" audience. The ordinary citizen may, if he chooses, proclaim that three times three equals ten, that the Declaration of Independence was signed in 1492, or that water is a compound of iron and nitrogen. The only prestige with which he can back up these statements is his own reputation for credibility, and that will not last long if he persists in his fantasies. No one is obliged to listen to him, and few will do so, except for merriment's sake. But the statements of a teacher are supported by the prestige of his office, and his pupils have little choice but to hear him out. The opinions he expresses in the classroom cease to be purely private opinions. Behind them, upholding and enforcing them, is the prestige of the professional position he occupies. He has assumed a responsibility which the private citizen does not assume. And if he is faithless to this responsibility, he is subject to penalties from which the private citizen is immune. This is true, not of the teaching profession alone, but of all professions. A physician would be guilty of malpractice if he prescribed the old wives' remedies that ordinary persons recommend with impunity (though hardly with prudence) to their neighbors. The armchair strategist is perfectly free to plan campaigns that a professional soldier would be court-martialed for attempting to carry out. The sidewalk superintendent can harbor ideas about building construction that would put an architect behind bars if he incorporated them in an actual blueprint.

What then is the professional responsibility which a teacher assumes? Essentially it is the same kind of obligation that every professional man and woman accepts. There are two parts to such an obligation. The professional man or woman, in the first place, is bound to work toward the achievement of the *purposes* or *ends* which society has prescribed for the profession in question. "Into whatever houses I enter," reads the Hippocratic Oath of the physician, "I will go for the advantage of the sick." This is the purpose for which the medical profession exists. It is the end defined by society itself. No physician has freedom to define his purpose in any manner inconsistent with this. The first part of any professional obligation is to carry out sincerely and conscientiously the fundamental task which society has assigned to the profession, accepting as part of the contract society's definition of purposes or ends.

But there is a second part to every professional obligation. This is a responsibility to the standards of the profession itself. The Hippocratic Oath again provides an illustration of this: "I will follow that system of regimen which, according to my best judgment, I consider best for my patients, and abstain from whatever is injurious." This is not an obligation to follow the behest of the patient or public opinion, where *methods* or *means* are concerned. Quite the reverse. The physician swears that he will resist every effort by persons who are not professionally trained to dictate to him the methods to be used. Society expects—nay demands—that he use his own best professional judgment. There would be no point whatever in having a medical profession, if the physician were obliged to prescribe what the patient or the by-stander wanted him to prescribe. So it is with every profession. The civil engineer does not build bridges wherever he pleases. He expects to be told where to build them. But he must use his best professional judgment in designing a bridge that will be useful and safe. If someone undertakes to tell him that a lesser factor of safety will suffice, it is his professional obligation to refuse to build the bridge.

Now the "best judgment" of a professional man is something quite different from personal opinion or private caprice. There are fairly objective standards by which its exercise can be judged. Professional malpractice is something of which the law takes cognizance. The professional man who fails, through wilfulness, carelessness, or ignorance, to exercise his judgment in a fashion that other well-trained members of the profession deem sound is liable to punishment. No body of professional men can be expected to agree on every detail connected with the practice of their profession, but every such body knows well the limits beyond which discretion becomes irresponsibility. Society is wise to employ the profession's own standards in guarding itself against incompetence and malpractice, for if it attempts to devise some other test it runs the grave risk of hampering the responsible members of the profession in their exercise of that very discretion upon which society relies.

Teaching is a profession, and it is subject to the same two-fold responsibility as any other profession. In the first place, its ultimate purpose, aim, or end is legitimately set by society beyond the rightful power of the individual teacher to alter or amend it. That purpose is clear: the teaching profession exists to produce, through instruction or training, intelligent men and women, that is to say, men and women who can employ effectively the various specialized skills—especially the intellectual skills—upon which civilized human life depends.

*How* to teach men and women to think is a professional problem, like the problem of *how* to keep them healthy. Society asks the teacher to employ his best professional judgment in deciding what regimen of study will most effectively produce the desired result, just as it asks the physician to use his best professional judgment in deciding what medical regimen to prescribe. In this second part of his obligation, the teacher is responsible for maintaining the standards set by his professional colleagues. Lapses from these standards are certainly punishable by society, just as malpractice in medicine or law is punishable. But the standard employed should be that applied to any other profession, namely whether the teacher, through wilfulness, carelessness, or ignorance, has abused the discretion properly vested in a teacher and has violated the standards of responsibility set by the profession itself.

Up to this point, I believe, the argument I have given would be accepted by professional educationists, as well as by scientists and scholars. But a crucial question now arises: What is the responsible professional group that can properly and safely determine the standards of competence and integrity beyond the limits of which a teacher is guilty of professional malpractice? The secondary school educationists are fond of arguing that public school teaching is a separate and independent profession, and that its standards are to be set by professors of education and their colleagues in the secondary school bureaucracy, without regard to the professional standards maintained by scholars and scientists. The argument is utterly fallacious. Such a faulty standard completely fails to guarantee the integrity of the secondary schools. Virtually all the irresponsible teaching that has brought the schools under attack is the consequence of subscribing to this misleading doctrine. To persist in accepting it is to endanger society on the one hand and freedom of teaching on the other.

Let us see why such a standard is false and inadequate. The question at issue is not methods of instruction in the narrow, pedagogical sense; that is, how to present matters to an elementary school child, how to use visual aids, how to administer a high school, and the like. The question is far more profound and searching than any of these; namely, what kind of intellectual training will produce men and women capable of thinking clearly and accurately? To answer it, one must know what clear and accurate thinking consists in. As we have seen, there are several different kinds of thinking: historical, mathematical, scientific, linguistic, philosophical, and the rest. The man who knows what constitutes clear and accurate historical thinking is the historian, the man who knows what constitutes clear and accurate mathematical thinking is the mathematician. The standard of what constitutes competent and responsible teaching in history can be set only by professional historians, if the standard is to have any validity. The same is true for each of the basic disciplines. Whether mathematical teaching is sound is a question for mathematicians to answer. What kind of scientific instruction will produce a genuinely scientific attitude of mind is a question for scientists.

The professor of education has no competence whatever in these matters, nor has the teacher who is trained exclusively in pedagogy. A glibness in the use of classroom techniques, an ability to seize the attention of youngsters and to keep them busy, provides no guarantee whatever that the instruction that follows will be sound or responsible. The teacher may conduct his class smoothly and expertly, but if he does not know what constitutes disciplined thinking in the field, he may be teaching the most arrant nonsense. And his administrative superior, himself a professional educationist, may recognize and reward the smoothness without being able to detect the nonsense. This, let us hope, is a rare occurrence. But there is no way to prevent its occurring save by insisting that every teacher of history shall be trained as an historian, shall think of himself as an historian, shall keep abreast of developments in historical interpretation, and shall consider himself bound by the standards of historical scholarship.

In the public schools today there are thousands of teachers of history who do look upon themselves as historians and whose teaching does meet the highest standards of historical objectivity. There are thousands of teachers of mathematics, of science, of language, and of the other disciplines whose work stands up to the most searching scholarly scrutiny. This kind of professional responsibility is not being developed or furthered, however, under existing systems of teacher training in the United States. Professional educationists are putting an ever-increasing strain upon the scholarly competence of teachers, by asking them to handle "integrated" courses which bring together some of the most complex and controversial disciplines that exist—those in the social sciences, for example. But they are denying to teachers the opportunity to develop real competence in these disciplines through intensive study of them. Instead, the educationists set up courses of their own in "Elementary School Core Programs" or "Fundamentals of Curriculum Development," [1] thus diverting more and more time into pedagogy at precisely the moment when prospective teachers need to develop greater scholarly competence than ever before if they are to teach these new and controversial fields responsibly.

A teacher trained mainly in pedagogy cannot bring to the discussion of controversial problems the kind of professional responsibility which the public has a right to demand. A teacher who is also a scholar endeavors to present conclusions that he has reached through original inquiry into the evidence or through critical examination of the researches of others. On matters which he is unable to investigate for himself, he at least obliges himself to present conclusions supported by the best judgment of competent scholars, which he ascertains through the study of contemporary publications in the field. The teacher who has not been trained as a scholar lacks the equipment necessary to reach warrantable conclusions by any of these methods. What he presents to his students are irresponsible opinions rather than responsible professional judgments. These opinions are irresponsible because the teacher who offers them is not capable of supporting them by reasoned argument of his own, acceptable to other scholars working in the field.

The teaching of unsupported conclusions is irresponsible teaching, regardless of the nature of the conclusions themselves. Genuine education consists in the communication not of conclusions but of the power to reach conclusions. "Indoctrination," as it is called, is thus a form of irresponsible teaching. It does not train the student to use valid processes of thought, it merely tells him the results he is expected to reach. It is as if one should teach arithmetic by ordering the pupils to memorize the answers in the back of the book. All will go well until a new problem is presented. But life is bound to present new problems, even if the teacher does not.

Indoctrination is no answer to the problem of teaching controversial subjects. The opinions which pupils carry out of the classroom will be perfectly "safe," no doubt, but the intellectual powers they carry out will be nil. And it is the intellectual power of the citizen which is the security of the state. The purpose of training for citizenship is to enable a man to deal intelligently with *new* controversial issues as they arise. Now the very fact that an issue is controversial means that there is conflicting evidence to be weighed, there are opposing arguments to be logically tested, there are alternative solutions to be explored. Authorized answers to old problems will not help him—only the experience he has gained in thinking old problems through to a rational conclusion. Indoctrination is a narcotic to kill the pain of thinking. And it prepares a student to face new problems in only one way—by reaching for the hypodermic needle.

So long as life itself is filled with unanswered questions, so long must the school face courageously the problem of teaching controversial subjects in a responsible manner. Such subjects cannot be excluded from the schoolroom any more than the air can be. Every issue that liberal education deals with is arguable. My own field of history is filled with disputed interpretations, back to the most ancient times. At its growing edge, every science and every scholarly discipline consists of a mass of unreconciled arguments. To train a man to think clearly and originally is nothing else than to train him to handle controversial issues.

To handle such issues, in the sense intended here, is to handle them according to the methods of free, objective, critical, scholarly inquiry. No other methods are legitimate and no others can safely be tolerated in an educational system founded on the principles of responsibility and freedom. We have no obligation—indeed, no right—to tolerate the intellectual methods of the communist who has abandoned free, critical investigation out of devotion to a party line. Similarly we have no obligation and no right to tolerate the methods of those who would suppress free, critical inquiry in order to root out communism.

There is, it seems to me, one perfectly valid ground for denying to a proved communist the privilege of teaching in an American college or school. The reason, to quote President Grayson Kirk of Columbia University, is simply that "such a person is no longer intellectually a free agent." [2] By virtue of his acceptance of the communist party line, he has subordinated his own judgment, in a professionally indefensible manner, to the dictates of an ideological directorate. He has repudiated the standards of scholarship in favor of the standards of a political bureaucracy. He has abdicated intellectual responsibility and has rendered himself incapable of communicating to his students any genuine appreciation of critical, objective, disinterested thinking.

The disqualification, be it noted, arises out of the processes of thought which the communist employs, not out of the specific conclusion he reaches. The distinction is a vital one. If we are to maintain freedom of thought, we must discriminate clearly and constantly between unsound reasoning and unpopular conclusions. No teacher has a right to the former; no teacher is free unless he has a right to the latter. Freedom means nothing unless it means freedom to criticize and freedom to reach unpopular conclusions. The freedom to conform is not freedom at all; the most tyrannical state that ever existed has granted *this* privilege to its subjects.

To scrutinize the methods by which a teacher has reached his conclusions, and to test those methods by the accepted standards of his profession is not to violate academic freedom. It is simply a means of enforcing academic responsibility. But to penalize a teacher for the opinions he holds, when he has reached them by independent, responsible, scholarly inquiry, is a totally different matter. Such a procedure will destroy free, objective inquiry in precisely the way in which the communists themselves have destroyed it. Academic freedom is not endangered, I believe, by the automatic exclusion of proved communists from the teaching profession. It is gravely endangered, however, if occasional coincidences between the views of a competent scholar and the views that may happen to be supported by the communist party line at a particular time are made the basis for condemning the former. We cannot fight communism by limiting and restricting the right of non-communists to think, to write, and to teach freely, for by so doing we are simply furthering the work that the communists themselves want to see accomplished.

I believe that we can defend ourselves against the communist threat to freedom of thought and of teaching, without ourselves becoming the destroyers of those freedoms. In the realm of education we can do so if we will remember at all times that the subversive teacher is not the one who is critical or who reaches unpopular conclusions, but the one who employs processes of reasoning that are unsound and invalid according to the standards of professional responsibility set by active and independent scholars in the field. The teacher we can trust is the one who possesses the ability to deal with evidence and with processes of reasoning according to the accepted critical methods of the discipline involved. The professional competence which society must require of the teacher of controversial subjects is not competence in pedagogy but competence in scholarship.

I am convinced that the loyal Americanism of our teachers and school administrators is exceeded by the loyalty and devotion of no other profession or group in the land. I am far less sure, however, that their knowledge, their critical judgment, and their scholarly competence are being sufficiently developed under existing programs of teacher training to equip them to deal in a genuinely informed way with the complex controversial issues of the present. And the training they possess is stretched perilously thin when they are required to range over many different fields of knowledge in a "common learnings" program or a "core curriculum," or when they are asked to give their teaching a wholly contemporary orientation.

It is ignorance rather than disloyalty which we ought to fear in our teachers. Ignorance can produce the same effects as disloyalty, if it means that a teacher cannot get to the factual heart of a matter, cannot discriminate between valid evidence and mere propaganda, or cannot analyze for himself by scholarly methods the issues that are presented. A loyalty oath is no protection against our most insidious enemy, ignorance. It is time for us to stop worrying about how loyal our teachers are, and start worrying about how much they know.

The discussion of controversial subjects in the classroom does create an opportunity for subversive teaching. The danger, I feel, is greatly exaggerated in current discussions. Whatever the degree of danger may be, however, it arises neither from discussing such issues nor from dealing with them critically but from allowing them to be taught by unqualified, incompetent, uneducated persons.

The nation has nothing to fear and everything to gain from the widest possible diffusion of knowledge about Russia and Russian policy. We need to understand, not to ignore, the character of Marxist ideology. We need to study objectively and realistically the evidence that exists concerning the plans and purposes of the international communist movement, for we need to know precisely what sort of threat it presents to the free world of the West.

Respect for American institutions and for American freedom is bound to increase in every rational mind with every increase in knowledge of the dread alternative which our opponents hold up to us. But it must be accurate knowledge, communicated by men and women who are informed, critical, and responsible. A teacher who is to discuss the Soviet Union cannot be merely one jump ahead of his class. He must bring to his teaching a deep and critical knowledge of modern European history, of political structures throughout the world, and of fundamental economic and constitutional principles. Without these he can be entirely well-meaning, yet he can become an easy dupe of the propagandists of the left or the right.

For similar reasons, the teacher who is to deal with contemporary economic problems in the United States must be thoroughly grounded in American history, in political science, in economics, and in sociology. He must be prepared to use the critical methods of these disciplines. He will not acquire the thorough knowledge and the intellectual skill that he needs by enrolling in courses on "the social foundations of education" or "the teaching of the social studies," as offered by professors of pedagogy in schools or departments of education. He can acquire it only through serious, scholarly work in the disciplines themselves, under the guidance of responsible scholars in the field.

This brings us back to our starting point: the necessity of basing our educational system, from top to bottom, upon the basic disciplines of science and scholarship. These are not only the tested means of acquiring intellectual power. They are also the tested means of preserving intellectual freedom. Let our totalitarian enemies fear the free, critical, well-trained mind; they have good reason to fear it. Precisely because *they* fear it, *we* must be careful to foster it. Let us not be timid in the avowal of our faith: "And ye shall know the truth, and the truth shall make you free."

# 13

## The Study of Our Own Civilization

In one of his boldest and most magnificent figures of speech, John Milton likened Truth to the good Osiris, whose body, hewn into a thousand pieces, was scattered to the four winds. "From that time ever since," wrote Milton, "the sad friends of Truth, such as durst appear, imitating the careful search that Isis made for the mangled body of Osiris, went up and down gathering up limb by limb still as they could find them." Though present-day scientists and scholars may not speak so confidently of Truth as Milton did, they are painfully aware of the difference, for intellectual life, between an animated body and a heap of disservered limbs. They know that life will not be restored to liberal education until some power "shall bring together every joint and member, and shall mould them into an immortal feature of loveliness and perfection." [1]

To restore to intellectual life the unity which the forces of modern life are threatening to destroy constitutes one of the most significant tasks to which thoughtful men and women are addressing themselves today. In the realm of research, the co-operation of

190

scholars and scientists from many disciplines in the study of a particular problem is one of the distinctive features of twentieth-century scholarship. In the realm of instruction, there has been a corresponding development of curricula that involve the correlated study of several disciplines, organized about some central theme. The integrated *course* has been discussed in an earlier chapter; the integrated *program* of study deserves a few concluding words.

Programs for the unified study of American civilization in its various aspects—historical, literary, aesthetic, economic, political, sociological—have been developed on many campuses to advance the great purposes of liberal education. The choice of such a theme is logical and sound, for the serious study of our own civilization not only possesses a self-evident relevance in the mind of the student, but it also carries out the ancient maxim, "Know thyself." So long as disciplined and enlightened scholarship presides over these curricula, their worth and integrity are unquestionable.

Now that programs of American studies have won recognition, however, can we be sure that their further spread will be for the right reasons? In these middle years of the twentieth century, I for one cannot reply with a confident Yes. The narrow and vicious nationalism that stalks the country today threatens liberal education in part by suppression, in part by infiltration and subversion. Against this latter danger, curricula in American civilization are ill-protected. To the jingoist how inviting such programs are! How apt for his purposes! In what other field of science or scholarship can the enemy of critical thinking bring greater pressure to bear? To a bigoted nationalist, afraid of the free and wide-ranging mind that compares and contrasts and judges for itself, how conveniently narrow an American studies program must appear! How little policing it should require to keep it safely within the bounds of our national frontiers and our national prejudices! If programs of American studies are to retain their good repute, their sponsors must be on guard against chauvinistic allies who offer support in return for a betrayal of liberal education itself.

But narrow nationalism is only one variety of intellectual strangulation. Men of fantastically limited minds have gained control over wide areas of modern education. And programs of

American studies, unfortunately, are likely to receive their sinister blessing. First of all there are the vocationalists. Like the fur trader who believes that a geyser exists only to poach his morning eggs, these men think of education only as preparation for employment. To them American studies are the best adjunct to job-training, for they orient a student quickly to the society in which he will work, without wasting his time on the larger contexts of human life. Then there are the pedagogues who deliberately narrow their vision to the trivia of contemporary daily life, the toothbrush and the traffic light. The study of American civilization is less important in their scheme of things than learning how to act on one's first date, but at least it is not so remote and hence so insignificant as philosophy or literature or mathematics. Next there are the educational theorists who attack all disciplined, cumulative training in such basic tools as languages and mathematics. Even without intellectual equipment, their students may be said to have a grasp of the essential fields of knowledge, if only the essential fields of knowledge are redefined as the things their students can grasp. And an American program, one must confess, can be made to appear the first step toward such a convenient redefinition.

To anti-intellectuals generally, American programs are appealing because thereby so many long perspectives and so much human experience can be excluded and disregarded. If we value the scholarly study of American civilization, we must beware of fair-seeming supporters, who, whether they realize it or not, are enemies of the out-reaching yet disciplined mind which it is the true object of liberal education to produce.

Can programs in American studies resist these ominous pressures? Can they form a reliable basis for the kind of education that strives to be liberating and hence liberal? I have faith that they can. But deliberate and conscious effort is necessary if we who are teaching in these programs are to keep them free from chauvinism and from the narrow cult of contemporaneity. To defend American studies indiscriminately is to betray them. What we must do, in these days of danger, is to define the characteristics which alone can render such programs intellectually defensible.

The scholarly study of American civilization can be the foundation of a genuinely liberal education, I believe, precisely because any serious attempt to understand our national life must inevitably carry the student into investigations of events that happened far outside our geographical boundaries and of ideas that arose long before the beginning of our separate chronology.

To a thoughtful student, American civilization is less self-contained than almost any other with which he might concern himself. Our first settlers were not wandering barbarians who painfully developed their culture out of nothing in the spot at which their migrations ended. They were inheritors of a civilization which they set about reproducing, as faithfully as conditions would permit, in the new home they had chosen. It was not recent ideas but ancient traditions which moved them most deeply—the Bible, whose earliest passages were at least twenty-five hundred years old, and the intellectual traditions of Greece and Rome, whose civilization as a living thing had ended a thousand years before.

In its later development, as in its origins, American civilization was part of a larger whole that knew no national boundaries. Even when the United States set itself up as a separate nation, its Declaration of Independence was deliberately phrased in terms of ideas and arguments that were the common currency of eighteenth-century cosmopolitan thought, and its fundamental Constitution embodied, and justified itself in terms of, political ideas whose history stretched back at least to Aristotle. In its material development also, especially during the last hundred years, the United States lived no life apart, but was caught up in an industrial revolution world-wide in its sweep. Finally, in our own lifetime, the American people have been forced to fight for their lives and liberties against vast conspiratorial despotisms rooted in continents far—but not far enough—from our own.

A study of American civilization that follows out these trails into other civilizations and other ways of looking at things cannot fail to be a liberating study. I am not talking, of course, about "background knowledge"—that vague and delusive term which genteelly implies a smattering of ill-understood information. I am talking about serious and disciplined study of those other histories and literatures, in their own terms and preferably in their own languages; study that will enable a student to make informed comparisons, to trace movements as they migrate across arbitrary

193

frontiers, to know what is common to many before venturing to decide what is unique with one.

It hardly seems possible that a student should not see for himself the opportunity, indeed the necessity, for seeking origins, for making comparisons, for putting American civilization in the perspective of ever wider knowledge. But we must not take it for granted that this will be the case. Too many students are likely to be attracted to programs of American studies because they want to escape the tough problems that foreign languages and foreign ideas present, or because they fear to see challenged the comfortable doctrines they already believe. No education can be liberal that permits them to avoid these tasks and these challenges.

Nor may we overlook the parochialism that is latent in all of us. Vigilance against this is one of our major responsibilities. Too many students take local and state history as a starting point only to reach, not the farthest boundaries of place and time, but the opposite, the stuffy closets of antiquarianism and genealogy. Too many students who delve into obscure frontier writings or folklore or hill-billy music lose, rather than gain, perception of what constitutes great writing and great art and what maturity means in the realm of ideas. No program of American studies, in other words, can be expected to become automatically a program of liberal education. Through formal prescripts, or through conscientious advice, every student must be required—explicitly, rigorously, undeviatingly—to follow the trails that lead outward, into the study of other histories and cultures, and especially into the study of those enduring monuments of human wisdom and artistic achievement that provide the only world-wide standards of judgment.

In a program of American studies guided by principles like these I see the possibility of a new flowering of humanistic studies, equal in grasp and profundity with the great work of the past, and more alive, perhaps, to the men of this present age. The stern challenges which American civilization is now being called upon to face from without are akin to the challenges which many times in the past have awakened peoples from provincial slumber and opened to them the spacious vistas of the mind that I have made synonymous with liberal education. After the Spanish Armada came Shakespeare and Bacon's *Advancement of Learning*. After the Crusades, Dante and Giotto and the university foundations of western Europe.

Most telling example of all, after the Persian Wars came the flowering of Athens. The father of history, Herodotus, wrote of that great conflict between East and West, so near to him in time and place. But he saw that to understand it, he must carry his researches outward in geographical space and backward in time to the very limits of what could be known. History had still much to learn by way of critical discipline from the later work of Thucydides, but Herodotus endowed history at its birth with that sense of broad perspectives, that ideal of seeing in recent events the play of forces deeply rooted in the past, which are the historian's peculiar inspiration. What Herodotus gave to history, moreover, was essentially what the other thinkers of classical Greece contributed to their respective disciplines—the sense that present phenomena have implications which must be pursued by the mind as far as they will lead. The steadfast adherence to this principle was what made the Greek mind for so many later ages the model of the disciplined mind which liberal education should strive to produce.

The events of Greek history were human events, no more and no less human than the events of other histories. Yet consider how many others, as rich in drama and the revelation of human character, have been told in such a way as to make them seem but parish chronicles. That which has given Greek history its hold upon the imaginations of men has been the insight and perspective which the human mind has brought to the study of it. To the study of American civilization we can bring the minds of antiquarians and annalists, or we can bring the disciplined imagination of men who can see in a blade of grass chemistry and biology and poetry, and in the smallest human event sociology and ethics and history. If we do the latter, no one will think to ask whether the study of American civilization can constitute a liberal education. The question rather will be, what the Renaissance humanist would have asked concerning the classics, can any other study be so liberating as this?

# Appendix

## Proposals for a Permanent Scientific and Scholarly Commission on Secondary Education

At the suggestion of Professor James G. Randall, President of the American Historical Association, the Program Committee of the Association invited me to deliver a paper on "Anti-Intellectualism in the Schools: A Challenge to Scholars" at the annual meeting held in Washington, December 28-30, 1952.

In connection with the paper it seemed wise to me to present certain concrete proposals for action. Accordingly I drafted a set of resolutions dealing with the matter. The first version was completed on November 26, 1952, and was circulated for criticism to a number of colleagues in various departments at the University of Illinois and elsewhere. Their suggestions were incorporated in a series of revisions, and a final version (actually the seventh) was completed on December 8, 1952. This text is printed as document ii below.

A group of sixty-two historians agreed to sponsor the proposed resolutions, which were submitted to the Council of the American Historical Association under date of December 17, 1952. The names of the sponsors are attached to the letter of transmittal, which is printed as document i below.

Beginning on December 4, 1952, mimeographed copies of the proposed resolutions were mailed to friends and acquaintances in a number of colleges and universities throughout the country for circulation among their colleagues. Two formulas for signature were provided, one by which members of the American Historical Association might urge the adoption of the resolutions, and a second by which scholars and scientists in other fields might indicate their support.

The response was prompt and overwhelming. On December 19, 1952 (fifteen days after the document was first mailed out), a press release was prepared, giving the names of 554 scholars and scientists whose signatures had been received by that date. Though only a fraction of the universities and colleges of the country had been addressed (and this in a very unsystematic way), no further circulation of the resolutions was attempted. Signatures continued to come in, and on December 24, 1952, a supplementary press release reported a total of 618 names.

The final count showed a total of 695 signatories, of whom 199 were historians (62 sponsors and 137 other supporters), 93 were in English, 86 in the biological sciences, 77 in mathematics, 64 in the physical sciences, 41 in the foreign languages, 34 in agriculture, 25 in engineering, and the rest scattered (17 in philosophy, 13 in economics, 11 in political science, 8 in psychology, 8 in sociology, 8 in journalism, 4 in geography, 4 in pharmacy, and 3 in art and music). A total of 56 colleges and universities, in 31 states and the District of Columbia, were represented. Members of most of the major learned societies of the country were among the supporters of the measure.

The Council of the American Historical Association, at its meeting on December 27, 1952, decided against adopting the resolutions in the form presented, but passed a resolution of its own authorizing the appointment of a committee to approach the other learned societies on the matter. This resolution was reported to the business meeting of the Association on December 29, 1952, and was there approved. The text is printed as document iii below. I myself spoke from the floor in support of the substitute resolution presented by the Council, on the ground that it represented a positive step toward initiating the cooperative effort by scholars and scientists which the original resolutions envisaged.

The proposed resolutions and the resolution actually adopted by the Council of the American Historical Association (documents ii and iii below) were published in full in *School and Society*, LXXVII, 68-70 (January 31, 1953). The actions were reported in the *American Histori-*

*cal Review,* LVIII, 759-760, 777, 781 (April 1953). Editorials dealing with the proposed resolutions were published in the following newspapers: Baltimore (Md.) *Sun,* Dec. 30, 1952; Champaign-Urbana (Ill.) *Courier,* Jan. 5, 1953; Champaign-Urbana (Ill.) *News-Gazette,* Jan. 7, 1953; Decatur (Ill.) *Herald,* Jan. 2, 1953; Louisville (Ky.) *Courier-Journal,* Jan. 3, 1953; Richmond (Va.) *Times-Dispatch,* Jan. 13, 1953; Rochester (N.Y.) *Democrat and Chronicle,* Jan. 5, 1953; Rockford (Ill.) *Morning Star,* Jan. 3, 1953; St. Louis (Mo.) *Post-Dispatch,* Jan. 2, 1953; San Francisco (Calif.) *Chronicle,* Dec. 30, 1952; Washington (D.C.) *Post,* Dec. 29, 1952; Washington (D.C.) *Evening Star,* Dec. 30, 1952; Winston-Salem (N.C.) *Journal,* Dec. 31, 1952.

i. LETTER OF TRANSMITTAL

December 17, 1952

To the Council of the American Historical Association:

We, the undersigned, believing that the time has come for scholars and scientists to take a united stand in defense of sound intellectual training in the public schools, wish to propose the attached resolutions for adoption at the annual business meeting of the American Historical Association in Washington on Monday, December 29, 1952.

The resolutions were originally drafted by Professor Bestor for incorporation in the paper which he will read to the Association on December 28. The text has gone through several revisions as the result of suggestions received from historians and from scholars in other fields. The list of supporters given at the end of the document indicates that the measure proposed is likely to enlist the co-operation of learned societies in many other fields.

We urge the Council to recommend the resolutions to the members of the Association for action at the annual business meeting. If the Council does not feel that it should take the step of recommending the resolutions, Professor Bestor will ask permission to present them from the floor.

Respectfully submitted,

DOUGLASS ADAIR, Associate Professor of History, College of William and Mary in Virginia

GEORGE L. ANDERSON, Professor of History and Chairman of the Department, University of Kansas

PAUL M. ANGLE, Secretary and Director, Chicago Historical Society

WILLIAM O. AYDELOTTE, Professor of History and Chairman of the Department, State University of Iowa

THOMAS A. BAILEY, Professor of History and Executive Head of the Department, Stanford University; member of the Council, American Historical Association

CHARLES A. BARKER, Professor of History, Johns Hopkins University

HOWARD K. BEALE, Professor of History, University of Wisconsin

SAMUEL F. BEMIS, Professor of History and Inter-American Relations, Yale University

ARTHUR E. BESTOR, JR., Professor of History, University of Illinois

RAY A. BILLINGTON, William Smith Mason Professor of History, Northwestern University

GRAY C. BOYCE, Professor of History and Chairman of the Department, Northwestern University

MERIBETH E. CAMERON, Academic Dean and Professor of History, Mount Holyoke College

MANOEL CARDOZO, Associate Professor of Portuguese and of Brazilian History, Catholic University of America

VERNON CARSTENSEN, Associate Professor of History, University of Wisconsin

THOMAS C. COCHRAN, Professor of the History of the People of the United States, University of Pennsylvania

RICHARD N. CURRENT, Associate Professor of History, University of Illinois

FREDERICK C. DIETZ, Professor of History and Head of the Department, University of Illinois

CHESTER V. EASUM, Professor of History, University of Wisconsin

CLEMENT EATON, Professor of History, University of Kentucky

JOHN T. FARRELL, Professor of History, Catholic University of America

HAROLD U. FAULKNER, Professor of History, Smith College

JOHN HOPE FRANKLIN, Professor of History, Howard University

FRANK FREIDEL, Associate Professor of History, University of Illinois

FLETCHER M. GREEN, Kenan Professor of History, University of North Carolina

LEWIS HANKE, Professor of Latin American History, and Director, Institute of Latin American Studies, University of Texas

FRED H. HARRINGTON, Professor of History and Chairman of the Department, University of Wisconsin

CARLTON J. H. HAYES, Seth Low Professor of History, Emeritus, Columbia University; Past President, American Historical Association

JOHN HIGHAM, Assistant Professor of History, University of California, Los Angeles

MERRILL JENSEN, Professor of History, University of Wisconsin

PAUL KNAPLUND, Professor of History, University of Wisconsin

MICHAEL KRAUS, Professor of History, City College, New York

RICHARD W. LEOPOLD, Associate Professor of History, Northwestern University

ARTHUR S. LINK, Associate Professor of History, Northwestern University

CHARLES H. McILWAIN, Eaton Professor of the Science of Government, Emeritus, Harvard University; Past President, American Historical Association

JAMES C. MALIN, Professor of History, University of Kansas

SAMUEL ELIOT MORISON, Jonathan Trumbull Professor of American History, Harvard University; Past President, American Historical Association

RICHARD B. MORRIS, Professor of History, Columbia University

GEORGE MOWRY, Professor of History, University of California, Los Angeles

CHARLES F. MULLETT, Professor of History, University of Missouri

ALLAN NEVINS, DeWitt Clinton Professor of American History, Columbia University

CHARLES E. NOWELL, Professor of History, University of Illinois

FREDERICK L. NUSSBAUM, Professor of History, University of Wyoming

STANLEY PARGELLIS, Librarian, Newberry Library, Chicago

GEORGE W. PIERSON, Professor of History, Yale University

GAINES POST, Professor of History, University of Wisconsin

JAMES G. RANDALL, Professor of History, Emeritus, University of Illinois; President, American Historical Association

ROBERT L. REYNOLDS, Professor of History, University of Wisconsin

WILLIAM L. SACHSE, Professor of History, University of Wisconsin

GEORGE SARTON, Professor of the History of Science, Emeritus, Harvard University

MAX H. SAVELLE, Professor of History, University of Washington; member of the Council, American Historical Association

ARTHUR M. SCHLESINGER, Francis Lee Higginson Professor of History, Harvard University; Past President, American Historical Association

ROBERT LIVINGSTON SCHUYLER, Gouverneur Morris Professor of History, Emeritus, Columbia University; Past President, American Historical Association

JAMES L. SELLERS, Professor of History and Chairman of the Department, University of Nebraska

FRED A. SHANNON, Professor of History, University of Illinois

KENNETH M. STAMPP, Professor of History, University of California, Berkeley

CHESTER G. STARR, JR., Associate Professor of History, University of
   Illinois
RAYMOND P. STEARNS, Professor of History, University of Illinois
WENDELL H. STEPHENSON, Professor of History, Tulane University
JOSEPH WARD SWAIN, Professor of History, University of Illinois
THOMAS J. WERTENBAKER, Edwards Professor of American History,
   Emeritus, Princeton University; Past President, American Histori-
   cal Association
C. VANN WOODWARD, Professor of History, Johns Hopkins University
LOUIS B. WRIGHT, Director, Folger Library, Washington, D.C.

ii. PROPOSED RESOLUTIONS CONCERNING PUBLIC EDUCATION

*Preamble.*—The American Historical Association is enjoined by its
Act of Incorporation to report on "the condition of historical study in
America," and it has always interpreted this mandate to include a con-
cern with the teaching of history in the public schools of the nation.

The American Historical Association stands ready, as it has always
done, to co-operate with educational administrators in devising sound
public-school programs in history and the social studies. It is alarmed,
however, at the growth of anti-intellectualist conceptions of education
among important groups of school administrators and educational
theorists. Such conceptions have led, in many instances, to public-
school curricula in which intellectual training has been pushed into
the background, to teacher certification laws and rulings that dangerously underemphasize training in the subjects to be taught, and to pro-
nouncements to the effect that the intellectual criteria employed by
scholars and scientists are inapplicable to the public schools. To the
degree that such anti-intellectualist conceptions gain headway in the
public-school system, the possibility of fruitful co-operation between
scholars and professional educators grows smaller.

Because of the serious danger to American intellectual life arising
from anti-intellectualist tendencies, the members of this association
believe that co-operation with professional educators in devising specific school programs should be supplemented by activity of another
kind, designed to uphold and strengthen sound, systematic, disciplined
intellectual training in the public schools. Such an effort presupposes a
clear-cut statement of the educational philosophy to which scholars
and scientists subscribe, and seems to call for co-operation among all
the learned societies of the country, acting through an independent,
interdisciplinary commission of their own creation.

*Therefore, be it resolved,* that the American Historical Association reaffirms its belief in the following educational principles:

1. An indispensable function of education, at every level, is to provide sound training in the fundamental ways of thinking represented by history, science, mathematics, literature, language, art, and the other disciplines evolved in the course of mankind's long quest for usable knowledge, cultural understanding, and intellectual power. To advance moral conduct, responsible citizenship, and social adjustment is, of course, a vital function of education. But, like the other agencies which contribute to these ends, the school must work within the context provided by its own characteristic activity. In other words, the particular contribution which the school can make is determined by, and related to, the primary fact that it is an agency of intellectual training.

2. The ability to handle and apply complex ideas, to make use of a wide range of accurate knowledge, and to command the means of effective expression is valuable not only to the scholar or scientist, but equally to the citizen, the businessman, the skilled worker, the farmer, the house-wife, and the parent. Their practical needs cannot be effectively served by vocational and utilitarian training unless such training includes a conscious intellectual component. Only if men are led to grasp the theory behind the practice can they achieve the superior efficiency in every activity of life which comes, as Horace Mann said, "where *mind* is a member of the partnership."

3. An educational philosophy is both anti-intellectual and anti-democratic if it asserts that sound training in the fundamental intellectual disciplines is appropriate only for the minority of students who are preparing for college and the professions, and if it proposes to deprive the rest of the children of our people of such training by substituting programs that minimize intellectual aims.

4. The content of the public-school curriculum is of such vital importance to the entire intellectual, scientific, and professional life of the nation that control of secondary-school educational policy ought not to be vested exclusively in a narrow group of secondary-school administrators and professional educators. Scholars, scientists, and other professional men must assume responsibility for advising the public clearly and continuously concerning the scientific and scholarly soundness of proposed changes in the curricula of the public schools. And universities and colleges must preserve and strengthen their entrance requirements in the basic fields of knowledge not merely to maintain their own standards but also to prevent, so far as possible, the deterioration of the secondary-school education which is provided for students not planning to enter college.

5. The great intellectual disciplines are not mere collections of facts and formulas, but ways of thinking with organized structures of their own. The learning of facts is not intellectual training, unless those facts are seen as the conclusions of systematic inquiry and as part of a larger structure of knowledge. Reorganizations of the curriculum are destructive if they cause the student to lose sight of the ordered relationships that exist, and of the methods of investigation that are employed, within each of the basic fields of knowledge. In particular, no genuine knowledge of history is imparted by an omnibus course that uses isolated historical facts merely as illustra-

tions, that presents no conception of historical development, or that treats history itself as irrelevant to an understanding of contemporary society.

6. "It being, of course, the first requisite of a teacher that he should himself know well that which he is to aid others in learning" (to quote the words spoken at the opening of one of the two original institutions for teacher training established in the United States), all programs for the training and certification of teachers must emphasize competence in the subject to be taught. Experienced teachers, in particular, ought not to be permitted to achieve professional advancement by piling up additional credits in pedagogical courses when their greatest need is to acquire a more thorough and advanced knowledge of the disciplines they are responsible for teaching.

7. Freedom implies responsibility, and freedom of teaching implies a responsibility on the teacher's part of knowing the facts and of applying the critical methods of scholarship to the subjects that come up for discussion in the classroom. The freedom of all teachers is placed in jeopardy whenever teachers who are inadequately trained in subject matter undertake to handle controversial topics. Especially in history and the social studies, where practically all topics are controversial, freedom of teaching can be convincingly defended only if teachers are held to rigorous standards of competence in the disciplines involved.

8. To insist that instruction must meet the exacting standards of scholarship is not to infringe upon freedom of teaching. Such infringements occur when pressure groups—whether reactionary or radical—force the schools to conform to their preconceived ideas, to limit the curriculum, to censor textbooks, or to forbid the teaching of controversial subjects. Scientists and scholars must vigorously resist such efforts to impose upon the schools any narrow dogma in politics, economics, religion, or science, for learning itself is thereby threatened with destruction. They must also resist anti-intellectualism in the schools themselves, for if freedom of thinking and respect for intellectual effort are undermined there, it will be easy for demagogues to convince a larger public that intellectual effort is of little value in any case, and that freedom of thought is not worth preserving.

*Furthermore, be it resolved,* that the American Historical Association calls upon its sister learned societies in every field to join with it in creating a Permanent Scientific and Scholarly Commission on Secondary Education, to be made up exclusively of scholars and scientists in the various disciplines of learning, to be affiliated with the scholarly and scientific societies of the country (as distinguished from professional educational associations and from non-professional general organizations), to be adequately financed and provided with an efficient secretariat, and to be charged with the following functions:

1. To analyze, with respect to their scientific and scholarly soundness, every major proposal (of the recent past, the present, and the future) affecting the content and organization of the public secondary-school curriculum;

2. To scrutinize programs of teacher training in order to ascertain their adequacy in giving teachers command of the disciplines they are supposed to teach;

3. To study the laws and administrative rulings governing the certification of teachers in order to determine whether these encourage excessive course work in pedagogy at the expense of thorough training in subject matter, and whether they operate to exclude from teaching well-qualified young men and women trained in the liberal arts and sciences;

4. To study the membership and the structure of Federal, state, and municipal departments of education and of publicly sponsored educational commissions to determine whether the scholarly and scientific point of view is adequately represented in the agencies that decide public-school policy;

5. To study college admission policies from the point of view of their efficacy in preserving and strengthening disciplined intellectual training in the secondary schools;

6. To organize subcommittees to work under its general direction on matters connected with one particular field of learning or on the problems of one particular state;

7. To make its findings known to as wide a public as possible, through publication and other means;

8. To recommend courses of action that might be adopted by the scientific and scholarly societies or by their individual members in order to further the ends in view;

9. To furnish information and professional opinion to governmental agencies, legislative and executive, concerning the scholarly and scientific implications of proposed public-school policies, and to offer specific recommendations if requested;

10. To co-operate with public educational administrators in devising sound programs for the public schools in the basic intellectual disciplines, on the understanding that the programs mutually agreed upon will actually be made the basis of curricular reorganizations in the public schools.

*Finally, be it resolved* that the council of this association is hereby requested to consider ways and means of furthering the purposes herein proposed; and that the executive secretary is instructed to transmit copies of this document to the officers of all the other national learned and scientific societies, to the executive staffs of the federations of such societies, and to such other persons as shall seem to him appropriate.

iii. RESOLUTION ADOPTED BY THE COUNCIL OF THE AMERICAN HISTORICAL ASSOCIATION, DECEMBER 27, 1952

The Council discussed sympathetically Professor Bestor's resolutions concerning public education. After careful consideration, it was the consensus in the Council that the problem presented by these resolutions is a serious one, meriting close and thoughtful study before any action by the Association. The Council felt, however, that adoption of these resolutions in their present text would be premature, since action by the Association must take into due account certain important implications of any such action.

For the Association should very carefully determine, first, precisely what the policy of the Association itself ought to be, relative to this problem. Secondly, it is thought that the Association should approach the other learned societies with a view of formulating some sort of common policy with them. Thirdly, it is thought that any effective implementation of the sense of the resolutions would best be forwarded by taking into consideration the mature thought of the professional educators who are conscious of this problem and would wish to collaborate in the formulation of any comprehensive statement on national educational policy.

The Council therefore authorizes the incoming president of the Association to appoint a committee to formulate and bring to the Association a statement of its policy, to approach the other learned societies and professional educators on the subject of a common position relative to the problem, and to discuss with them the possible setting up of the proposed interdisciplinary educational commission.

# Acknowledgments

Parts of this book have appeared in the *William and Mary Quarterly* (January 1952), *The American Scholar* (Spring 1952), the *Scientific Monthly* (August 1952), the American Association of University Professors *Bulletin* (Autumn 1952), the *New Republic* (January 19, 1953), *School and Society* (January 31, 1953), and the *Christian Register* (March 1953). I am grateful to the editors and publishers of these journals for permission to reprint the material here, some of it in considerably altered form.

I likewise acknowledge with thanks the permission of The Macmillan Company to print the extracts from John Dewey contained in chapter 4, and the permission of Time Inc. to reproduce the article which constitutes note 13 to chapter 7.

I have profited greatly from conversation and correspondence with hundreds of persons throughout the United States, to all of whom I express sincere thanks. I also appreciate the opportunity that has been afforded to me to present my views before a number of different bodies in a number of different states. Needless to say, the ideas expressed in this book are not necessarily those of any group which has extended to me the courtesy of its platform or its pages.

What perhaps does need saying is that the problem I am discussing is nationwide in its scope. I have had in mind the situation in no one university nor in any one state. Such examples as I have given could be duplicated in any part of the United States; in presenting them I have had no intention of singling out for criticism any particular region or institution.

This disclaimer should be made specific for my home state of Illinois and for its state University, on whose faculty I am proud to serve. Only the last quarter of my twenty-three years of teaching has been spent at the University of Illinois, and many of the ideas expressed in this book derive from experiences, observations, and discussions at the seven other major universities, in seven widely separated states, at which I have been privileged to teach: Yale, Columbia, Stanford, Wisconsin, Minnesota, Northwestern, and Wyoming.

The non-localized character of my argument is best indicated by the fact that during the past year I have spoken on the subject by invitation before national and regional organizations or under the auspices of colleges in seven states besides my own and in the District of Columbia, namely: the American Historical Association; the Michigan College Association; the Arizona College Association; the Mahoning County (Ohio) Teachers Association; the City Club of Rochester, New York; St. John's College, Annapolis, Maryland; the Arkansas State Teachers College, Conway; the University of Wyoming; the AAUP chapter of the Catholic University of America, Washington, D.C.; and the Phi Beta Kappa chapter of the University of Buffalo. I have delivered only one public address on the subject on my own campus, and this at a considerably earlier date.

# Notes

## 1. THE VANISHING SENSE OF PURPOSE IN EDUCATION

[1] The quoted phrases are from various letters of Jefferson, dated between 1786 and 1822. They are easily accessible in *Thomas Jefferson On Democracy*, ed. by S. K. Padover (New York: Penguin Books, 1946), pp. 89, 149, 87, 90, 118, 89, 90.

[2] U. S. Office of Education, *Biennial Survey of Education in the United States, 1948–50*, Chapter 2, *Statistics of State School Systems* (Washington, 1952), pp. 28-29, Table 1, "Statistical Summary of Public Elementary and Secondary Schools: 1870–1950." The precise figures are as follows. Columns and rows marked with an asterisk contain derived figures, calculated from but not actually presented in the original tables.

| | 1869–70 | 1949–50 | *Figure for 1949–50 as a multiple of figure for 1869–70 |
|---|---|---|---|
| Pupils enrolled | 6,872,000 | 25,111,000 | 3.65 |
| Percent of children 5-17 years of age (inclusive) enrolled | 57.0% | 81.6% | — |
| Total expenditures | $63,397,000 | $5,837,643,000 | 92.08 |
| Total expenditure per pupil in average attendance | $15.55 | $258.85 | 16.65 |
| *Total expenditure per pupil in average attendance, adjusted for purchasing power of 1949–50 dollar | $28.95 | $258.85 | 8.94 |
| Average number of days attended by each pupil enrolled | 78.4 days | 157.9 days | 2.01 |
| Total teachers | 201,000 | 914,000 | 4.55 |
| *Average number of pupils enrolled, per teacher | 34.2 | 27.5 | — |
| Value of school property | $130,383,000 | $11,396,804,000 | 87.41 |

209

| | | | |
|---|---|---|---|
| *Average value of school property per pupil enrolled | $18.97 | $453.86 | 23.92 |
| *Average value of school property per pupil enrolled, adjusted for purchasing power of 1949–50 dollar | $35.53 | $453.86 | 12.77 |
| Pupils enrolled in public high schools | 80,000 | 5,707,000 | 71.3 |
| Percent secondary enrollment is of total enrollment | 1.2% | 22.7% | — |

The adjustment for the value of the dollar, which has been made in the fifth and the eleventh rows of this table, employs the Bureau of Labor Statistics Wholesale Price Index (all commodities), which stood at 86.7 in 1870 and at 161.5 in 1950. U.S. Bureau of the Census, *Historical Statistics of the United States, 1789–1945* (Washington, 1949), series L 15; and supplements in the *Statistical Abstract*.

The last two rows in the table indicate the tremendous expansion of enrollment at the secondary school level. Educationists prefer to concentrate attention upon these figures, rather than upon total enrollment. Unfortunately no separate figures for secondary school expenditures alone are available, the administration of the two levels of the system being inextricably entwined. Consequently no calculation of total expenditure per pupil in average attendance *in high school* is possible. Since higher teachers' salaries, more expensive buildings, and greater overhead for transportation and the like are characteristic of secondary education as compared with elementary, it is reasonable to assume that high school expenditures constitute more, not less, than 22.7 percent of total school expenditures today. There is no evidence whatever to suggest that the total expenditure per pupil in high school has increased less rapidly since 1870 than the total expenditure per pupil in the system as a whole.

[3] See, for example, William H. Burton, "Get the Facts," *Progressive Education*, XXIX, 89-90 (Jan. 1952). The educationists, it seems to me, draw the wrong moral from these quotations out of the past. The persistent and unchanging criticism of the inadequate training afforded by the public schools in the basic skills of reading, writing, and arithmetic constitutes the one clear mandate which educational authorities have received from the public—a mandate to devote the full resources of the schools to improving and intensifying training in the fundamental intellectual disciplines.

[4] Earl H. Hanson, "Today's SCHOOLS Are Better, Too—The Facts Are on Their Side," *NEA Journal*, XL, 619-621 (Dec. 1951). A more extensive statement is Archibald W. Anderson, "The Charges Against American Education: What Is the Evidence?" *Progressive Education*, XXIX, 94-96 (Jan. 1952).

2. THE IDEAL OF DISCIPLINED INTELLIGENCE

[1] Edwin H. Reeder, "The Quarrel Between Professors of Academic Subjects and Professors of Education: An Analysis," American Association of University Professors *Bulletin*, XXXVII, 514 (Autumn 1951).

[2] Ralph Waldo Emerson, "The American Scholar" (1837), in his *Complete Works*, ed. by Edward W. Emerson (12 vols., Boston, 1903–04), I, 111-12.

## 3. IS A GOOD EDUCATION UNDEMOCRATIC?

[1] William Ellery Channing, address at Taunton, Mass., reprinted (from a newspaper report) in Henry Barnard, *Normal Schools* (Hartford, Conn., 1851), pp. 96-97.

[2] *Henry Barnard on Education*, ed. by John S. Brubacher (New York, 1931), p. 96.

[3] Archibald W. Anderson, "The Cloak of Respectability: The Attackers and Their Methods," *Progressive Education*, XXIX, 70 (Jan. 1952). In an anonymous letter to the editor of a local newspaper, some remarks of mine in favor of intellectual training for *all* children in the public schools were attacked on the ground that they involved "acceptance of the nineteenth century ideal of class education." Champaign-Urbana (Ill.) *Courier*, March 10, 1952.

[4] Philadelphia *National Gazette*, July 10, Aug. 23, Aug. 25, Aug. 19, 1830; reprinted in John R. Commons and others, eds., *A Documentary History of American Industrial Society* (10 vols. and supplement, Cleveland, 1909–11), V, 107-8, 112, 114, 112.

[5] Alexis de Tocqueville, *Democracy in America*, Part II (1840), revised translation by Phillips Bradley (2 vols., New York, 1945), II, 35.

[6] Horace Mann, "Twelfth Annual Report" (Nov. 24, 1848), in Massachusetts Board of Education, *Annual Reports*, XII (1849), 55, 59-60.

[7] *Ibid.*, pp. 67-68, 71.

[8] *Ibid.*, pp. 76-78.

[9] Horace Mann, "Fifth Annual Report" (Jan. 1, 1842), *ibid.*, V (1842), 116, 117, 118.

[10] George S. Counts, *Dare the School Build a New Social Order?* (New York, 1932).

## 4. PROGRESSIVE EDUCATION AND REGRESSIVE EDUCATION

[1] At the conclusion of a long series of public statements concerning public education, made at various times during the spring of 1952 by the heads of the departments of mathematics and English and by professors of botany, sociology, English, and history at the University of Illinois, the Dean of the College of Education at that institution dismissed the matter with the remark: "No serious student of education pays any attention to these arguments or gives them any weight." Champaign-Urbana (Ill.) *Courier*, June 18, 1952.

[2] Hughes Mearns, *Creative Youth: How a School Environment Set Free the Creative Spirit* (New York, 1925).

[3] John Dewey, *Experience and Education* (New York, 1938), pp. 86-87, 89-90, 96, 98-99, 102, 105-6. Quoted by permission of The Macmillan Company, publishers.

[4] William James, *Principles of Psychology* (2 vols., New York, 1890), I, 488.

[5] A. H. Lauchner, "How Can the Junior High School Curriculum Be Improved?" *Bulletin of the National Association of Secondary-School Principals*, vol. XXXV, no. 177, pp. 299-300 (March 1951). I am responsible for the indicated omissions at the *end* of certain paragraphs. The three dots that occur in the *middle* of sentences, however, are the original author's substitutes for conventional punctuation.

I have quoted this passage on several occasions. Many educationists profess to be horrified by it, but none has seen fit to follow my suggestion of writing a forthright critique in some professional educational journal. In other fields when a man writes arrant nonsense his colleagues promptly pin his ears back, for they are aware that silence on the part of the profession constitutes assent. My defense of intellectual training in the schools brought down upon me a 37-page attack in the pages of the very journal which, two years before, had published Mr. Lauchner's anti-intellectualist remarks without a murmur of protest. I pointed this out in my reply, and asked "Can any candid observer doubt which way the wind is blowing in Educationdom?" See Harold C. Hand and Charles W. Sanford, "A Scholar's Documents," *Bulletin of the National Association of Secondary-School Principals,* vol. XXXVII, no. 194, pp. 460-504 (April 1953), especially p. 500; and A. E. Bestor, "Reply to 'A Scholar's Documents,'" communicated on Sept. 2, 1952, to the editor of that journal for publication.

⁶ Kenneth L. Heaton and G. Robert Koopman, *A College Curriculum Based on Functional Needs of Students* (Chicago, 1936), p. 64. The volume describes an actual experiment involving the Central State Teachers College at Mount Pleasant, Mich.

⁷ *Ibid.,* p. 148.

⁸ U.S. Office of Education, *Biennial Survey of Education in the United States, 1948–50,* Chapter 5, *Offerings and Enrollments in High-School Subjects* (Washington, 1951), pp. 107-8, Table 7, ". . . Percentage of pupils enrolled in certain subjects in the last 4 years of public secondary day schools, 1889–90 to 1948–49." This table shows that in 1899–1900 exactly 50.6 percent of all high school students (as defined in the heading of the table) were enrolled in courses in Latin. In 1948–49 the following percentages of the student body were enrolled in the various foreign languages: Spanish, 8.2 percent; Latin 7.8 percent; French, 4.7 percent; German, 0.8 percent; Italian, 0.3 percent; others negligible. The total of all comes to only 21.8 percent. This total would include duplications (that is, students studying more than one language), whereas the figure for Latin alone would presumably not; hence the disparity between the two dates was doubtless even greater than the figures indicate. If one adds up the percentages for 1899–1900 in all the various languages the total comes to 72.7 percent.

⁹ See the passages from John Locke and others collected by Benjamin Franklin in a footnote to his *Proposals for the Education of Youth in Pennsylvania* (1749), ed. by R. G. A[dams] (Ann Arbor, Mich., 1927), pp. 14-17. Note that none of the writers disparages grammar as such.

¹⁰ U.S. Office of Education, *op. cit.,* p. 29, paragraph 13. As late as 1909–10 no less than 56.9 percent of all high school students were enrolled in courses in algebra alone, and 30.9 percent were studying geometry. Today (1948–49) only 54.7 percent of the students are taking any sort of mathematics. Even "general mathematics," the hybrid that is supposed to appeal to the "real-life" needs of pupils, enrolls only 13.1 percent of the student body. *Ibid.,* pp. 107-8, Table 7.

¹¹ *Ibid.,* pp. 26-27.

¹² *Ibid.,* p. 27, paragraph 5.

## 5. THE SCHOOL AND THE PRACTICAL NEEDS OF YOUTH

¹ The situation which normal schools were founded to correct was clearly

stated in numerous contemporary documents. According to William Russell, writing in 1823, "The common schools for children, are, in not a few instances, conducted by individuals who do not possess one of the qualifications of an instructor; and, in very many cases, there is barely knowledge enough 'to keep the teacher at a decent distance from his scholars.'" Quoted by Henry Barnard, *Normal Schools* (Hartford, 1851), p. 9, who considered this statement of Russell's the earliest plea for normal schools in Connecticut.

² University of Illinois, *Undergraduate Study, 1952–1953* (University of Illinois *Bulletin,* vol. 49, no. 82, July 1952), p. 317. This course is *Education 234.* To illustrate the retardation to which students in education are subjected, it is amusing to note the courses that bear the same number in two of the genuinely scientific departments: *Chemistry 234* is Organic Chemistry (p. 294); *Theoretical and Applied Mechanics 234* is Laboratory in Fluid Mechanics (p. 441).

³ University of Illinois, *Catalog, Urbana Departments, Graduate College, 1952–1954* (University of Illinois *Bulletin,* vol. 50, no. 8, Sept. 1952), pp. 104-7. Courses numbered 400 and above (as all these are) are open to graduate students only.

⁴ Ralph Waldo Emerson, "The American Scholar," in his *Complete Works,* ed. by Edward W. Emerson, I, 102.

⁵ National Association of Secondary-School Principals, *Planning for American Youth: An Educational Program for Youth of Secondary-School Age* (Washington, 1944), p. 10; the ten points are stated more verbosely on p. 43. This pamphlet is a summary of *Education for All American Youth,* published by the Educational Policies Commission of the National Education Association. The pamphlet is quoted here, rather than the longer work, because it was the one more directly addressed to the public at large and more widely circulated.

⁶ *Scientific Monthly,* LXXV, 109-116 (Aug. 1952). Passages from this article are incorporated in the various chapters of the present book.

⁷ Quoted in Ellwood P. Cubberley, *Public Education in the United States* (Boston, 1919), p. 146.

⁸ Horace Mann, "Twelfth Annual Report" (Nov. 24, 1848), in Massachusetts Board of Education, *Annual Reports,* XII (1849), 78-79.

6. "LIFE-ADJUSTMENT" TRAINING: A PARODY OF EDUCATION

¹ U.S. Office of Education, *Life Adjustment Education for Every Youth* (Office of Education, *Bulletin, 1951,* no. 22; Washington, 1951), p. 16, n. 2. The resolution was drafted by Dr. Charles A. Prosser.

² President's Commission on Higher Education, *Higher Education for American Democracy* (1947–48), as excerpted in Gail Kennedy, ed., *Education for Democracy* (Boston, 1952), p. 20.

³ Illinois Secondary School Curriculum Program, Bulletin No. 9, *New College Admission Requirements Recommended* ([Springfield, Ill.], Jan. 1950), p. 3. The agency responsible for this series will hereafter be abbreviated ISSCP.

⁴ Florence B. Stratemeyer and others, *Developing a Curriculum for Modern Living* (New York, 1947), pp. 76, 89.

⁵ *Life Adjustment Education for Every Youth,* pp. 11-12.

⁶ *Ibid.,* p. 7.

[7] ISSCP, Bulletin No. 13, *How the Illinois Secondary School Curriculum Program Basic Studies Can Help You Improve Your High School* (May 1951), pp. 8-9.

[8] *Ibid.*, pp. 11-13.

[9] ISSCP, Bulletin [No. 1], *Guide to the Study of the Curriculum in the Secondary Schools of Illinois* (Aug. 1948), p. 33.

[10] ISSCP, Bulletin No. 11, *How to Conduct the Follow-Up Study* (Aug. 1950), pp. 30-32.

[11] *Ibid.*, p. 11.

[12] *Ibid.*, p. 33.

[13] *Ibid.*, pp. 11, 12, 13.

[14] *Ibid.*, pp. 30-32, items B2, C3, E3, G1, B9, F6, F7.

[15] *Ibid.*, item H8.

[16] ISSCP, Bulletin [No. 1], p. 10.

[17] ISSCP, Bulletin No. 11, pp. 34 *et seqq.* In defending the "Follow-Up Study," Professor Hand denies that "the initial poll results are to be taken as a warrant for doing anything whatsoever in respect to the curriculum," and points out that instead they "are to be utilized as the beginning point for group discussions among patrons, teachers, and pupils in which choices *among the problems suggested by the Study* are to be made" (Harold C. Hand and Charles W. Sanford, "A Scholar's Documents," *Bulletin of the National Association of Secondary-School Principals*, vol. XXXVII, no. 194, p. 483, April 1953; italics added). In view of the words I have italicized, it is difficult to see what difference this makes, unless it be a difference for the worse. My objection is that no sentiment in favor of systematic training in the basic intellectual disciplines can appear in the answers to Professor Hand's questionnaires, because none of the disciplines are mentioned in the questions. The circumstance that these answers are to be "the beginning point for group discussions" merely means that more people are going to be misled by the biased data furnished to them.

[18] *Ibid.*, p. 10. Note also the following statements: "The central purpose underlying the use of this questionnaire is precisely that of securing factual evidence which can be used to persuade a larger proportion of the pupils, teachers, and school patrons of the necessity of thus functionalizing the high school curriculum" (p. 13, repeated almost verbatim on p. 27). "The Follow-Up Study . . . is designed to yield opinion data . . . which will be helpful in 'engineering' an improved, broadly based consensus regarding what the local high school should be doing for its students" (ISSCP, Bulletin No. 13, p. 14).

[19] ISSCP, Bulletin [No. 1], p. 35.

[20] ISSCP, Bulletin No. 11, pp. 30-32, items E8, E10.

[21] Letter from Harold C. Hand, Urbana, Ill., Feb. 25, 1952. Quoted with the writer's permission, the indicated elisions being authorized by him.

[22] ISSCP, Bulletin No. 13, p. 11.

[23] ISSCP, Bulletin No. 11, p. 15.

[24] *Ibid.*, p. 17.

[25] *Ibid.*, p. 9.

[26] ISSCP, Bulletin [No. 1], p. 6.

[27] *Ibid.*, p. 35.

[28] ISSCP, Bulletin No. 9, pp. 5-6.

[29] *Ibid.*, pp. 13-14.
[30] ISSCP, Bulletin [No. 1], p. 25.
[31] ISSCP, Bulletin No. 9, p. 13.
[32] ISSCP, Bulletin No. 13, p. 15.
[33] *Ibid.*, pp. 16-18.
[34] ISSCP, Bulletin No. 16, *The Schools and National Security* (May 1951), p. iii.
[35] *Ibid.*, p. 1.
[36] *Ibid.* The italics are in the original.
[37] *Ibid.*, pp. 2-3.
[38] *Ibid.*, p. 3.
[39] *Ibid.*, p. 4.
[40] *Ibid.*, pp. xi-xii.
[41] *Ibid.*, p. 221. The italics are in the original.
[42] *Ibid.*, p. 230.
[43] *Ibid.*, p. 229.
[44] *Ibid.*, p. 230. This recommendation was mentioned as an example of anti-intellectualism in the schools in an address which I delivered to the American Historical Association on Dec. 28, 1952. Two defenders of the Illinois Curriculum Program objected that the quotation was "unrepresentative" (Harold C. Hand and Charles W. Sanford, "A Scholar's Documents," *Bulletin of the National Association of Secondary-School Principals,* vol. XXXVII, no. 194, p. 470, April 1953). I do not consider it so. "Life-adjustment" education is presented as something new, therefore something different from the traditional program of systematic training in the intellectual disciplines. To determine the new direction it is proposing, one must look at the *novel* objectives it avows, and the quoted item is justly representative of these. I am happy that "life-adjustment" educationists still hope to lead young people to "understand the historical development of the democratic tradition and also that of other ideologies" (quoted *ibid.*, p. 469), though it seems to me that they submerge this objective in such a miscellany of activities that it stands little chance of being achieved. Be that as it may, one learns nothing about the *new* direction that "life-adjustment" education is taking by noting the objectives (like this one) which it professes in common with traditional programs. The thing that *differentiates* the two philosophies of education is the preoccupation of the new one with "reducing the tensions of young people." And this kind of emphasis can easily lead, as I point out, to employing the discipline of history for such purposes as making "studies of how the last war affected the dating pattern in our culture."

The matter can be looked at in another way, for the quotation actually forms part of an argument of the type denominated *reductio ad absurdum*: "the refutation of a proposition by demonstrating the absurd conclusion to which it would inevitably lead when logically developed." I consider the definition of the "major tasks" of a social studies teacher, offered in *The Schools and National Security,* inadequate, contorted, and misleading. Many sound and defensible kinds of instruction are doubtless *possible* within its terms. But an adequate statement of educational aims needs to be discriminating as well as inclusive, and this one is not. It opens the way to trivial and even worthless programs of instruction. To show that this is true I had only to quote the report itself, which reached conclusions that are perfectly logical but at the same time patently ridiculous. I know of no rule in logic or historical criticism which forbids one to quote the absurd conclusion of a writer as evidence that his orignal assumptions were faulty.

## 7. THE INTERLOCKING DIRECTORATE OF PROFESSIONAL EDU-CATIONISTS

[1] Illinois Secondary School Curriculum Program, Bulletin No. [1], p. 15.

[2] *Ibid.*, p. 42.

[3] The list of members of the steering committee is published in each of the Bulletins. The following analysis of its membership was supplied by Dean C. W. Sanford, Director of the Program, under date of March 5, 1952: "There are 27 superintendents, principals, professors of education, and representatives of the State Department of Education; 15 high school teachers of agriculture, art, biology, business education, chemistry, English, French and Spanish, home economics, vocational industrial education, mathematics, physical education, and social studies; seven representatives of lay groups; three college teachers of geography, music, and speech; two presidents of liberal arts colleges; one dean of girls in a high school; one librarian in a high school; one director of teachers' welfare in an education association; and one head of a parochial school unit."

[4] These three college professors, moreover, sat as representatives not of the national learned societies in their fields, but of teachers' organizations: the Illinois Council of Geography Teachers, the Illinois Music Educators Association, and the Illinois Speech Association (the representative being the chairman of a university Department of Speech Education). ISSCP, Bulletin No. 13, pp. 27-28.

[5] See pp. 209-10, above.

[6] *Report of the Committee of Ten on Secondary School Studies* (New York: Published for the National Educational Association by the American Book Co., 1894), pp. 4, 10.

[7] *The Social Studies in Secondary Education* (U.S. Bureau of Education, *Bulletin, 1916*, no. 28; Washington, 1916), pp. 6-7.

[8] One outstanding exception, of course, was the *Report of the Commission on the Social Studies*, published in 16 vols., from 1932 to 1937, under the editorship of August C. Krey. It numbered among its contributors many of the most distinguished scholars in the various fields covered. Nevertheless (whether because of its generality, its length, or the character of its recommendations), the report cannot be said to have exerted upon actual school programs an influence comparable to that of the late nineteenth and early twentieth century reports.

[9] Ward G. Reeder, *A First Course in Education* (revised ed., New York, 1943), p. 370.

[10] In the three-year period from July 1947 to May 1950 the *Education Index* listed twenty-nine articles under the heading "Life Adjustment Education Program." A careful check of these has failed to reveal any searching criticism of the underlying assumptions of the proposal, save for a few reservations by Catholic periodicals with respect to its predominantly secularistic character. A number of educationists, in discussions with me, have asserted that they agreed with many criticisms of the program that I

have made in a preceding chapter, and thence have argued that it is unfair to hold educationists collectively responsible for the anti-intellectualist tendencies implicit in the proposal. But one of the functions of professional journals is precisely that of subjecting new ideas to vigorous and continuous criticism from within the field, in order to dissociate the profession as a whole from the vagaries of its individual members, and to protect the general public from being misled by assuming, as it is bound to do in the absence of professional criticism, that a given idea has passed muster with those professionally charged with the responsibility of weighing it.

[11] National Congress of Parents and Teachers, "National Bylaws," art. III, sec. 3; published in its *Proceedings*, LIV (1950), 269.

[12] These phrases were actually used in a public address at the University of Illinois by the Dean of the College of Education, and were applied to a professor of botany at the same institution who had published an article critical of educationists in an official journal of the American Association for the Advancement of Science. See Champaign-Urbana (Ill.) *Courier*, Jan. 9, 1952. The article in question was Harry J. Fuller, "The Emperor's New Clothes, or Prius Dementat, " *Scientific Monthly*, LXXII, 32-41 (Jan. 1951).

Another example of the *argumentum ad hominem*, involving also a disingenuous suppression of relevant evidence, is analyzed in my "Reply to 'A Scholar's Documents,'" communicated on Sept. 2, 1953, to the *Bulletin of the National Association of Secondary-School Principals* for publication in answer to an article which appeared in that journal, vol. XXXVII, no. 194, pp. 460-504 (April 1953).

[13] The most appalling instance of this occurred recently at the University of Nevada. With the permission of the publishers, I reprint the account which appeared in *Time*, June 15, 1953, p. 50:

**THE RIGHT TO BE A BUTTINSKY**

On most campuses, no one would think there was anything very strange about the ideas of Frank Richardson. A mild-mannered man with a distracted, scholarly air, he is chairman of the biology department at the University of Nevada, has never done anything more unorthodox than ride to class on a motorcycle. But Richardson happens to believe in high academic standards and intellectual discipline. It was that belief that got him into hot water with Nevada's new President Minard W. Stout.

A former professor of education who was principal of the laboratory high school at the University of Minnesota, President Stout does not put too much store by conventional academic standards. He thinks that an emphasis on such "discipline" subjects as mathematics, languages and history is little more than "intellectual snobbery." Last fall, acting under this credo, Stout announced that Nevada would henceforth have no entrance standards at all, would take in any Nevada high-school graduate no matter what his ability or preparation. With that, the Stout *v.* Richardson battle was on.

"**Mind Your Own Business.**" As head of the local chapter of the American Association of University Professors, Biologist Richardson felt he had a duty to protest. After one Stout speech, he made some pointed criticisms, during the question period, of the new policy. He was also critical when Stout abolished the faculty's Academic Council. Later, he committed what to Stout seemed the most serious offense of all: he began distributing about the campus reprints of an article by Historian Arthur Bestor Jr. (TIME, Jan. 5) of the University of Illinois. The article was called "Aimlessness in Education," and it echoed Biologist Richardson's opinions completely. It denounced the brand of education that many modern pedagogues are preaching, called for a restoration of intellectual content to the U.S. curriculum.

A few days after that, Stout summoned Richardson to his office, told him that he had been hired to teach biology, that he should "mind your own business and stop being a buttinsky all over the campus." Richardson, still convinced that it is a professor's business to be concerned about educational philosophy, went right on discussing the matter with his colleagues. To President Stout, such talk amounted to a "vicious conspiracy." Last March he ordered Richardson and four other like-minded professors to show cause before the board of regents why they should not be fired.

Stout eventually changed his mind about the other four, but his attempt to dismiss Richardson raised an academic hue & cry far beyond Nevada's borders. At the University of Illinois, dozens of facultymen signed a petition of protest; other petitions went the rounds at Stanford and the University of California. Meanwhile, four Reno lawyers offered to fight Richardson's case without fee. This week the case was up before the board of regents.

"I Will Defend . . ." At the hearing the administration's special counsel, Harlan Heward, did his best against Biologist Richardson. To help prove that Richardson was nothing but a troublemaker, counsel tried to get Harold N. Brown, professor of education, to denounce the distribution of the Bestor article as an effort to split the campus. Surely, said Lawyer Heward, the article had angered Professor Brown. No, said Brown, it had not. "Well," cried Heward, "you must admit that the article wasn't any good." Answered Brown: "I never did agree with it, but that's a matter of opinion. [Richardson] had every right to send it, and I will defend the best I know how that right."

At week's end, the board of regents was still trying to decide about that right— the right of a professor to hold to his own educational principles and to be a buttinsky when he feels those principles are endangered. But whatever their decision, some facultymen felt that Stoutism had already carried the day. Said Author Walter Van Tilburg Clark (*The Ox-Bow Incident*), as he turned in his resignation as lecturer in English: "It appears to me that the administration is seeking to reduce the university to a manageable mediocrity." [Copyright Time Inc., 1953.]

The Board of Regents voted on June 9, 1953, to dismiss Professor Richardson, and an appeal has been taken to the Nevada Supreme Court. (See *New York Times,* June 11, 1953, and *Time,* June 22, 1953, pp. 43-44.)

I am happy to report that a memorial on the case, addressed to the Board of Regents before the hearings, was signed by members of both the education and the liberal arts faculties of the University of Illinois. The document, which I drafted, included the following statement of principles:

1. Every member of the teaching staff of a university is engaged in education, and has an equal right with every other to express his considered opinions on educational policies, whether of his own department, of the university, or of the public schools of the state and nation of which he is a citizen. Who can possibly have a better right to discuss public educational policies than the men and women who are professionally engaged in teaching?

2. .The admission standards of a university directly affect the work of every member of its faculty, hence every member has a right to express his judgment concerning their adequacy. In a state university, certainly, where such matters are of public concern, he has a clear right to express that judgment publicly.

3. The university has a responsibility for upholding in the state and the community the highest standards of science and scholarship. Every member of the faculty shares that responsibility. In a democracy free discussion of educational policies is essential if such standards are to be understood and maintained. To deny any educator—that is to say, any faculty member—his right publicly to discuss

educational policies thus undermines the integrity not only of the university but of the public educational system as a whole.

4. Dismissal of a university professor merely because he has criticized the educational policies of the university administration and has refused to be silenced on a matter clearly within his professional responsibility is so unheard-of a violation of academic freedom and tenure that we find it hard to believe that such action could even be contemplated in an American university.

[14] See pp. 131-33, above, and note 3 to chapter 8, below.

[15] See pp. 149-54, above.

[16] Two publications were called to my attention as a result of the request for evidence to the contrary. Neither reported any studies which came close to meeting the specifications. Indeed, the evidence of any correlation between training in pedagogy and good teaching was exceedingly slight, and the educationists' own studies showed that there was actually a somewhat higher correlation between academic course work and teaching efficiency. The two publications are analyzed in the remainder of this note.

The more recent study is William A. McCall, *Measurement of Teacher Merit* (North Carolina, State Superintendent of Public Instruction, Publication No. 284; Raleigh, 1952). Successive tests were given to 2,164 sixth-grade pupils in North Carolina, and the data were used to rate or score the 73 teachers involved on the basis of "the teacher's proved ability to produce growth in pupils" (p. 11). These ratings were then compared with various other measurements that are commonly used in judging the merit of teachers and the correlations were found to be low. In particular the following conclusions were reached: ". . . there is very little relationship between training and merit, for 90 per cent of the difference in merit among teachers must be ascribed to something other than the amount of training" (p. 21); "The college marks, mostly those in education courses in many institutions, were averaged for each of the 73 teachers, and the validity index was computed. *It was −28 per cent.* The r [product-moment coefficient of correlation] between college marks and criterion is −.11. Thus both methods show that college marks ["mostly those in education courses," as stated above] do not indicate whether students have made progress toward becoming competent teachers, and cannot, therefore, be used to guide prospective employers of teachers. The measurement and guidance provided are, in fact, erroneous" (p. 28, italics in the original).

The second publication which educationists considered relevant was A. S. Barr, "The Measurement and Prediction of Teaching Efficiency: A Summary of Investigations," *Journal of Experimental Education*, XVI, 203-283 (June 1948), which analyzes approximately 140 previously published studies. None is a controlled experiment of the type specified in the letter I have quoted in the text. In general, each study commences with a predetermined criterion of teaching efficiency, applies it to a group of teachers, and at the same time measures other qualities and qualifications of the teachers in question. The findings are then correlated with one another. The largest group of studies (and the one which includes most of those mentioned below) used "supervisory in service ratings of teacher efficiency as the criterion." Ten studies in all are particularly relevant to the question in which we are interested, for these ten present correlations of teaching efficiency both with grades in pedagogical courses and with grades in academic courses, thus making comparisons possible. Of these ten studies, five show a *greater* correlation between academic study and teaching efficiency than between pedagogical course work and teaching efficiency; only three show the opposite (and two of these are rather ambiguous); while two show equal correlation.

The actual correlations with teaching efficiency in these ten studies are as follows. In many studies a large number of different measures are correlated with teaching efficiency. In the following list, the measure that represents most directly the standing in academic courses and the measure that represents most directly the standing in pedagogical courses (as distinguished from practice teaching) are presented. The references are to Barr's numbered summaries; the citation of the original study can be found in his article.

*Group I, Summary No. 2* (p. 227): general honor point ratio (all subjects), .46; honor point ratio in the major, .45; honor point ratio in education, .27. *Group II, Summary No. 5* (p. 233): professional educational grades, .19; academic other than professional, .19. *Summary No. 17* (p. 236): total university grade point average, .44; mark in educational psychology, .15. *Summary No. 19* (p. 237): final grade in educational methods, .05; mean grade in three education courses, .40; four-year grade point average, .24. *Summary 21* (pp. 237-38): all college grades, .45; college professional grades, .40. *Summary No. 22* (p. 238): four-year grade point average, .31; major grade point average, .23; education grade point average, .27. *Summary No. 25* (pp. 239-40): college marks, .29; subject matter marks, .28; education marks, .26. *Summary No. 33* (pp. 241-42): mark in science of education, .17; average mark in five subjects (including science of education), .25. *Summary No. 42* (p. 245): academic marks, .30; professional marks, .30. *Summary No. 46* (p. 247): academic marks, .07; professional marks, .14.

These correlations are too small, and the samples tested too limited, to justify any generalization save one: The iron-clad requirement of pedagogical course work as a prerequisite for teaching is justified by no experimental evidence whatsoever, and by no statistical evidence that is significant, tending to show that it contributes to the making of a good teacher.

[17] University of Illinois, *Undergraduate Study, 1952–1953* (University of Illinois *Bulletin*, vol. 49, no. 82, July 1952), pp. 315-21. Professors emeriti are excluded from the count.

[18] University of Illinois, *Catalog, Urbana Departments, Graduate College, 1952–1954* (*ibid.*, vol. 50, no. 8, Sept. 1952), pp. 101-8 (courses in Education numbered 400 or above); pp. 73-75, 77-78 (Chemistry and Chemical Engineering, same).

[19] University of Illinois, *Undergraduate Study, 1952–1953*, p. 291. Note that each *comparison* in the text involves data from the same catalogue.

[20] Orville T. Bright, "Changes—Wise and Unwise—in Grammar and High Schools," National Education Association, *Journal of Proceedings and Addresses*, XXXIV (1895), 277.

[21] Edwin H. Reeder, in American Association of University Professors *Bulletin*, XXXVII, 520 (Autumn 1951).

[22] American Association of University Professors *Bulletin*, XXXVIII, 645, 646-47 (Winter 1952-53).

[23] The original letter was shown to me, the circumstances recounted,

and a transcript furnished, by the Professor of English who was the student's adviser. Permission to quote the letter has been granted by the writer of it.

Additional evidence of discrimination against prospective teachers because of *high* grades in academic subjects comes from Virginia. The student's letter printed on pp. 118-19 of this book was quoted in an address of mine and was reprinted therefrom in the Richmond *Times-Dispatch*, Aug. 6, 1953, p. 10, col. 2, with the following editorial comment:

The foregoing strikes us as little short of insane. It is obvious, of course, that some men and women who make very high grades are poorly equipped for the teaching profession, but who ever heard of arguing that *because* a student has made such grades, he or she will not be adequate, or promote "democracy in the classroom" . . .

We haven't heard of any such idiocies in the public school system of Virginia. It is fervently to be hoped that none will put in their appearance.

Three days later (Aug. 9, p. 2-B, cols. 1-2) the *Times-Dispatch* gave top position to an editorial entitled "Philosophy That Deplores Scholarly Teachers Has Spread to Some Virginia Public Schools," and which read in part as follows:

The assumption advanced by THE TIMES-DISPATCH in this place on Thursday that no public schoolteacher, or would-be teacher in Virginia would be deemed to be less effective by virtue of having made good grades in college, turns out to have been grievously incorrect. We are amazed, and ashamed, to confess that "it can happen here." Indeed, it has happened already, and teachers have been told that good grades are undesirable.

The letter we publish at the top of today's Voice of the People [quoted below] is one of several received almost immediately after our editorial appeared, and all of them say approximately the same thing. There are public school officials in Virginia, according to these teachers who have written us, who hold the positive belief that a college graduate who has made straight "A's" in his or her chosen subject, is not likely to make an effective teacher!

The letter referred to was from a teacher in Charlottesville, and it read in part as follows (*ibid.*, col. 3):

My principal personally lectured to me during a two-day orientation period because I had been graduated cum laude and had made "A's" in my subjects in college. He insinuated I was doomed to be a failure as a teacher. He maintained that a thorough knowledge of the subject matter which I was to teach (English) was not necessary. On the contrary, the best teachers, according to him, are those who have only a slight knowledge of subject matter.

I love teaching and plan to make it my life's work. . . . But the sad thing is that I and numerous others like me are being driven from Virginia's schools by such idiocies as you refer to in your editorial. . . .

I am writing this as a letter to you personally in the hope that you will continue to fight for "qualified," not "certified" teachers in our public schools.

The evidence continues to be presented, and courageously commented on, in the *Times-Dispatch* as this book goes to press. The matter has also been taken up editorially by the St. Louis *Post-Dispatch*, Aug. 26, 1953, p. 2C, col. 2.

[24] See quotations on p. 83. An ardent apostle of "life-adjustment" education has published an article with the frank title "The Real Barrier to a More Realistic Curriculum: The Teacher"; Richard A. Mumma in *Educational Administration and Supervision*, XXXVI, 39-44 (Jan. 1950). He com-

plains that teachers "have no desire to switch from French to a course in human relations, or from trigonometry to consumer education" (p. 42).

25 Willard B. Spalding, "The Education of Teachers," *Journal of Educational Research*, XLIII, 600 (April 1950).

26 Henry Chauncy, "The Use of the Selective Service College Qualification Test in the Deferment of College Students," *Science*, July 25, 1952 (vol. 116, no. 3004), p. 75, fig. 3. According to the author: "The results for sophomores, juniors, and seniors (not shown) are . . . surprisingly similar to those for freshmen." A total of 339,000 candidates took the tests during the spring and summer of 1951.

27 The degree to which teachers are intimidated by their administrative superiors was revealed in the communications received by the Richmond *Times-Dispatch* in the course of the discussion mentioned in note 23 above. The following excerpts are from an editorial in that paper, Aug. 12, 1953, p. 16, col. 1:

It is bad enough to have teachers in the Virginia public schools saying that they know of instances where teachers, or would-be teachers, have been penalized because they had made high grades in college. It is even worse to find that so many teachers in the Virginia public schools seem to be afraid to discuss this or any other controversial aspect of the school system, unless their names are kept secret. . . .

Does it occur to our school boards and school administrators that this is a most alarming phenomenon? Are they fully aware that it is a travesty on freedom of inquiry and freedom of expression to have teachers who write to us in good faith, in order to participate in a serious discussion of the school system, regularly asking us not to give their names to anyone? This has been going on for some years now, and there is no question that teachers in the public schools are afraid of reprisals, if they criticize the status quo—or even if they defend it, as in today's letter. . . .

If the public school people are such profound believers in "democracy in the classroom," why don't they try "democracy in the profession," to the end that the teachers, who constitute the backbone of the system, may be permitted to voice their conscientious opinions of existing practices and principles?

All of us are seeking the same objective, namely, the best possible system of public schools. Such a system can't be built on a group of teachers who are terrorized into silence, and who are handed edicts from on high without being able to express themselves as to their wisdom or unwisdom.

## 8. FIRST STEPS IN EDUCATIONAL REFORM

1 *The School Code of Illinois, Enacted by the Sixty-Fourth General Assembly,* compiled by N. E. Hutson (Springfield, 1945), p. 204; and *Supplement* (1947).

2 This text differs slightly from that suggested to the Commission on March 6, 1952.

3 The standard compilation is Robert C. Woellner and M. Aurilla Wood, *Requirements for Certification,* 17th edition, *1952–53* (Chicago: University of Chicago Press, 1952). Under date of Nov. 12, 1952, I circulated to the various state departments of education a questionnaire designed to elicit supplementary information concerning minimum requirements in history and the social studies for teachers assigned to courses in those subjects. Prompt and courteous replies were received from the officials of all forty-eight states, the District of Columbia, and certain territories. The actual

figures given in reply to some of the questions were not strictly comparable, state by state, hence I was unable to devise a form of tabulation that would not be misleading and unfair in certain respects. Valuable information was furnished, however, and a few generalizations, corroborated by a careful check of Woellner's compilation, can be drawn. Every state requires a minimum number of hours in education for certification; the median is eighteen semester hours. Several states do not deal with specific subject matter preparation in their certification requirements. The reply from Vermont, for example, read: "We have general certification rather than subject certification and do not find that the privileges offered by this procedure are subject to abuse by superintendents or principals." (Parenthetically, I should like to raise the question whether the elimination of fixed pedagogical requirements from state certification would be any more likely to lead to abuses by local school authorities.) Most states make provision for majors and minors in teaching fields, but some of these have a policy like that of California, stated as follows in the reply to the questionnaire: "The general secondary credential permits the holder to teach *any* subject from the 7th grade through the junior college." Three states (Florida, Idaho, and New Hampshire) and the District of Columbia gave an affirmative answer to the following question: "In order to obtain a certificate entitling him or her to teach HISTORY in the public high schools of the State, must a teacher pass a state-administered examination in the field of HISTORY?"

The following statement from a member of the Illinois State Teacher Certification Board sums up the conception of certification and its function which I presume prevails in most of the states: "We do not issue certificates as teachers of mathematics, or history, or chemistry or of any particular subject. This is not the function of certification. The certificate is a license to teach, and like the license to practice medicine or law, it does not prescribe the specialties (with a few exceptions). The requirements to teach a particular subject, like history, are left to other controls." (Letter from Robert B. Browne to the author, Champaign, Ill., April 7, 1953; quoted with the writer's permission.)

The regional accrediting associations deal with a teacher's preparation both in pedagogy and in the subject taught, hence their criteria furnish the clearest indication of the relative importance which is attached, under the present system, to these two different types of preparation. The North Central Association, which comprises the schools of nineteen states, bases its approval of secondary schools upon a set of written "regulations," of which the third deals with the "qualifications of staff members." This regulation sets a minimum standard, phrased in semester hours, both for "professional preparation" (that is, course work in pedagogy) and for "preparation in teaching areas." This basic minimum in each case is the same, study amounting to fifteen semester hours. ("Policies, Regulations, and Criteria for the Approval of Secondary Schools," *North Central Association Quarterly*, XXVI, 135; July 1951). The requirement of fifteen semester hours in the field which a teacher proposes to teach could be fully satisfied by an introductory freshman course in the subject and three half-year courses picked up at some time or other during the three remaining college years. A college graduate who does not intend to teach or make other professional use of a subject is required to take far more than this in order merely to major in it.

Public school teaching is the only profession I know where training in how to perform professional tasks is given equal weight with command over the knowledge which the profession exists to apply or impart. The point of view is not that of a profession at all, but of a trade. Even so, the equality which the accrediting agency appears to grant to training in the discipline taught, as compared with training in pedagogy, is more apparent than real. The minimum of fifteen semester hours specified in the rules does not refer to an individual subject, but to a whole cluster of subjects, that is to say, an "area." The precise wording of the criteria of the North Central Association should be noted:

... the minimum preparation is fifteen semester hours at the college level in any one of the following areas: language arts, a foreign language, social studies, science, mathematics, business, health and physical education, music, art, home economics, agriculture, and industrial arts, and adequate preparation in each subject taught. In the case of a teacher who devotes a minor fraction of his time to the teaching of a particular subject, a reasonable deviation from the minimum preparation may be accepted. ...

In the case of unified courses which draw their subject matter from two or more teaching fields, the minimum preparation expected will be twenty semester hours on the college level, appropriately distributed among the teaching fields concerned. (*Ibid.*)

The social studies embrace history, political science, economics, sociology, and anthropology. According to the criteria, a social studies teachers is prepared in the area if he has taken an introductory freshman course in one of the subjects, say history, and a half-year course in each of three others. And if he is responsible for an "integrated" course in the social studies and the language arts, for example, he can slice the bologna even thinner.

### 9. THE REORGANIZATION OF TEACHER TRAINING

[1] The questionnaire mentioned in chapter 8, note 3, included the following: "Would a course in the teaching of history offered by a department of history (not a department of education) be accepted as fulfilling part of the requirement in EDUCATION [for a teacher's certificate]?" The answer of twenty states was an unqualified "yes"; of thirteen other states, an unqualified "no." Various kinds of qualified answers were given by thirteen states and the District of Columbia; examples are: "Yes, providing it is a course called methods or techniques of teaching history" (Calif.); "Yes, but only when recognized by the Education department as an education course and so listed" (Ill.); "No, unless the Dept. of Ed. approves it as an Ed. Methods course" (Utah). Two states did not reply to this particular question.

[2] University of Illinois, *Undergraduate Study, 1952–1953* (University of Illinois *Bulletin*, vol. 49, no. 82, July 1952), pp. 317-18. No other philosopher or book is mentioned in the description.

### 10. THE RE-ESTABLISHMENT OF STANDARDS THROUGH EXAMINATION

[1] Wilford M. Aikin, *The Story of the Eight-Year Study, With Conclusions and Recommendations* (*Adventure in American Education*, vol. I; New York, 1942).

[2] *Ibid.*, p. 104.

³ *Ibid.*, p. 109.
⁴ *Ibid.*, p. 112.
⁵ *Ibid.*, pp. 110-11.
⁶ The Committee on the Strengthening of Mathematics Teaching of the Illinois Section of the Mathematical Association of America in a Report dated May 9, 1953, went on record as follows: "Moreover, it emphasizes the need for making teachers, school officials, and patrons aware of the statistical flaws in the now notorious Eight-Year Study, flaws which render its conclusions of little value" (Report, mimeographed, pp. 6-7). In an article on "Mathematics and the Educational Octopus," in the *Scientific Monthly* LXXVI, 237 (April 1953), Prof. Stewart S. Cairns, head of the department of mathematics of the University of Illinois, refers to the eight-year study as "a gold mine for those seeking samples of statistical fallacies," and points out the amazing bias admitted in the opening pages of the official report of the study: "Everyone invited to serve on the Commission was known to be concerned with the revision of the work of the secondary school and eager to find some way to remove the obstacle of rigid college prescriptions" (Aikin, p. 2). The other side of the argument is presented by Archibald W. Anderson, "The Charges Against American Education: What is the Evidence?" *Progressive Education*, XXIX, 99-102 (Jan. 1952). Since I am not a statistician I shall not attempt to enter into this controversy. My argument concerns not the reliability of the study but the fallacious interpretations placed upon it.

⁷ In its Bulletin No. 9, *New College Admission Requirements Recommended*, the Steering Committee of the Illinois Secondary School Curriculum Program and the Illinois Life Adjustment Education Program gives more space to quotations from the eight-year study (pp. 9-13) than to any other "findings." All the research studies cited, in fact, long antedate the inception of the "life-adjustment" program.

⁸ Aiken, pp. 144-45. The quotations are from the original "Proposal," dated May 1932. The other five sections of the statement of underlying ideas bear the following headings: "Release of creative energies," "Clearer understanding of the problems of our civilization, and the development of a sense of social responsibility," "Revision of curriculum materials and their organization," "Guidance of students," and "Teaching."

⁹ *Ibid.*, pp. 118-19.
¹⁰ *Ibid.*, p. 118. Printed entirely in italics in the original.
¹¹ *Ibid.*, p. 122.
¹² *Ibid.* The end result of this way of thinking is the set of criteria which the Illinois Curriculum Program recommends "for admission to general college work in place of any other set of entrance requirements." The five criteria it lists are totally inadequate. They are as follows: "1. Score on a scholastic aptitude test; 2. Score on a test of critical reading; 3. Score on a test of writing skill; 4. Score on a simple mathematical test; 5. Evidence that the student has an intellectual interest and some effective study habits as shown by his having taken at least two years of work in one field in high school in which his grades were better than average." (ISSCP, Bulletin No. 9, *New College Admission Requirements Recommended*, p. 14.) One has an uneasy feeling that the Committee borrowed these, without acknowledgment, from the list of requirements for admission to the seventh grade in

some private school that was surreptitiously lowering its standards to gain enrollment.

¹³ B. Othanel Smith, William O. Stanley, and J. Harlan Shores, *Fundamentals of Curriculum Development* (Yonkers, N. Y., 1950), p. 615. The passage concludes with this amazing statement: "The issue of the best form of curriculum organization is not fully settled and the need for research is urgent. *In the meantime, the burden of proof is distinctly on the defenders of traditional practices*" (p. 616, italics added). In the curious jurisprudence of the educationists, any program they accuse—any program that is "traditional"—is to be presumed guilty until its innocence is proved beyond reasonable doubt. Thank God it is the life of the mind, and not the life of the body also, that hangs in this weighted balance!

¹⁴ *General Education in School and College: A Committee Report by Members of the Faculties of Andover, Exeter, Lawrenceville, Harvard, Princeton, and Yale* (Cambridge, 1952), p. 14. This exceedingly important report recommends combining the eight years of high school and college into a seven-year program for able students, because of the duplication and waste that a really well-prepared student is subjected to in the university—which (though the report discreetly avoids saying so) is fully engaged during the first year or two in bringing the poorly prepared student up to snuff.

¹⁵ The report cited in the preceding note recommends an experiment "to see whether it is possible to get sufficient agreement on the content and objectives of certain college freshman courses to make feasible the construction of valid tests for advanced placement" (p. 129). A well-developed program of this kind is in effect at the University of Buffalo. See Mazie E. Wagner, *Anticipatory Examinations for College Credit: Twenty Years Experience at the University of Buffalo* (University of Buffalo *Studies*, vol. 20, no. 3, Dec. 1952).

## 11. THE STRUCTURE OF LIBERAL EDUCATION

¹ Despite its many strong points, the so-called "great books" program seems to me at fault in this respect. It tends to emphasize dialectical argument at the expense of all those intellectual processes which involve the sifting of multifarious evidence and the drawing of conclusions therefrom.

² The principles I have in mind are admirably exemplified by the series of *Select Problems in Historical Interpretation* prepared for use in undergraduate courses by various members of the Department of History at Yale, and by the proposals for scientific instruction embodied in President James B. Conant's *On Understanding Science*.

## 12. FREEDOM OF TEACHING

¹ University of Illinois, *Catalog, Urbana Departments, Graduate College, 1952–1954*, p. 104.

² Grayson Kirk, address at the University of Puerto Rico, March 12, 1953, as reported in *New York Times*, March 13, p. 12, col. 4.

## 13. THE STUDY OF OUR OWN CIVILIZATION

¹ John Milton, *Areopagitica*, ed. by William Haller (New York, 1927), pp. 49-50.

# Author's Supplementary Note
## to the Second Edition

This book is a reprint and therefore necessarily dated. In planning the republication both the author and the publisher agreed that the text, appendix, and notes should be reproduced exactly as they stood in the original edition of 1953. To have cited new statistics to support old conclusions, or to have searched out new quotations to justify old strictures, would have been to make a patchwork out of a fabric of argument that was originally all of a piece.

The object, however, has not been to preserve a period piece, designed to occupy a space on the shelf alongside facsimiles of old Sears Roebuck catalogues and other mementos of a quainter era. The book is republished because it is felt to have some relevance for 1985.

Whether it does is for the reader to decide. In support of the view that educational standards are still endangered as they were in 1953, and that deterioration remains unchecked, some present-day evidence may properly be appended to the original work. Here then are eighteen of the thirty-seven findings about the cur-

227

rent state of American education which the National Commission on Excellence in Education reported in its publication of April 1983 titled *A Nation at Risk: The Imperative for Educational Reform:*

○ International comparisons of student achievement, completed a decade ago, reveal that on 19 academic tests American students were never first or second and, in comparison with other industrialized nations, were last seven times.

○ Average achievement of high school students on most standardized tests is now lower than 26 years ago when Sputnik was launched.

○ The College Board's Scholastic Aptitude Tests (SAT) demonstrate a virtually unbroken decline from 1963 to 1980. Average verbal scores fell over 50 points and average mathematics scores dropped nearly 40 points.

○ Many 17-year-olds do not possess the "higher order" intellectual skills we should expect of them. Nearly 40 percent cannot draw inferences from written material; only one-fifth can write a persuasive essay; and only one-third can solve a mathematics problem requiring several steps.

○ There was a steady decline in science achievement scores of U.S. 17-year-olds as measured by national assessments of science in 1969, 1973, and 1977.

○ Between 1975 and 1980, remedial mathematics courses in public 4-year colleges increased by 72 percent and now constitute one-quarter of all mathematics courses taught in those institutions.

○ Secondary school curricula have been homogenized, diluted, and diffused to the point that they no longer have a central purpose. In effect, we have a cafeteria-style curriculum in which the appetizers and desserts can easily be mistaken for the main courses. Students have migrated from vocational and college preparatory programs to "general track" courses in large numbers. The proportion of students taking a general program of study has increased from 12 percent in 1964 to 42 percent in 1979.

○ This curricular smorgasbord, combined with extensive student choice, explains a great deal about where we find ourselves today. We offer intermediate algebra, but only 31 percent of our recent high school graduates complete it; we offer French I, but only 13 percent complete it; and we offer geography, but only 16 percent complete it. Calculus is available in schools enrolling about 60 percent of all students, but only 6 percent of all students complete it.

○ The amount of homework for high school seniors has decreased (two-thirds report less than 1 hour a night) and grades have risen as average student achievement has been declining.

○ In many other industrialized nations, courses in mathematics (other than arithmetic or general mathematics), biology, chemistry, physics, and geography start in grade 6 and are required of *all* students. The time spent on these subjects, based on class hours, is about three times that spent by even the most science-oriented U.S. students, i.e., those who select 4 years of science and mathematics in secondary school.

○ A 1980 State-by-State survey of high school diploma requirements reveals that only eight States require high schools to offer foreign language instruction, but none requires students to take the courses. Thirty-five States require only 1 year of mathematics, and 36 require only 1 year of science for a diploma.

○ One-fifth of all 4-year public colleges in the United States must accept every high school graduate within the State regardless of program followed or grades, thereby serving notice to high school students that they can expect to attend college even if they do not follow a demanding course of study in high school or perform well.

○ Too few experienced teachers and scholars are involved in writing textbooks. During the past decade or so a large number of texts have been "written down" by their publishers to ever-lower reading levels in response to perceived market demands.

○ In England and other industrialized countries, it is not unusual for academic high school students to spend 8 hours a day at school, 220 days per year. In the United States, by contrast, the typical school day lasts 6 hours and the school year is 180 days.

○ In many schools, the time spent learning how to cook and drive counts as much toward a high school diploma as the time spent studying mathematics, English, chemisty, U.S. history, or biology.

○ A study of the school week in the United States found that some schools provided students only 17 hours of academic instruction during the week, and the average school provided about 22.

○ The teacher preparation curriculum is weighted heavily with courses in "educational methods" at the expense of courses in subjects to be taught. A survey of 1,350 institutions training teachers indicated that 41 percent of the time of elementary school teacher candidates is spent in education courses, which reduces the amount of time available for subject matter courses.

○ Half of the newly employed mathematics, science, and English teachers are not qualified to teach these subjects; fewer than one-third of U.S. high schools offer physics taught by qualified teachers.[1]

The commission went on to offer some thirty-eight "Implementing Recommendations."[2] The reader may wish to examine them, noting parallels to proposals for educational reform advanced in the present work.

One reform urged in this book has not been implemented in the form proposed, although some elements in it have been realized. A brief account of developments in the matter since 1953 is perhaps in order here.

The resolutions that are printed in the Appendix of the present volume were offered at a meeting of the American Historical Association in December 1952, sponsored by sixty-two historians (including myself, the actual draftsman), and endorsed by a total of approximately seven hundred scholars and scientists from a variety of fields. Our hope was that the learned societies of the country would join in establishing a Permanent Scientific and Scholarly Commission on Secondary Education, which would bring to bear on educationl policymaking the point of view of men and women professionally concerned in the advancement and dissemination of knowledge in the basic scientific and scholarly disciplines.

A united effort by groups so diverse proved impossible to bring about. What the specialized societies could—and in many instances did—do was take steps to bring about more effective teaching of their particular disciplines in the lower schools. Thus the American Historical Association (to which the resolutions in question were originally addressed) expanded its honorable tradition of aid to school instruction by creating a Service Center for Teachers. This has enlisted eminent historians in the production, thus far, of more than seventy pamphlets describing for teachers the historical materials available for illuminating particular historical topics. Similar efforts in other fields have been too numerous to catalogue here.

Closer to the proposal set forth in the resolutions of 1952 was the founding in 1956 of the Council for Basic Education, now completing nearly thirty years of leadership in the effort to restore to the school curriculum a badly needed emphasis on the fundamental disciplines of modern intellectual life—science, history, mathematics, foreign languages, literature, and the arts.

To the late Mortimer Smith belongs the credit for initiating the effort that led to the creation of the Council for Basic Education. He brought together in the mid 1950s a number of us who had voiced concern about the state of American education. As it became apparent that a federation of learned societies was not likely to take the leadership in a movement to challenge the anti-intellectual drift of so much public-school policy, the group that Mortimer Smith had assembled undertook to create an independent organization that would work for the raising of intellectual standards in the schools. Headquartered in Washington, D.C. (at 725 Fifteenth Street, N.W.), the Council for Basic Education has published a stream of reports on educational developments, evaluating schools that are exhibiting special promise, reviewing curricular proposals and offering proposals of its own, and presenting in varied forms the argument that serious, rigorous, disciplined intellectual training is indispensable in a democracy and hence in its schools.

The slogan "Back to basics!" has sometimes been understood as a call to cut back the school program to some minimum of elementary skills—a minimum all too likely to become accepted as the maximum for most pupils. The Council for Basic Education uses the word "basic" in a totally opposite sense. Far from advocating a diminished school program, cut back to "the three R's," the council stands for a program constantly enriched, as the student moves upward, through the introduction of more and more of the concepts, the techniques, and the data that are fundamental (or basic) in mature intellectual life. The council (like the present book) recognizes these great intellectual disciplines as cumulative in character, never completed or exhausted at some initial level, but opening up a constantly broadening range of knowledge, of power, *and* of genuine excitement.

## NOTES

1. National Commission on Excellence in Education, *A Nation at Risk: The Imperative for Educational Reform. A Report to the Nation and the Secretary of Education by the Commission on Excellence in Education* (Washington, D.C., 1983), pp. 8-9, 18-23. The first six of the paragraphs quoted above are from the section of the report headed "Indicators of the Risk"; the next two are from the commission's "Findings Regarding Content"; the next five from "Findings Regarding Expectations"; the next three from "Findings Regarding Time"; and the last two from "Findings Regarding Teaching."

2. *Ibid.*, 24-33.

# Retrospective One
## Clarence J. Karier

I

The guns in Korea had just fallen silent when Arthur E. Bestor first opened the pages of his new, most significant critique of American education, *Educational Wastelands: The Retreat from Learning in Our Public Schools* (1953). The book quickly assumed its position as the most serious influential educational criticism of the decade.[1] Although there have been many critiques of American education in the last thirty years, none, it seems, made such a solid case for the life of the disciplined mind in a democratic context as did Bestor's *Educational Wastelands*. Much of what he said rang true for his day and continues to ring true for our day.

The reader will find much that is relevant to the current discussion of education, in part at least because many of the problems with which Bestor wrestled were fundamental problems which have not been resolved and remain very much with us. Over the past thirty years, many of these unresolved problems not only have intensified and deepened but have broadened in their scope to affect the entire educational system from the elementary school

to the general university. It is not easy to change the course of
an educational system. Yet that is what Arthur Bestor in *Educational Wastelands* and his follow-up work, *The Restoration of
Learning* (1955), intended to do. He disagreed with the course
American education had taken and stood up to change it by attempting to open a dialogue on the issues that he saw as most
crucial.

From today's perspective, when most critiques of education are
either government- or foundation-commissioned reports, Bestor's
book appears as uniquely different. Over the past three decades,
much of the critical dialogue surrounding education has been financed, directed, and sold to the American public through media
campaigns directed by philanthropic foundations. The names of
James Bryant Conant, Charles Silberman, and Ernest L. Boyer
immediately come to mind. Their work, whether it was *The
American High School Today* (1959), *Crisis in the Classroom*
(1970,) or *High School* (1983), all reflects the influence of expert reports and the expenditure of large sums of money. The
result of these Carnegie-sponsored projects read like committee
reports, a kind of brokered consensus upon which certain views
turn up acceptable and others muted. At least two of these reports ended up on the "best seller" list. They did so, in no small
measure, because of the expensive media campaign orchestrated
by the Carnegie Foundation to "sell" their product.[2] In contrast,
*Educational Wastelands* reached large numbers without the assistance of a massive advertising campaign. It was not written by
a committee or a commission lavishly supported by government
or foundation grants, but by an individual professor of history who
was committed to an intellectual view of the life of the mind and
who understood the importance of that life for a democratic society. The result was a landmark work.


## II

*Educational Wastelands* was published in 1953, the year, as
earlier noted, the Korean War armistice was signed. That war was
but an extension of the larger cold war which began almost immediately after the close of World War II. Many of the veterans
returning from that war went to college on the G.I. Bill, settled

in the newly built suburbs to rear their families, and became part of a growing middle class who saw their future and their children's futures in terms of educational opportunity.

Within this context, America underwent a second red scare. In 1946 a conservative eightieth Congress was elected which included Senator Joseph McCarthy from Wisconsin, and the House Un-American Activities Committee broadened its reach to seek out subversive activities in the entertainment and communications industry. Through the process of cultivating fear of Communists, political careers such as those of Joseph McCarthy and Richard Nixon were advanced overnight while the careers of other people such as Whittaker Chambers, Owen Lattimore, and many other victims were just as readily destroyed. This was the time of spy trials, Fifth-Amendment Communists, and blacklists. By January 1949, China fell to the Communists and by September of that same year the Soviet Union exploded their first atomic bomb. The mood of the country was ripe for conspiracy theory as Senator McCarthy, in February 1950, delivered his famous Wheeling, West Virginia, speech in which he charged the State Department with coddling Communists. From that time until early in 1954 when the televised Army-McCarthy hearings discredited him, McCarthy remained a powerful force in American politics. The fear of Communism and the growing "red menace" hung heavy over the land. By 1950, James B. Conant became actively involved in the "Committee on the Present Danger" as the C.I.A. began making and issuing reports on Soviet education and their manpower development as opposed to American education.

Within this growing and developing cold war context, new and more critical voices began to be heard regarding the state of American education. Mortimer Smith published *And Madly Teach: A Layman Looks at Public School Education* (1949), and Bernard Iddlings Bell produced *Crisis in Education* (1949), which were quickly followed by Albert Lynd's *Quackery in the Public Schools* (1953) and Arthur Bestor's *Educational Wastelands* (1953). Progressive education and, indeed, much of the educational establishment was now under attack. There can be little doubt that much of the criticism was stimulated by cold war considerations, but there were other factors as well. Lawrence Cremin in *The Transformation of the School* (1961) made

235

a persuasive case that professional educators, especially those associated with the progressive education movement, became separated from the lay public and by the postwar period had lost touch with the growing middle class which sought a better education for their children. Equally persuasive was the case that Arthur Bestor made in arguing that professors of education and colleges of education and their courses had become too far separated from the academic disciplines which have traditionally defined the meaning of an educated person. Both trends appear to have been occurring simultaneously. Both the lay public and professors in the academic disciplines since the early decade of the century had lost ground to the new pedagogical professionals who drew strength through the state certification systems, their professional associations, and the colleges of education which trained them.

Through the 1930s and 1940s, the center of this development was Teachers College, Columbia University. Teachers College, with its sparkling array of talented leaders, including John Dewy, William Heard Kilpatrick, George S. Counts, John L. Childs, Harold Rugg, Edward L. Thorndike, and a host of others, tended to dominate not only the development of the Progressive Education Association but also the general direction of the relatively new network of professional associations. Never before or since has America been so close to having a national college for the training of its teachers. By mid-century Teachers College had come to be viewed as the "mecca" of teacher education in America. From that center flowed a new generation of teacher trainers who tended to reproduce the training they received at Columbia in other colleges of education. One such college was at the University of Illinois and at this Bestor took sharp aim.[3]

The strength of Teachers College was found, to a large extent, in its strong-willed, intellectually powerful, charismatic teachers. The courses taught by Kilpatrick and the team-taught foundations courses became legendary. In many ways the new pedagogical professionals had just recently gained in power and in respectability. All seemed well as they savored the height of their influence. However, there were problems emerging. Few took note that many of the original cadre that led Teachers College to its heights were originally trained, not in education courses, but in

the disciplines. Fewer still could believe that the problem of re-
placement of this illustrious but aging cadre would prove so difficult if not insurmountable. The problem was further accentuated
by the fact that these forceful leaders tended to cast an intellectual shadow over the next generation which, rather than stimulating growth as they had hoped, in fact inhibited its development.
As societies were formed to honor the memory of these great men
and women, even before they had passed from the scene, many
of the younger generation slipped deeper into the quagmire of
educationist jargon. The reification of the educationist language
was rapid. At Teachers College the separation of the academic
disciplines from education courses was near complete. While the
graduates of Teachers College spoke of 120th Street (which sepa-
rates Columbia University from Teachers College) as the widest
street in the world, that separation tended to be reproduced on
other campuses as well.

While the "Interlocking Directorate of Professional Educationists" of which Bestor spoke seemed securely in place, in many
ways they were particularly vulnerable. They were vulnerable in
the sense that they had lost touch with the growing middle class,
a significant segment of which were the recipients of the G.I. Bill.
It was that class which increasingly voted heavier bond issues for
new suburban schools and who were most concerned with preparing their children for college. The educationists were vulnerable, not only on the lay public side but also on the academic discipline side as well. The popular educationist's child-centered
rhetoric of teaching the child rather than the subject often appeared as strangely out of place to the lay public interested in
sending their children to college to learn those subjects as it was
to the academic professionals in the colleges who taught those
subjects.

By the 1950s the aging cadre of powerful educational leaders
began retiring from Teachers College and passed from the educational scene. When the attack on progressive education, life adjustment education, and educationists in general eventually came,
it came when many of the voices upon which a generation of
educationists had grown to depend were no longer available to
engage the critics.[4] Thus, when Lynd took on the "world of professor Kilpatrick" as just so much "neo-pedagogue's palaver," it

was clear that the strength of the old guard was going to be tested. With the rapid decline of the progressive education movement, as well as Teachers College dominance over teacher education in America, came the clear recognition that the educational directorate, at which Bestor aimed his criticism, appeared to be considerably weaker than many expected.

As earlier noted, the educationist who spoke out for "progressive education," and "life adjustment education" appeared increasingly out of place in the postwar, cold war period. While Charles A. Prosser, as a member of the Commission on National Aid to Vocational Education, proposed "life adjustment education" for 60 percent of the American public, consisting of a practical, down-to-earth, hands-on, nonintellectual curriculum designed to help people adjust to the trivial dimensions of life, and others proudly boasted of teaching the child rather than the subject, the time for Bestor's criticism was ripe.

Within the field of pedagogy there have always been child-centered educators such as Jean Jacques Rousseau who romanticized the child's nature and looked to that nature for educational guidance. Alongside those child-centered educators have also stood the practical vocational educators such as Johann Henrich Pestalozzi who usually thought in terms of a practical "hands-on," "how-to" educational curriculum. The historical roots of the twentieth-century life adjustment curriculum lie intermingled in those nineteenth-century trends. The child-centered education which often appeared interminged with the practical life adjustment education was usually also anti-intellectual in basic orientation. Both strains emerged when western societies were just beginning to move toward mass systems of schooling. In both cases, these traditions tended to underestimate heavily the intellectual potential of the average child. Whether it was in the nineteenth century or the twentieth century, these educators often justified their educational recommendations in terms of meeting the individual needs and differences of children.

Some educators, however, carried their anti-intellectualism to such an extreme as to make Pestalozzi look like an old-fashioned academic. The Champaign, Illinois, junior high school principal, A. H. Lauchner, whom Bestor quotes extensively as a sample of anti-intellectualism in the schools, is one such educator. In meeting the needs and individual differences of children, Lauchner argued that all children need not learn to read, write, and spell any more than all children need to learn to bake a cherry pie. Lauchner believed he was meeting the individual needs of children. Although some educationists insisted that Bestor was wrong and that Lauchner's position was not representative, others insisted that it was more representative than most were willing to admit. However, the many teachers who sat through progressive child-centered curriculum courses and attended the various association meetings knew that Lauchner's line of argument was not unusual. Many professional educationists, under the guise of individual differences and meeting the needs of the individual child, often appeared ready—and, indeed, willing—to write off a sizable segment of the population to a inferior education if not to a life of illiteracy.

Bestor correctly pointed to the historical roots of the problem in turn-of-the-century America, when secondary education not only took on some new and different students but, more important, some very different aims and goals. The differences between the "Committee of Ten" (1892) report, which assumed everyone would take a similar high school curriculum, and the *Cardinal Principles of Secondary Education* (1918) report, which assumed a differentiated curriculum, are highly significant. As Bestor correctly noted, the "Committee of Ten" report was dominated by college and university personnel who assumed that the college disciplines were to be the guiding light for the high school curriculum regardless of the ultimate destinies of the students. In contrast, the *Cardinal Principles of Secondary Education* (1918) was written by educationists who saw the goal of the secondary school not in academic terms but in such social efficiency terms as: 1. health, 2. command of fundamental processes, 3. worthy home-membership, 4. vocation, 5. citizenship, 6. worthy use of leisure time, and 7. ethical character. As Edward Krug noted in *The Shaping of the American High School 1880–1920,* the "command of fundamental processes," the only goal supporting the academic disciplines, was added as an afterthought.[5]

Behind all these fundamental changes in the purpose of the high school was a cadre of educationists who saw themselves as democratically meeting the individual needs of all children. Out of this key issue involving individual differences and meeting the needs of all children in time would grow the differentiated curriculum or tracking system, the testing movement, and the professionalization of the educationists' field in state departments of education as well as in the normal schools and colleges of education at the university level. Bestor was historically correct when he tied the emergence of much of professional education to the development of the differentiated curriculum and tracking system earlier in the century. He also correctly identified the historical roots of Prosser's life adjustment movement at mid-century with Strayer's and Snedden's work on the National Education Association committee, "The Commission on the Reorganization of Secondary Education" (1918), which had produced *Cardinal Principles.*

Bestor clearly and persuasively pointed to the shift in purposes of secondary education as the key event in helping to show the rise to power of the educationist establishment as separate from the liberal arts college. He hit the critical issue when he charged that the educationists' differentiated curriculum was not based on democratic principles but rather on an elitist assumption about who could and could not be educated. Like Mortimer Adler and Robert Maynard Hutchins before him, he argued that a liberal education designed to teach people to think in a democratic society must be made available to all and not to just the economically and socially privileged few. One cannot read Bestor's *Educational Wastelands* without the clear recognition that the author was a democrat. Generations of teachers-in-training were taught that the "Committee of Ten" was dominated by conservative elitish concerns while the committee which created the *Cardinal Principles* was on a more democratic track. Thus the professionalization which followed could also be viewed as moving in a more democratic direction. Bestor charged that the reverse was actually true. If one carefully studies the tracking system as it historically evolved and the assumptions made in the process, it is clear that Bestor had the stronger case.[6]

Bestor went on to charge that the academic disciplines have been cut off from what took place in the public schools. This was done, he believed, by educationists in colleges of education and state educational agencies and by public school administrators working at the local level. The result, Bestor argued, was a growing anti-intellectualism in the public schools. Bestor believed the solution was to be found in the reinstatement of the academic disciplines to their rightful place in directing the goals and purposes of a high school education. Bestor effectively made the case for the learned disciplines which went to make up the heart of a liberal arts education. Like Alfred North Whitehead in *Aims of Education,* Bestor made the distinction between subject matter as inert ideas and the living process of the disciplines as ways of knowing, which he believed made up the real heart of the disciplines. His argument proceeded by suggesting that the public school teachers ought to be liberally educated, not in terms of absorbing more subject matter, but rather to be liberally educated in the ways of thinking and knowing. He clearly understood the liberal arts disciplines and how they ought to function in their very best sense.

Bestor also clearly had studied the way many professors of education think, especially those like William Heard Kilpatrick and Florence Stratameyer, who had advocated an integrated core or common learning curriculum.[7] As he pointed out, these attempts at curriculum integration were often not integration at all, but rather superficial attempts by educationists to put together disciplines of knowledge which they did not fully understand or appreciate. As a consequence, they often assumed the arrogant position of creating a new discipline of knowledge almost at the stroke of a pen. Unable to do so, they repeatedly turned to superficial inert bits of information and called them subject matter and, in turn, missed the more important principle of the living knowledge which emerges out of a disciplined study of a field of knowledge. Thus failing to appreciate how living knowledge was produced, educationists put together the artifacts of the disciplines called subject matter in new and strangely different combinations. As a result, the curriculum usually advocated by these people often looked more like an impromptu abstract collage rather than any systematic coherent body of knowledge. The outcome was often a trivialized, highly popularized curriculum which required little thought and equally little substance. To the hundreds of thousands of American teachers who sat through heavily laden, trivialized education courses requiring little thought and much memorization and wondered why, Bestor's explanation will seem most persuasive. Thus, Bestor not only took the "democratic" mask from the educationists's ideology but, in redefining the purpose of education in terms of disciplined knowledge, he critically undercut the educationists' propensity to create their own popularized curriculum.

Bestor made it clear that he was not arguing against improved methods of instruction. His quarrel, he insisted, was with those educationists who constructed curricula at the elementary, secondary, and college level of instruction, without the aid of the disciplines. The educationists who posed as curriculum experts were, he insisted, the true corrupters of intellect. As many of these curriculum experts became involved in the public schools by advising school boards and parents, they also became involved in the process of engineering social consent. Bestor's critique of Harold Hand and the Illinois secondary school curriculum program and the way the experts engineered public consent for their programs is, today, still a highly relevant critique of the way much American public opinion and support are managed through expert evaluation processes. Today, however, we are far more sophisticated in engineering public consent at every level of both the political and the educational spectrum.

## III

How solid was Bestor's critique of American education? In some respects he was on target and in certain respects he seemed to have missed the mark. When he argued that the separation of the liberal arts from teacher education was damaging to the education of the American teacher, it seems he was clearly on target. The same seemed to be the case when he analyzed the anti-intellectual tendencies of college of education professors, especially when they professed to meet the needs of all youth and became involved in curriculum reform rather than improved methodology. He well understood the problem of vocationalism which, from the *Cardinal Principles* (1918) to the life adjustment movement in 1950, repeatedly attempted to direct American education toward a "how-to," practical, "hands-on" training to the detriment of a liberal education for all. He accurately pointed to the undemocratic nature of the differentiated curriculum and well understood how it was that so many education courses so often turned out to be trivia-laden, meaningless experiences. He correctly analyzed the political network of educationists whom he called an "interlocking directorate" and how they had grown to protect their own vested interests. In this analysis, however, he appears to have missed the significance of philanthropic foundations and the role they have played throughout the twentieth century. In many ways he seemed to have had an understanding of part of the political network but missed a very important side which was connected to the major foundations. It was that side which in the next thirty years tended to occupy center stage in the national educational dialogue. By the end of the decade, Bestor's criticism was virtually completely upstaged by James B. Conant and his Carnegie Foundation campaign to shape the public dialogue on education.[8]

Much of what Bestor said about teacher education was true enough; the problem with his critique is that he did not go far enough. He was realistic when analyzing the work of educationists, but he tended to be idealistic when he looked at the liberal arts college. With minor reservations aside, Bestor's liberal arts college was basically an ideal. Herein lies a serious weakness in his critique. He seemed to sense this problem as he turned to some of the problems of a liberal arts education at the end of his book. Nevertheless, teachers are educated not only by education professors but, more important, by liberal arts professors as well. The question of how much difference educationists make in the training of teachers was unanswered in his day as well as in our own. At the undergraduate level the pedagogical component of high school teacher training has remained at approximately 25 percent for secondary school teachers and approximately 50 percent for the elementary school teachers. The question of what was taking place in the 75 percent of liberal arts courses taken by secondary school teachers remains highly relevant. Were those students receiving Bestor's liberal ideal as ways of knowing, or were those young people inducted into a world of inert "subject matter"? When Bestor suggested that the American public had not been adequately educated to understand, appreciate, and do mathematics, most would agree. When he suggested, however, that this

243

is caused by not having had enough math courses, many would disagree. An investigation into the way math is taught in the liberal arts college would, it seems, be more appropriate.

Bestor's hard-hitting critique of educationists tends, at times, to overemphasize their influence. For example, when Bestor suggested we might get qualitatively better teachers by reducing certification requirements, he failed to realistically face the fact that in 1953, as in 1984, it was not certification requirements which hampered the flow of the most talented into a career of teaching; rather it was financial rewards.[9] A similar problem arose with his analysis of the implications of the Eight Year Study. His tendency to assume an idealistic rather than a realistic eye toward the liberal arts college seemed to get in the way of his logic when he suggested that the proper conclusion to draw from the Eight Year Study, in which students from experimental high schools generally did as well as those from the traditional high schools in their four years of college, was to adjust college admission requirements.[10] One might more logically conclude that there was something wrong with what was going on in the liberal arts college. The failure to critique realistically what passed for a liberal arts education represents Bestor's blind side. It was a serious shortcoming. At the time Bestor wrote, higher education was already taking on many of the social functions the high school had taken on earlier in the century. In the next thirty years, not only did the colleges massively expand and assume problems similar to those the high schools had faced, but they were overwhelmed with some of their own unique difficulties. The problems of specialization versus generalization and vocationalism were never as easily resolved as Bestor seemed to suggest might be possible at the time.

Bestor correctly sensed a decline in the standards of American intellectual life. He thought he found the culprit in the public schools and the way the teachers were trained. He seemed to have gotten hold of part of the problem, but failed to sense the extent to which all of the universities and America's culture-producing industries were involved. Bestor nostalgically looked back on the high school training he received in 1922 to 1926 at the Lincoln School at Teachers College, Columbia. He considered the teachers who taught him truly outstanding progressive educators and noted their intellectual sophistication. One might ask who trained those teachers and what kind of liberal arts college education they had received? For the most part, one suspects he was taught by teachers who were trained by teachers still very much in the classical education tradition. There is a kind of educational capital, or legacy, which one generation inherits from another through its teaching cadre. The literary classical educational legacy which began its steep decline during the first two decades of the century had by mid-century begun to run out. Generations of teachers were now being cycled through the system with less and less of that legacy in their educational repertoire. Bestor had the benefit of that earlier generation of teachers; his children and their children would not. By mid-century that educational tradition, which for a thousand years defined the meaning of a liberal education and thereby steadied the intellectual life of many generations of teachers, had run out.

It was not enough simply to suggest as Bestor had done that: "The classical languages, it is true, were sacrificed to modernity—a serious mistake, I believe—but the promise that they would be replaced by sound training in the living foreign language was honestly fulfilled."[11] There was far more, however, in the classical-language tradition than modern-language instruction could replace. In many ways the classical tradition set literary standards and cultural tastes that tended to influence if not permeate the teaching cadre as well as the general culture. With that tradition went the very definition and purpose of a liberal education. As the classical tradition gave way, that meaning and purpose were clearly in trouble, as the neo-humanist Irving Babbitt pointed out in *Literature and the American College* (1908). Although one might be repelled by Babbitt's elitism, his analysis of what would take place in the liberal arts college once the classical tradition disappeared was nothing less than propehetic. Babbitt's analysis of what he termed Rousseaunian romanticism and Baconian scientism as he believed he saw it overrunning higher education, in retrospect, appears highly relevant to the modern malaise in higher education. While there were many attempts to redefine the idea of a liberal education in modernist terms, and few attempts were as impressive as Harvard's *General Education in a Free Society* (1945), none ever seemed to come to grips adequately with the central problem which Babbitt posed with respect to Baconian scientism. Babbitt argued throughout his professional career that the Ph.D. training which placed so much emphasis on the production of new knowledge and the cultivation of the narrow specialty was not only ill suited for the training of a liberal arts college professor but was, in fact, disfunctional. Much of what he predicted in *Literature and the American College* and elsewhere has painfully come to pass. A Baconian scientism reflected in the Ph.D. experts cultivating their own narrow field of knowledge pervades the ruins of the modern liberal arts college.

Bestor was part of a generation of educators who themselves benefited from the classical legacy, intellectually lived off its capital, and were committed to the reconstruction of the ideal of a liberal education in the modern world. As gallant as their attempts were, the results for the most part must be recognized as a failure. In large part this was due to the failure to heed Babbitt's warning. Although Babbitt's argument about the disfunctional training of the Ph.D. expert for a liberal culture was recognized by William James, Jacques Barzun, Gilbert Highet, Robert Maynard Hutchins, and many others, American higher education continued to replace its older retiring liberal arts professors with highly skilled Ph.D. specialists. The disciplines, themselves, were losing their liberal ideal.[12]

Since Arthur Bestor wrote *Educational Wastelands* (1953), Irving Babbitt's prediction of a growing Baconian scientism cultivating a vocationalism fed by a Rousseauist sentimentalism, in large part, has pervaded not only the high school but, more important, the liberal arts college itself. The questions, then, of what constitutes a liberal education today and what is taking place in the liberal arts students' curriculum and classroom are most important factors to be considered in any assessment of teacher education in America.

Some of the recent criticism of the high school today points to the tendency on the part of high school teachers to do all the talking and deliver what appears to be massive doses of inert knowledge rather than to cultivate student thinking. While one must find fault with any system which tolerates such practices, one ought to look carefully at the way those teachers were educated or should one say "trained." In some cases it may be that the problem lies in their pedagogical methods courses or their practice teaching experience or in-service experience. More serious, however, is that it might just be the way they have come to learn what they know of their discipline from their liberal arts education. It still may be true, as most classicists used to argue, that teachers tend to teach as they were taught. As one travels about the liberal arts colleges and observes the huge sections of listeners carefully writing down inert bits of knowledge to be fed back on standardized examinations, one might be close to an answer as to why so many high school teachers behave as they are said to behave. If one pauses to listen to the content, one is likely to hear highly vocationalized material being delivered by a young Ph.D. aspirant who appears to relate well to those few students who might some day follow in his or her own narrower footsteps. If one carefully examines what a student studies under the rubric of a liberal education, one cannot help but be impressed with the vast array of "how-to" courses that have come to take the place of the arts and humanities courses. However, if one looks more closely at the content of the arts and humanities courses, strange configurations emerge. Arthur Bestor's idealized world of a liberal education seems remote.

At Bestor's old institution, the University of Illinois, the power of the educational establishment has since been noticeably lessened; nevertheless, the course on John Dewey is still popular and offered regularly on an elective basis.[13] The problem, however, of vocationalism which Bestor so correctly analyzed as pervading the college of education now pervades the entire university. At somewhat less than dignified graduation ceremonies at that institution, the graduates from the College of Engineering rise and chant in unison, "We've got jobs," while the graduates from the Liberal Arts College chant in return, "We want jobs," thus symbolically reflecting the vocationalism which has come to pervade the entire university. More upsetting is the increasing general lack of historical knowledge which is reflected when otherwise reasonably bright liberal arts upper-level students appear confused by such terms as Renaissance and Reformation. It seems safe to say that many liberal arts degrees today do not represent what Bestor thought they should.

The day has long passed when one might safely assume, as

Bestor had assumed, that our teacher training can be easily straightened out by limiting education courses and simply adding more hours of training in the disciplines. The disciplines, themselves, need careful attention, as does the very meaning of a liberal education and its reality. Irving Babbitt's criticism, although seldom considered, ought to be included in any reassessment of a liberal education.

Many of the problems we face today had not yet materialized when Bestor wrote; others were just beginning. When Bestor wrote *Educational Wastelands,* America was just beginning to enter the television era, as well as the era of declining scholastic aptitude test scores. The relationship between the two phenomena is still debatable. However one decides that issue, reasonable observers will agree that there has been an overall decline in the general intellectual culture and standards of America's "higher" learning as well as the culture-producing industries from the days when Arthur Bestor attended Lincoln School at Columbia University. Bestor himself was keenly sensitive to that decline and clearly was reacting to that trend. A number of studies of the level of intellectual requirements reflected in the textbooks used in the 1920s as opposed to those used in the 1950s significantly bear out this trend.[14] The problem of standards for textbooks published for use in the public schools is most serious and, then as now, clearly reflects the separation of the leaders in the academic disciplines and learned societies from the ongoing curriculum of the public schools. As fewer and fewer textbooks used in high schools are written by leading professors from the disciplines, the problems of which Bestor had written have only become exacerbated.

Whether one chooses to call it popularization of culture, modernity, or a general decline in intellectual culture, it is clear that America has lost a significant literary and humanistic legacy. Arthur Bestor stood in the midst of that decline and forcefully reacted by attempting to recall his fellows back to an ideal meaning of a liberal education. The result was one of the best critiques of American education of the period. It should be read along with Harvard's *General Education in a Free Society* as well as Irving Babbitt's *Literature and the American College.*

While *Educational Wastelands* was thought out and developed in the midst of much cold war hysteria, the book is surprisingly free of such rationalizations. Four years later, however, Sputnik went up and Bestor along with many others rationalized America's failure in space by blaming the public schools rather than the military and civilian leaders in the federal government who were actually responsible. By the end of the decade, other cold war voices such as those of A. G. Rickover and James B. Conant, who spoke in terms of manpower training programs, were heard. In many ways it was Conant who brought to a close a decade of criticism of the educationists. He did it not only through a professionally orchestrated campaign backed by the Carnegie Foundation, but he did it also through the actual support of the educational establishment that Bestor was criticizing. Conant was viewed as a friendly critic. Most educationists breathed a sigh of relief when his *American High School Today* (1959) assumed its place on the best-seller lists. As Charles Burgess and Merle Borrowman put it, "Throughout the 1950s public school educators, ever more sorely pressed by opponents, were repeatedly to express thanks to the deity for Conant."[15]

Conant managed to co-opt many of the critics' arguments and turn public attention toward creating a more efficient system utilizing the power and influence of the educational establishment that was already in place. Conant was more interested in perfecting the tracking system for developing cold war manpower needs than he was in destroying the educationist's power and producing a liberal education in which all might develop in a democratic society, as Bestor had dreamed. By the closing years of the decade, massive federal funds became available for such useful cold war manpower fields as science, math, foreign languages, and guidance training, but little for the arts and humanities. While Bestor continued to seek changes by investing considerable time and effort in organizing the Council for Basic Education, these efforts tended to be overshadowed by the rising power of a new national educational establishment which combined the power of the federal government with a network of key foundations to form a new "interlocking directorate." As attention turned in the following decade to the civil rights movement and antiwar movement. Bestor's criticism of the educationists seemed to fade from the scene.

Arthur Bestor's *Educational Wastelands,* nevertheless, remains one of the more serious critiques of the American educational establishment in the decade of the 1950s. In many ways his critique, with all its limitations, was hard-hitting, fundamental, and accurate. Especially was he on target when he analyzed the anti-intellectualism cultivated by many college of education professors working under the guise of curriculum expertise. Contrary to the many educationists who quickly classified him as opposed to "democratic" education, he was far more democratic than many of his educationist opposition, who seemed ready and willing to write off large sections of the population to illiteracy, or minimal literacy, in the name of individual differences. In certain respects some of what Bestor said about educationists and education courses is sadly still true. It still is not easy to change that system, although some improvements have been made.

Bestor had his blind side, which was to be found in his idealism regarding higher educational institutions themselves. There was a reason why educationists so quickly came to power and influence in the first half of the century. A significant part of that reason lies in the failure of leaders in the academic disciplines to invest their time and effort in public education problems for any sustained length of time. The lack of leadership in textbook publishing is but one sad case in point. More important, however, is the continuing decline and loss of the liberal educational ideal within many institutions of higher learning in the past thirty years. It is not enough to recommend, as many of the current critics of teacher education have done, that teachers ought to take more liberal arts courses before entering a teacher education program. It is more important to look critically and seriously at the total education of the American teacher. Any serious examination will require both a realistic and an idealistic appraisal of the liberal education component in the education of that teacher. Bestor's *Educational Wastelands* is loaded with his educational ideals. For the current generation engaged in such an appraisal, some of those ideals may yet prove worth considering.

## NOTES

1. For a somewhat similar estimate, see Lawrence A. Cremin, *The Transformation of the School* (New York: Alfred A. Knopf, 1961), p. 344.

2. While many have asked the question, who controlled American education, the more relevant question to ask might be, who controls the dialogue about public schools? For an analysis of the media blitz used in the selling of *The American High School* (1959), see Stephen Preskill, "Raking from the Rubbish: Charles W. Eliot, James B. Conant, and the Public Schools" (Ph.D. diss., University of Illinois, 1984).

3. Many of the faculty at Illinois were graduates of T.C., Columbia and tended to attempt to reproduce the Teacher College program. In its later years, the P.E.A. *Journal* was published at Illinois.

4. I am using the term "educationists" throughout as Bestor defined the term, to include school administrators, principals, and state educational agency personnel, as well as professors of education.

5. See Edward A. Krug, *The Shaping of the American High School 1880-1920* (Madison: University of Wisconsin Press, 1969), pp. 378-406.

6. See, for example, Paul Violas, *The Training of the Urban Working Class* (Chicago: Rand McNally Co., 1978).

7. See pp. 52-55.

8. See Preskill, "Raking from the Rubbish."

9. See p. 134.

10. See p. 154.

11. See p. 45.

12. See Irving Babbitt, *Literature and the American College* (New York: Gateway Editions, 1956), p. 89.

13. It is noteworthy that Bestor's treatment of John Dewey in this book is reasonable and restrained. It was only later in the midst of polemical debate that Bestor appeared to have fallen into a highly questionable interpretation of Dewey.

14. See, for example, Gail Armstrong Parks, "Adolescence in the Twenties as Represented in American Novels, Popular Magazines, and Literature Anthologies of the Decade" (Ph.D. diss., University of Illinois, 1977); also see James Warren Olson, "The Nature of Literature Anthologies Used in the Teaching of High School English 1917–1957" (Ph.D. diss., University of Wisconsin, 1969).

15. Charles Burgess and Merle L. Borrowman. *What Doctrines to Embrace* (Glenview, Ill.: Scott, Foresman and Co., 1969), p. 130.

# Retrospective Two
## *Foster McMurray*

The republication of Arthur Bestor's *Educational Wastelands* may be greeted warmly even by those whom Bestor would place in the camp of the enemy, for it is conceivable that a fascinating controversy about important educational issues may be resurrected with some degree of force and of public participation. Conceivable, but by no means certain. In this time when conservatism is rampant, Bestor's traditionalist viewpoint may attract the zealous and the bigoted, for Bestor is something of a Jerry Falwell among educators. If that should happen, the resulting controversy may be marked by animosities even stronger than Bestor's own. In hopes that this could be avoided, I am pleased to represent here the way an educationist opponent of Bestor's ideas would look at some of the issues upon which we differ. Differences are interesting in themselves, and they point to a need for further inquiry and more of insight than is available just now, rather than for ferocious jousting. By all means, let controversy continue until better insights have taken away the occasion for it.

*Educational Wastelands* is controversial in a way which needs

253

to be better understood. There is a kind of controversy which supporters of Bestor's educational doctrine might think is Bestor's own. It is a kind in which the virtuous and enlightened do battle against the forces of outer darkness. In this case, the forces of outer darkness, presumed to be arrayed in great number and strength, are the small bands of educationists who devote their careers to the study of educational problems and to making proposals of new ways to conduct schooling. How bad (or good) they are remains for future determination, but even now it must be said that they are not a unified army of anti-intellectuals, as Bestor would have you believe. In their attitudes toward educational values, educationists are spread over a wide spectrum, such that almost any kind of position about schooling, from conservative to progressive, is to be found represented among them. Their thinking on educational issues is often different from Bestor's, but, as I shall try to show, not less enlightened. Another kind of controversy occurs when extremists refuse to accept normal standards of logic and evidence in their zeal to dispute points of view which men of good will are inclined to accept. However, Bestor's role is *not* one of upholding normal standards of logic and evidence against unreasonable zealots. Among enlightened men of good will there are some who side with him, and others who side with his opponents. The situation is such that appeals to criteria of good reasoning and to evidence are not sufficient to bring opinion closer to agreement. This observation serves to introduced the concept of "legitimate controversy."

A controversy is legitimate when participants are unable to reach agreement, because beliefs and values which divide them cannot be proven true or false, right or wrong, wise or unwise, by any means known and accepted within intellectually responsible publics. At his best, when he is not misrepresenting or maligning, Bestor is a skilled partisan in legitimate controversy. He writes as if he *knows* that he is right and his opponents wrong, but this is characteristic of most partisans in the heat of dialectic exchange. Even if he believes firmly in what he may think of as "the truth" about education, a fair-minded person is capable of agreeing that differences of opinion from those of educationists are just that; a warfare of opinions, not of assertions that are open to proof or of conversion into assured knowledge. To be sure, between

Bestor and the educationists there are many differences of a factual kind; is it the case, for example, that the schools of America are controlled by educationists and their allies? Or that educationists as a group and on the whole are anti-intellectual? But these factual claims are not the heart of Bestor's contribution to educational literature. His major concerns are to bring about changes in teacher training, in schools of education, and in schools, and most of all to change the public's acceptance of aims for schooling. These concerns are a product of opinion, and his arguments in their support are controversial in the way which I am calling legitimate.

My intent goes beyond that of merely granting Bestor a right to his opinions, and beyond that of suggesting that the views of his opponents be accorded the same right. My hope is to prod the kind of controversy in which Bestor was so active into renewal or continuation, thinking that if it should engage the minds of educationists and anti-educationists in further search for enlightened opinion, then a better understanding of educational goodness may result. In what follows, therefore, I shall limit my remarks to a consideration of opinions, and I shall resist the temptation to criticize Bestor for what I think are unwarranted claims about matters of fact. I am not concerned to present evidence nor to document with intent to establish credibility, but rather to present a contrast between Bestor's opinions and those which I think are superior.

To assert a legitimate controversy here is to imply that Bestor is not necessarily a fool or a knave. Indeed, I am granting thereby that on this or that issue, Bestor may some day turn out to have been right. Even so, it seems to me that where he is most clearly in the right, his adjacent views are sadly wrong. Three examples are offered below.

(1) Some educationists have a tendency to ask schools to play a role in too many affairs, or to do too much, or to do that which is not properly a part of the school's responsibility. Those who were called "life adjusters" were principal sinners. They expected the schools to help learners to solve all of their life problems. Against this gargantuan view, Bestor argued that the institution of the school has specific and limited responsibilities. The responsibilities of the school are those which are appropriate to its nature

255

as school. In this, Bestor was certainly right, and the life adjusters
wrong. But the life adjuster group was never fairly representative
of educationist opinion, and it is now gone from the scene. (Since
much of Bestor's ire is directed against a kind of educationist who
is no longer around, it may be that a part of his dialectic is out-
moded.) Although a lunatic fringe of educationists seems to have
withered away, a need to argue for the idea of a limited and specific responsibility of the school remains pressing today. It seems
to me that educationists, even the best of them, have not achieved
clarity concerning the unique institutional function of the formal
school. Furthermore, I would agree with Bestor that one's thinking about, say, the aims of education is bound to go wrong if one
is not aware of what that institutional role ought to be. What is it?

Bestor's answer is that schools exist to teach "the power to
think." (p. 10) They seek to accomplish that objective by teaching the organized disciplines. The teaching of organized disciplines is the central work of schooling, because "The disciplines
represent the various ways which man has discovered for achieving intellectual mastery and hence practical power over the various problems that confront him." (p. 19) The quoted material
represents the most extraordinary and wrongheaded of Bestor's
opinions. A consideration of that claim will follow later. At this
point, it is introduced to make clear the nature of Bestor's position
concerning the ultimately practical reason for teaching people how
to think. It is so that they may apply the power to think, acquired
through the study of the disciplines, to whatever problems they
may confront. In effect, schools exist to give persons the power
to solve life's problems. In this Bestor is surprisingly like the life
adjusters whose views he detested. They, too, believed that a primary responsibility of the schools is to teach people how to solve
whatever problems they might encounter. Toward that end they
contributed catalogs of typical problems, and then units of instruction designed to teach how to solve them, problem by problem. For that latter idea, which encouraged a "how to" approach
to instruction, Bestor was scornful (as anyone might well be),
thinking that the best way to accomplish the ultimately practical
end is by teaching how to think in general, leaving it to the well-
educated mind to consider what, for any specific problem, should
be done to solve it. In that regard, Bestor and the life adjusters

were far apart. But in their thinking about the major task of the school, they were alike.

To be critical of that position, observe a difficulty which seems obvious: for many of the more serious and chronic problems of modern life—problems like the onset of mental illness of certain types, a rising crime rate, the decline of big cities, uncontrolled fluctuations in the economy, unemployment of millions who seek jobs, the threat of war, the hegemony of administrators—no solutions are known. Does that mean that the school has no responsible role with respect to the kinds of problems which no one knows how to solve? If one says that schools exist to teach how to be an intelligent problem solver, then that would seem to follow. The problem here is twofold. In the first place, let it be noted that human intelligence, or the mind, is not only, or perhaps not even primarily, an instrument for solving problems. The larger role of the mind is to direct one's behavior toward the realization of worthy ends, and to seize upon the qualities which this world offers to those who are aware of their extent and location, and who appreciate them. Concerning problems, it is the function of the mind not necessarily or always to solve them, but to realize problems in their fullness and connectedness, and to do what one can. If resolution is not possible, then it is the function of the mind to manage, anyway, and to preserve continuity and personal integrity.

A second difficulty arises in view of the arts and the humanities. If the task of schooling is to teach how to think through teaching the organized disciplines, then it would seem that the arts and the humanities have no place in schooling proper—unless, of course, you assert that the arts and the humanities are organized disciplines. There could be a small loophole in that direction. By tradition, the discipline of logic is classified as belonging to philosophy, and philosophy as one of the humanities. Let it be granted: logic is a discipline. The trouble here is that the more purely formal and disciplined logic becomes, the more clearly it is perceived as belonging to mathematics rather than to philosophy (when conceived as one of the humanities). No doubt Bestor would want to assert that the study of philosophy has a favorable influence upon one's ability to think, and that may be granted as true. But if philosophy teaches how to think, it is a special kind of thinking. Philosophic thinking is dialectical, a consideration of arguments for and against alternatives, in a never-ending controversy. Philosophic discourse never reaches resolution of the problems which it engages. Problems come and go in fashion, but the continuation of dialectical discourse is the heart of philosophy, a fact which is found most unsettling by those beginning students who want to learn the "right" answer. Philosophy, and the arts and the humanities in general, have a role in the curriculum that is different from teaching how to think and to solve one's problems.

Let me suggest that the place of these materials in a liberal education is one of helping to cause changes, changes like the cultivation of esthetic sensibility, like a growing capacity for the enjoyment of products which exist primarily for esthetic reasons, and the enlargement of awareness about relations to the rest of a complex world, especially with an eye to responsibility for one's part in it. This viewpoint could be expanded and modified, and thereby vastly improved, but the mere gist of it is enough for this discourse. There is an educational contribution from deepening acquaintance with the humanities and the arts which is tremendously important, but which is different from teaching how to think. Indeed, it is more central to liberal education than a more limited effort to cultivate the power to think. Cultivation in the humanities helps to shape the preferred ends toward which a power to think is directed. It modifies the role of deliberate intent in human affairs.

If a liberal education includes a deepening acquaintance with the arts and humanities, and if the educated result of such acquaintance is something different from learning how to think, then the task of the school is necessarily different from that which Bestor proposes. What could it be?

An available route toward finding a better position is by way of asking what is common to the kinds of materials—namely, the arts, sciences, and humanities—from which the contents of a liberal education are drawn. Each of these is so different from the others that it may seem the only thing they have in common is their belonging in a liberal education. But there is a common quality. They are alike in that they transcend common sense, that part of a culture which is most widely distributed within a society

258

and is a least common denominator among socialized persons. The arts, sciences, and humanities are not communicated through mundane interactions of ordinary daily life, and so, if they should enter the culture in a significant degree, it is only because of the formal school. The common sense, on the other hand, is so very common because it deals with the obvious features of the environment, with those environmental presences that command immediate attention and which must be taken into account just to get along and to be accepted as a civilized member of society. The common sense is so ubiquitous and necessary to survival that children cannot wait to acquire it through institutionalized courses of instruction. This may suggest that the arts, sciences, and humanities are not absolutely necessary for living acceptably in our kind of world, and this is indeed the case. A person who is largely ignorant of school-taught culture may get along reasonably well by ordinary standards, and even economically prosper by selling used cars or playing football professionally. It is this uncomfortable fact which is seized upon for justification by school dropouts and the self-consciously lowbrow, and which contributes much to the difficulty of teaching. If, for vast numbers of people, the arts, sciences, and humanties have little to do with ordinary day-to-day living, then what could be important about them, important enough to justify years of work in school learning?

The functional value of a liberal education derives from this characteristic of the materials in question: they enable us to perceive objects and forces in the environment which are otherwise hidden from ordinary perception. In some cases, environmental forces are hidden from ordinary perception because they are subtle rather than obvious, like the musical qualities which differentiate serious music from the popular music favored by callow youth. In other cases, environmental forces are not capable of being perceived by the naked senses unless through the intervention of special equipment, like microscopes and scientific meters. Examples would include gravitational fields, atmospheric radiation, and vitamins in food. In still other cases, environmental forces are not evident because their force is exerted indirectly or through intervening and circuitous processes, as in the influence upon the present of long-ago historic events. The purpose which this acquaintance serves is to enable a well-educated person to become more sensitive to those often hidden or intricate and subtle forces of his environment.

There are many reasons why it is better to be aware of and sensitive to the subtle environmental forces, rather than insensitive, but the most important of them is that a person's relationship with the environment comes to a greater degree under deliberate control. A person is more in command, less taken by surprise, less likely to be overwhelmed by what happens, and in a better position to arrange for the best available quality of life. The world of an educated person is more complicated and more stimulating than the world of the poorly educated, and at least potentially more interesting, offering more to see and do, and more for which one must accept responsibility.

There is a tendency for educators to overstate the case for education, making claims of advantages that are not really a necessary consequence of having been well educated. The truth is that one may be well-educated and yet unhappy; one may be sensitive to what goes on around him and yet a miserable failure. There is nothing in the nature of liberal education which assures a person of happiness or virtue, or even of behaving intelligently in all spheres of life. Nevertheless, there are certain kinds of positive effect upon experience of having been educated and which are essential to what we mean when we speak of education. Some of those have been adumbrated in the preceding paragraph, and more of them could be unearthed by diligent analysis. The point is that the reason for the existence of liberal education is different from that of acquiring the power to think. Bestor's proposals are overly simple and insensitive to what is required for the achievement of sound educational doctrine. Research in theory of education is waiting to be done, but if Bestor were right, then there is no need for it.

(2) Much to his credit, Bestor realized that children go to school with differing degrees of preparation for the subsequent school experience and its challenges. There is, for example, a difference in home backgrounds. Some children are encouraged by parents to respect books and learning, while others are conditioned to loathe and fear them. Concerning this inequality, Bestor proposed that the school "must make up, so far as it is able, the

deficiencies of background which it finds in its students." (p 36) This is a corollary of his belief that a good liberal education should be provided to everyone, not alone to those who are college bound. In these respects Bestor's position is admirable. It is also surprising to find it espoused by anyone of the educational right wing. It was the reviled educationists who did the most to champion the idea of taking responsibility for deficiencies in the background of their students, and who won a degree of understanding and acceptance for school action, as in the popular "head start" program. From traditionalists we have come to expect a different kind of position. These people are more likely to say, in effect, "Give me students who are bright and willing to work hard, and I will do my best to teach them." In marked contrast, one of the distinguishing marks of progressive educationists in their differences from conservatives is their belief that schools are responsible for the academic motivation of students. A failure of motivation may be attributed as a failure of schooling rather than of learners. A progressive educator believes that teaching the importance of academic learning, teaching students to place a high value upon the potential contribution of schooling, is to be given priority over teaching the particulars of various subjects; for, without the first, the second is of little account. Furthermore, educationists who have reached this stage of responsibility are especially sensitive to the many obstacles, broadly cultural as well as familial, which need to be overcome, and what a difficult assignment they have accepted.

Somehow, I doubt that Bestor is aware of this. He sometimes writes in the manner of his fellow traditionalists: "As a *public* school, its responsibility is to offer such training to every man or woman who has the capacity and the will to apply intellectual means to the solution of the problems that confront him." (p. 16) This is more like it; here we have the kind of position we would expect from Bestor. On the one hand, the task of schooling is to teach everyone how to think, but on the other hand, the responsibility of the school is to teach those who have "the capacity and the will to apply intellectual means." If a conservative is not self-consistent, that should not be too surprising. He is in no position to recognize the fact that equal educational opportunity is a radically liberal ideal. If this ideal came to be realized in a large society, the processes used to get there would have been radical in character.

The need for change of a radical character arises from a prominent characteristic of our society: popular culture contains many parts which work against the educability of almost everyone. It is held, for example, that "real" boys are expected to be obstreperous or mischievous in school, to put up a good fight against the influence of teachers and the higher levels of culture. This presumed attribute of masculinity is reflected in literature, in movies, in popular television programs, and in casual conversations everywhere. It is usually the case that fictional heroes and others who might be taken as models to be emulated are those who would much prefer to watch football than to read a book or go to a concert. In thousands of ways, our culture communicates models of personality which are at odds with the personal attributes which support the capacity to be educated. If schools are to succeed, they must work against those parts of the cultural fabric that demean schooling and the acquisition of higher culture. Bestor thinks that the enemy is the supposed anti-intellectualism of educationists. In actuality, anti-intellectual forces are abroad in the land, pervasive in our society and linked everywhere to popular culture. Can a conservative be expected to fight against entrenched culture?

(3) Bestor seems to have realized that schooling is linked to the cultivation of the mind, or that it has something to do with intelligence. His usual way of conceiving this relationship is expressed by saying that schools are responsible for teaching how to think, a regrettable conception that I have criticized in the foregoing. Nevertheless he is right, I think, in supposing that the teaching of schools is designed to stimulate the powers of the mind to reach their maximum development.

This doctrine contrasts with a kind of belief often encountered among humanists which holds that what matters most in schooling is the particulars of knowledge acquired through a curriculum of the right materials. "The best that has been thought and said" syndrome is typical here. Let it be granted that when a curriculum maker is helping to choose specifics of content that are most useful for instruction, the task of choosing rightly is difficult and important. From any given subject or science, the choice of some portions rather than of others is accomplished by having a good reason in support of the choice. One says, in effect, that it is more important for students to understand this than that, since not everything can be taught, and some materials have greater educational value than others from the same field of knowledge or the same branch of the humanities. But what is it that makes one bit of instructional content more desirable than some other?

In some of the examples that might pop into mind, it would seem that chosen items of knowledge are particularly important in themselves, just as knowledge, and must be learned by anyone who is to become educated: for example, that the earth is round, or that democratic governments are responsive to the will of the people, or that matter is composed of molecules and atoms. Being ignorant of such particulars of knowledge is incompatible with being educated. But there is a reason why such particulars are essential, which is that they are needed in order to think within a given discipline or domain. If a person has not understood the roundness of the earth, he cannot think astronomically. If he has not learned about elements and compounds, he cannot think in chemistry. With respect to any given discipline, the aims of education include that of teaching how to think within it. This has precedence over teaching the particulars of knowledge. On this issue, Bestor would agree. Does this mean that to teach the disciplines is to teach how to think?

There is at least one sense in which it surely does. To teach chemistry in the most educationally valuable way is, as mentioned above, to teach how to think in the manner of a chemist at work. An understanding of a science as a cultural object requires that one be able to look at phenomena in the way a scientist does, and to understand what is required by way of further experience to establish scientific validity for a cognitive claim. Bestor goes further. He claims that the study of the disciplines teaches how to think not only in the way that characterizes a scientist within his discipline, but also how to think in general, and even more, how to apply this power to the solution of practical problems that confront one. In this, it seems to me, Bestor is way off the mark. His mistake, I think, lies in his conception of a "discipline."

Unfortunately, there is no empirical science which undertakes research into the nature of a discipline, and this gap in our knowledge makes it easy for anyone to suffer some confusion in thinking about the role of the organized disciplines in education. If the republication of *Educational Wastelands* were to stimulate new inquiry into this problem area, the renewal of controversy would be justified. In the meantime, there is only a conflict of opinions. Let me step in brashly to offer mine.

A discipline is not so much a way of thinking as it is a way of doing research in the pursuit of knowledge. What gives any discipline its distinctive character is that it offers a way of narrowing and focusing a researcher's attention upon a limited part of the phenomena which appear in experience. In physics, for example, one may attend to matter in motion, ignoring the color and kind of substance which is observed moving. In biology, one concentrates upon the kind of organization of matter which supports life. In sociology, one concentrates upon social facts as related to other social facts. To learn how to participate in research is to learn how to limit and focus one's attention upon the kinds of objects that are defined within a discipline, and to ignore the rich mixture of other stuff which appears in experience on the level of common sense. In the second place, a discipline offers a vocabulary and a batch of technical concepts which aid not only in concentrating attention, but also in theorizing and designing tests and procedures for observing and verifying. And, finally, a discipline includes a cluster of instruments and techniques for use in research, some of which are common to various disciplines, and others of which are distinctive for any given discipline.

If this sketchy but (I think) correct account of what makes a discipline is understood, then it seems to follow that the study of a discipline, if it is said to teach how to think, teaches only how to think about the kinds of refined objects and events which that disciplines locates. To learn biology is to learn how to think about and to discern biological events. In this there is no necessary connection with learning how to think in general. The fact is, an ability to think in general is presumed *as a necessary prerequisite* to the study of a discipline. What is learned in that study is how to use, in thinking, the special instrumentalities which a discipline offers, and how to organize knowledge in a logical structure. I see no reason to claim that one learns how to think, and above all no reason to believe that one learns how to apply academic talents to the practical problems of living. The difference between pure science and applied science is rather large, and, in any event, the ability to do well in either is a form of professional specialization.

What, then, is a right understanding of how schooling is related to mind and intelligence? Rightly conceived and conducted, schooling stimulates and encourages a power to think which almost everyone brings to school from the beginning, and then helps everyone to advance in thinking from dealing with a simplified and narrowed environment to a complex reality in its manifold connections. If that kind of change takes place, then an educated person is possibly in a better position to deal with problems of living, but the improvement, if there is one, is an indirect result. It comes indirectly from having been encouraged to use informed intelligence (as different from untutored native talent) in dealing with environmental forces to which one has become sensitive, and from having learned about the resources which a civilization makes available, and from having learned how to read or otherwise communicate with those resources.

The main responsibility of the school is to stimulate the mind into action and to give it support and encouragement to perform at a high level. This differs from Bestor's position most obviously in that it presumes a mind already able to think and needing only the right kind of stimulation, encouragement, and help when it falters or goes off the track. (Also, it does not presume that we *know* how to think, nor that we know how to teach how to think.) But there are further differences, and they are big enough to require a substantial change in the patterns of schooling which we inherited from the past.

To encourage the mind to grow in its own natural paths of development, to help it to succeed in confronting environmental challenges of increasing complexity and to accomplish tasks of graduated difficulty, these are the responsibilities of the school. They make a teacher's job difficult, for they run against natural tendencies to put forth the least amount of effort that one can get by with and to enjoy the present rather than to labor now in behalf of a later and long-delayed good. But there are other equally natural tendencies which are a teacher's ally: namely,

265

curiosity about intriguing phenomena, a pleasure in being stimulated to a condition of alertness and brightness, and a pleasure in having achieved new insights and skills. These helps and hindrances are welcome and acceptable, because they go with the territory, as it were. Unfortunately, the traditions of schooling are a further hindrance which need not exist, except for the conservatives and traditionalists who have inertia and fear of change on their side.

Observe, please, that the school first appeared and developed its traditions in societies where schooling was associated with a governing elite. Formal education was one of the privileges of an elite. Given that kind of of status, schooling could be tough, disciplined with an iron hand, and competitive, for it was commonly thought that schooling was a proving ground to try one's mettle and to locate the best minds. Difficulties were magnified as part of the constant testing. The teaching of Latin after it had become a dead language was thought especially suitable. An integral part of these characteristics was the belief that persons who are not of an upper class are less in need of schooling than those who are. The enjoyment of a cultivated mind seemed to require a certain level, above the average, of wealth, power, and leisure. Concerning this tradition, the pertinent question is, did schooling of that kind succeed in stimulating and encouraging the mind to reach its maximum development?

It may have, for some students and in some instances. Those whose academic abilities permitted them to stand above their peers were stimulated, perhaps, by honors and distinctions, and encouraged to maintain their places at the head of the class as competition grew stiffer. But the very reason for that kind of success is alike the reason why traditional schooling tends to discourage the mind and to depress intelligence for the majority. Even for those few who found it stimulating, the kind of motivation employed was not very worthy. It worked because of pride and fear of shame. For the majority of students it taught a false modesty about one's mental abilities, a belief in one's intellectual inferiority, and reliance upon other kinds of ability than ability to learn school-taught culture. In those days when all students were of the elite, it became necessary to emphasize the playing field and sports in order to salvage the pride of the majority and to give potential administrators confidence in their aggressions. When the public schools of America admitted all children from all classes of society, the tendency of traditionalist schooling to discourage the mind was accentuated. Educationists have been sensitive to this, and they have been trying hard to introduce changes which offer a hope of stimulating the available intelligence of all children and youth rather than of only the few brightest, but opposition from traditionalists and conservatives has been very great. It is odd, is it not, that a person from the latter group should be writing in support of universal education and of teaching, presumably, *everyone* how to think?

There is a further topic which appears prominently in Bestor's book which may be expected to appear again if controversies resume with erstwhile passion. *Educational Wastelands* is an extended attack upon educationists; that is, upon persons who specialize in the study of educational issues as their lifework. If Bestor were to have his way, educationists would be deprived of their influence, their jobs, and their field of inquiry. There would remain only a few specialists in pedagogy. His reason for this is that the study of educational aims and policies is everybody's concern, and the structuring of school programs should be done primarily by professors in the liberal arts and sciences.

In one respect Bestor is right: the consideration of aims for education is everybody's concern. And it seems that everyone is ready and eager to tell us what the aims of education (that is, of deliberate education, or schooling) should be. But, as you would expect, there is no agreement. There are hosts of special-interest groups urging their special concerns and fighting for a place in the schools for whatever it is they especially value. It is impossible for the schools to satisfy all of these interests. There are too many, and a realistic scheduling cannot accommodate more than a few. Also, some are logically incompatible with others, and to try to satisfy one demand would work against the realization of conflicting values urged by others. In this jumble of discordant voices, Bestor and those who share his academicism are probably sure that they are right and that their educational values are the ones which all right-thinking persons would uphold if they were to realize where their best interests lie. Alas, so think all the others. What happens is that those who can muster enough power to in-

267

fluence politicians and educational administrators are given some voice in school programming, and others are left crying. We are a long way from giving everybody a legitimate part.

Schooling at any given time is the product of multiple pushes and pulls from pressure groups, combined with academic traditions that are too firmly entrenched to have been modified by rational judgments. If the result is not very satisfactory to anyone, that is hardly surprising. The question is, how can we introduce a greater degree of rationality and logical coherence? To an objective observer it may be evident that the problem of how to determine and to secure the true public interest in schooling is difficult in the extreme and, therefore, a proper subject matter for intense specialized examination. Not so to academics like Bestor. They urge us to turn educational problems over to those who spend their lives in school. After all, they claim, who knows more about schooling than professors who have never left schooling since their childhood? But this is like turning over the protection of the hen house to the foxes. A conservative might reply that the same observation applies to giving it over to the educationists. But that would not be fair. Although, like everyone else, educationists have their own vested interests to protect, the nature of what it is they want to protect is different from that of other interested groups. Their concern is not to win a place in schooling for their own special interests; it is to win a place for the professional study of educational issues.

Educationists are people who believe that the determination of educational aims and the securement of public interests in schooling is a very difficult matter. They believe that an issue of such difficulty and complexity calls for the efforts of people who are especially devoted to educational inquiry and to new research in the hope of finding a way to respect the legitimate interests of everyone and to blend them or to work them into a self-consistent and logically organized school program. Their guilt, if they share any, is that they are self-appointed guardians of the public welfare. The public neither invites them to their role nor certifies their conception of responsibility. But ask yourself: how would you prefer the public to protect its sense of educational value? They (the public) can have only two choices: they can be thankful that there are some persons who are willing to devote their careers to seeking the resolution of educational problems and then scrutinize closely the literature which results; or, they can turn to people who devote their professional lives to something altogether different but who are willing to think about education as a form of moonlighting on occasional evenings and weekends. To a non-educationist, that part-time effort should be enough, because what we need for educational reform is to return to education of the past. What got us into this mess, they might say, is the elaboration of new ideas. But the past is a past of many different approaches to schooling, both in theory and in practice. Going backward offers no escape from having to deal with a great variety of conflicting ideals and alternative ways of conducting school. If educationists were to believe, as some do, that the right ideas are already there, waiting for renewed appreciation, they would also think that the call for intensive research to establish just which of them is right (and why some others are wrong) is sufficiently demanding to require full-time professionals. In trying to destroy the professional study of educational problems, Bestor is guilty of a particularly boorish kind of anti-intellectualism.

For the balance of this short introduction, I would like to indicate how an educationist might view the situation of controversy about educational aims and programs referred to above. There is no typical educationist doctrine for which I might claim to be a spokesman. Theories and concepts advocated by educationists are numerous and diverse, a rich and fragrant mixture of alternatives. Like any other educationist, I can speak only for some of us.

The heart of the problem concerning educational aims is philosophic. For, when alternatives in value and valuation are examined critically, the process of critical appraisal and of search for self-consistent value schemes is necessarily a philosophic activity. To admit this might seem to be admitting that the determination of a single policy for public schools is impossible. Philosophers have never been able to achieve an insight upon which all could agree. The best that centuries of dispute have turned up is a continuous conflict among many schools of philosophic thought, and each philosophic giant has found it necessary to slay a predecessor before taking over the mountain. For this reason many educational theorists in the recent past were champions of a preferred philosophic system: idealism, realism, existentialism, and even (by mistake) pragmatism had their well-known advocates. Disputes among them were interesting and, to some degree, productive of sound educational thought; but, obviously, no solution to the search for a universally acceptable school doctrine could ever have been forthcoming. There is no reason to suppose that an entire nation can come together in allegiance to a single philosophic stance. How then can philosophically educational problems be resolved?

If there is a solution, it cannot be reached through the acceptance of any particular philosophic system. That leaves only philosophic method as a possible resource. But the true nature of philosophic method is itself controversial. It has been fashionable to say that philosophic method is one of analysis applied to our language habits in order to gain clarity and to avoid confusion in asserting what we mean or intend. For some, there is an underlying assumption that if we can be unambiguous in our use of language, then philosophic problems simply disappear or are avoided. For some time the linguistic-analytic fashion triumphed, not only in academic philosophy, but also in philosophy of education. Unfortunately, when educational theorists turned to doing linguistic analyses of educator's language, they might have gained a mite of academic respectability, but at a cost of becoming sterile as far as anything useful for educational doctrine was concerned, and philosophy of education lost its intellectual excitement and the support of educators. There is, however, a more fruitful concept of philosophic method.

Let me propose that there is a way of conducting philosophic inquiry which comes now to the aid of educational theorists. Consider a philosopher engaged in, say, metaphysics. What he is doing is attempting to bring into clear consciousness the criteria we all employ in distinguishing what is real from what is not. An assumption the metaphysician makes is that criteria of the real are implicit in our efforts to come to grips with reality. Another assumption is that by looking into their minds, philosophers might be able to discover those criteria and bring them in the bright light toward recognition. This, it is thought, would result in a better understanding of reality. The practical advantages to be gained from such understanding are an ability to separate the real from the unreal in a consistent manner, thereby avoiding certain problems which appear when criteria are only dimly perceived; also, the enlargement of a sphere for deliberate intellectual mastery. Other branches of philosophy are thought to use the same method. A logician, for example, seeks to make explicit the criteria we have, somewhere in our minds, for telling when reasoning is sound. This is the conception of philosophic method which holds some promise of helping us to reach an acceptable doctrine concerning the aims of education and related issues.

Among the many values which we find controversial and to be cherished are those which may be called "educational" values. It would be correct to say, for example, that to educate is to achieve the realization of educational values. If there be something properly called philosophy of education, it is an enterprise which includes the persistent effort to make explicit the criteria of educational value, or the criteria by which we could recognize an educative event and distinguish it from similar-looking but non-educative events. If those criteria can be made explicit, then a further responsibility of educational philosophy is to construct a concept of school program designed to achieve the practical realization of educational values. A tall order, certainly, but if schooling were to proceed under the direction of a rationally justified doctrine (something which has not yet happened anywhere), the analytic and the synthetic halves mentioned here would be minimal prerequisites.

It is easy to imagine a kind of event which could be called "educational." A teacher reads a sonnet to a class in a way that reveals meaning and emotional qualities, and thereby changes students' perception of the sonnet and, perhaps, of poetry more generally. This, I think, would qualify as an educative event; but, if you suppose that you could easily say why it qualifies, then you are overly optimistic or else unaware of pitfalls in the path of an analyst. An obvious difficulty is the presence in our society of persons (like, say, military officers) who believe that poetry is for women and children only. Some of these persons might claim that the presumed educative event is really miseducative. But suppose we could say, as a result of philosophic analysis, that an educative event requires that students encounter some part of the culture which transcends the level of common sense or which represents a refinement of cruder sensibilities. In that case, the poetry reading would qualify as an educative event, and would do so even if we were to accept the Philistine judgment about poetry.

Consider a different example. A young man—let us say his name is Arthur—takes a course in analytic geometry with a teacher who usually succeeds in getting his students to understand the subject matter at a more than superficial level and to gain a newfound respect for it. Some even get to like it. But not Arthur. He finds that even when he manages to do well on tests and to feel that he understands what analytic geometry is about, he is not favorably disposed toward learning more. Analytic geometry is not his cup of tea. Does this mean that in his case educational values were not realized? Certainly not. For anyone to discover, after fair and adequate exposure to a facet of school-taught cultural heritage, that it is not for him is an acceptable educational outcome. In thinking of examples like this, an educational theorist slips into a related task: namely, to specify the criteria by which we could say that instruction constituted a "fair and adequate exposure" from which a person might reach a negative conclusion. These tasks for educational theory are manageable, but they are more complex and difficult than anti-educationists can understand.

Furthermore, a successful passage at making explicit the criteria of educational value may turn out to violate the usual thinking of many Arthurs. Nearly everybody whose career places him or her outside of a school of education is eager to impose selected values upon the school and to inject into school programs that kind of cultural bias which is his or hers. Academicians are especially guilty of this, for they have a confidence in their judgments about academic values which their professional devotion might seem to justify. But even a small step in philosophic analysis would reveal that schooling must remain nonpartisan toward values which are in any degree legitimately controversial. If teachers were to teach their students that certain evaluations are to be accepted as the truth—for example, that Shakespeare is the greatest of poets—this would be in effect a misrepresentation. It would mislead by teaching students to accept the validity of a judgment which cannot be established so. And we would not want to call "educative" a kind of teaching which misrepresents the cognitive status of what is taught. If this simple truth is generalized, the result is a universal educational principle: toward all matters of legitimate controversy, the school must remain nonpartisan. Any departure from this principle results in, at best, propaganda.

Let it be confessed at once that this principle is likely to make almost anyone uncomfortable in its presence. It is difficult to accept and even more difficult to honor through the design of a school program which could satisfy its requirements. But it is fundamental. There is no way around it, even though it has never yet been acknowledged and accepted and is always violated. Even now, schools are trying to extend into the new generations certain attitudes and beliefs which support traditional institutional arrangements. Some, at least, of these attitudes and beliefs are inconsistent with the idea of universal educational opportunity, with the result that one portion of school effort is at odds with another. This fact is not self-evident, and it requires further explanation.

Suppose we were to take seriously the proposal that all persons, or at least all persons who have normal intelligence, are to be educated in such a way that their minds are stimulated to maximum development. For this it would be necessary to encourage all persons to rely upon their intelligence and their capacity to learn. But our traditional approaches to schooling, as we said before, are such that only the academically gifted are encouraged and everyone else is more or less discouraged. In school, merely average persons are taught to look upon themselves as merely average in a world where that degree of intelligence is not enough to get ahead in the race for opportunities and rewards. They are taught to be humble, to expect very little from their feeble minds, and to look for ways of getting along in the world which do not depend upon academic intelligence. Everyone is at least dimly aware that this is true of our schools. Why, then, is it tolerated and even actively supported?

Conservatives are inclined to say that the results described above are right and proper, because they teach everyone to know and accept the reality of our world. Let us face it, they might say, this is a world in which the race goes to the swift, and everyone ought to know it. Persons with modest intelligence must accept

273

their limitations and become emotionally prepared for a world in which their quality of mind is, after all, mediocre. This is logically compatible with a further set of beliefs about social, political, and professional strata in a properly organized society. To simplify for the sake of quick exposition, these further beliefs are those which support an hierarchically ordered social structure—one in which the most capable are at the top, the least capable at the bottom, and everyone else arrayed somewhere in between in accord with just desserts. Those who work hard will win for themselves levels in the hierarchy which are suited to their talents. The more important any job is, the more necessary that it be filled with the most capable. That way, the big decisions are made by the brightest and best. This idealization of hierarchical structuring is used to justify tradition.

This is not the place for a critical examination of that tradition. In this context, a pertinent observation is that the hierarchical ideal goes along with a corresponding educational ideal: the ideal according to which educational privileges are to be distributed unequally, the most of schooling for those who are likely to occupy the higher levels and the least to those who will sink to levels suited to their poor abilities and slovenly ways. This accords with tradition and with the conservative frame of mind. One reason for bringing it up here is to point out that it does not go with the ideal of universal education in which all are to be provided with a good liberal education. For this latter ideal, the benefits to be expected from a good education would have to be freed from association with high placement in the hierarchy. If everyone is well-educated, then being well-educated is no longer related to a place in the hierarchy, either high or low. A good education becomes indifferent to hierarchical placement. There would be a further consequence. For self-consistency, we would find it necessary to conceive the rewards of schooling, the contribution that schooling makes to life, in a new and different way. Instead of supposing that the more one profits from the opportunity to become educated, the more one may expect big rewards or high status, we would have to say that the rewards are related only to quality of life and quality of being human, completely apart from high or low placement economically and professionally. And for consistency with this, we would find it necessary to admit that quality of life is not necessarily a function of competitive striving to get ahead of others; that a nonaggressive, noncompetitive person might very well be one of high quality in tastes and talents. These self-consistent realizations are incompatible with conservative beliefs and values.

In pointing out these concatenations my intent is to suggest, as may be obvious, that Bestor's conservatism is incompatible with schooling which aims to encourage intellectual development in everyone. It is also to suggest that simple-minded and tradition-bound thinking about education needs to be overcome by the thinking of persons who specialize in the study of education—that is to say, by educationists, who are likely to be more sensitive to complex realities and more daring in seeing where new invention is needed.

To say that philosophy of education or educational theory ought to employ the methods of philosophy might seem to offer Bestor and his followers a weapon to use against me. If there can be such a thing as educational philosophy, they might say, then would it not be better to turn its problems over to trained philosophers rather than to educationists? This is a tack which Bestor would surely use.

In reply, let it be admitted that any philosophers who are eager to devote their time to thinking about education are welcome. Whatever they might have to say is almost sure to be received gratefully and with more than usual interest and respect. But a couple of reservations are in order. From time to time a major philosopher has published his views on education. Typically, he writes (like Whitehead, for example) about those of his ideals which are especially related to schooling. He might propose, at considerable length, an ideal picture of academic learning as an exciting, adventurous, and creative kind of activity, in contrast to the imitative and plodding kind of learning which unimaginative professors might try to provoke. This is praise for apple pie. Even the dull and plodding professor himself believes that he agrees wholeheartedly with the philosopher's ideal, and even, so help me, that he serves it. Who does not? What an educationist would like is some help in figuring out how to promote an adventurous and creative spirit among the dull clods one finds in school these days. From nearly all philosophers, including even the greatest

(Immanuel Kant, for example), we get no help in practical ways. Problems of curriculum design and of teaching method which are especially acute in trying to educate the masses are left to educationists. As for the typical academic philosopher, his thinking about education is likely to be nothing more than the repetition of bromides and the rejection of bold and innovative ideas.

A few times in Western history it has happened that a philosopher turned his devoted attention to educational theory and therefrom contributed an impressive and practically useful educational doctrine; that is to say, a comprehensive theoretical treatment of why and how to organize schools for the best results, and what to do in practically useful ways to implement a clarified concept of educational aims. J. F. Herbart and John Dewey were the most recent and most notable of such contributors, and their proposals were adopted with zeal and enthusiasm by educators all over the world. If it should happen again that a philosopher offers new and stimulating ideas about how to improve schooling, his or her proposals will be received with hospitality by educationists. Depending on how radically new and stimulating, perhaps *only* by educationists, who then become the vanguard of educational reform.

A related kind of Bestor-like criticism is to protest that educationists have no trained competence in philosophy. For some that is probably true; for others, certainly not. Those who specialize in educational theory are likely to be well-educated in philosophy. However, it would be a serious mistake to think that training in philosophy makes it easy to do philosophy of education. There had been a time in the recent past when some educational philosophers thought that an educational doctrine, blessed with the profound wisdom which popular imagination attributes to philosophy, could be derived by logical deduction from the metaphysical and epistemological doctrines of the great philosophers. This was absurd, as some of us pointed out. More recently, the futility of it has become so evident that little is heard from that camp. Educational theorizing requires intellectual labor devoted to finding creative solutions to complex educational problems. From metaphysics, nothing whatsoever is implied about education, and even the most learned of philosophers is not necessarily in any better position than any other learned person to create good ideas about education. If he or she happened to offer such, that may be taken as evidence of having accepted the challenge of educational theorizing as a unique arena for the application of philosophic method. Most philosophers lack either the interest or the ability, finding it easier to do the kind of work that everybody else in academic philosophy is doing.

In summary, I am proposing that the determination of aims for education is a problem for philosophic inquiry, and that it may be expected to yield most readily when theorists search for criteria by which we distinguish educative events from other kinds of events and bring those criteria into explicit awareness. Although this activity operates on an assumption that such criteria are already implicit in our understanding, it is not likely that inquiry will be terminated successfully after a limited number of hours, even years, devoted to it. Philosophic method is not of a kind which can reach universally accepted results. As I say, philosophic inquiry is never-ending, or ceaselessly dialectical. From this acknowledgment, therefore, it follows that the determination of aims for education is not to be accomplished in the near future in such manner that we can accept those results and thereafter direct our inquiries only to the tasks of devising methods of approach and capture. Is this nonterminating quality to be tolerated, or does this reveal a flaw in my conception?

Ask yourself: what could be wrong with a conception of educational theory which acknowledges that its mission is never completely satisfied, its work never done, and the tubes not twisted and dried? This is recognition of human fallibility and of progress as a function of change in conceptions of the good and how to reach it. It is straightforwardly realistic to see that over time our ideas about education will grow in unanticipated directions and toward novel insights. This is true even of that which is implicit and residing deep within the subconscious mind. What we can hope from philosophic inquiry is that we can achieve enough of clarity to support a rational educational doctrine, for today and tomorrow, and until better insights can replace old half-seen glimpses. Furthermore, the pursuit of educational aims is not exclusive of anyone's interests. Whatever we can bring to light about the nature of educational events is necessarily that which advances the public welfare, not according to controversial values of the kind which divide us into factions and partisanship, but according to a newly found realization that this or that kind of proposed education will favor the legitimate interests of everyone rather than of only Republicans and Baptists.

This needs further consideration. We have in our cultural heritage a kind of achievement that may be taken as a model to follow in education. What I have in mind is the principle of separation of church and state and the constitutional guarantee of freedom of worship. This protects the legitimate religious interests of all the many conflicting and often violently warring religious groups. Although each one is marked by a belief that it alone possesses the keys to the kingdom, and most are zealous in trying to convert the heathen, the principle of religious freedom says, in effect, that no one may force religion upon another nor deny another's freedom to see religious matters in a different way. Intensely religious persons may look at this with mixed feelings. They may realize, especially if their sect is in a minority, that democracy protects their religion and allows it to flourish unimpeded. But they may feel unhappy that they are required to leave the heathen, who do not understand salvation, to go on being damned, and they may fight for some kind of advantage over others in the religious wars, like school prayer and tax support for parochial schools. If they can manage to accomplish these, they score heavily against the godless. They are by no means sure that they want the principle of religious freedom to continue in force. Here, one kind of interest is in conflict with another, and the principle which protects everyone is something which some partisans may be willing to give up. In return for giving up that protection, the zealous gain a possibility of forcing their faith upon others, serene in their belief that it is good for them. In these respects, the principle of nonpartisan education is like the principle of religious freedom.

If we were to make some progress in the clarification of educational ideals and in understanding what is required of democratic schooling, it may turn out that some educators cannot accept a school that is nonpartisan. Feeling very strongly that their preferences about education are right and the educationists wrong, they might reject an effort by schools to treat legitimate and controversial values fairly. In that case, we should be able to make evident that what they want is parochial education, not public schools. On some matters dear to their hearts, they feel obligated to place first the indoctrination of children and youth in a pre-ferred set of values and beliefs, or faiths, and this need to indoc-trinate takes precedence over loyalty to any truly educational values. Could this be true of the Bestors?

Conceivably, Bestor could object that his ideal is one of teach-ing everybody how to think, and this does not include teaching everybody *what* to think. If everyone learns how to think, then everyone is in the best possible position to protect valid interests and to be properly aware of where they may be found. This is an appealing idea, and it does seem that a public in which everyone reaches a capability for maximum intelligence is a public which can be expected to reach maximum realization of pluralistic values. With that I would agree. So then, you might say, why not go along with schooling created primarily to teach people how to think?

Up to this point I have been objecting that Bestor's educational ideal rests upon a misconception of "disciplines," and upon a failure to realize that the encouragement of thinking demands certain changes in school traditions of a radical sort. Now it is time to consider head-on the question of whether we know how to think and how to teach how to think.

As you read *Educational Wastelands* you may form an im-pression of its author as a man of learning who respects knowl-edge and shuns ignorance. How surprising it is, then, to find that on this key question, Bestor makes no apparent effort to employ available cognitive resources about thinking. There are at least three disciplines or branches of disciplines which offer materials with import for educators. One is psychology, which is the only empirical science to investigate thinking in an effort to understand how it works. Closely related to the scientific study of thinking is that branch of psychology which studies intelligence, seeking to determine its nature and to answer such questions as whether intelligence is a unitary quality of behavior or, instead, the prod-uct of several factors. Of these two branches of psychology, the second is much better developed than the first, but neither one has produced very much of verified knowledge. I think it rea-sonably correct to say that we do not yet know much, scientifically, about the nature of thinking, and we cannot yet put to rest most of the controversies about intelligence and the degree to which we may hope to change upward a native endowment.

Another discipline which might have something to offer for consideration of how we think is philosophy. Because it is not an empirical science, philosophy cannot offer knowledge about thinking, but it has something valuable nonetheless: namely, the philosophy of mind. Philosophers have asked a variety of questions about the mind, not all of which seem closely related to an educator's interests. But they have speculated about the mind as knower, considering whether the mind can transcend the limits of experience and whether the mind has a way of knowing which is other than the method of science. Even more closely related to an educator's concerns is the product of philosophers, like Descartes and Dewey, who speculated about how the mind works. In this century there was one book, by John Dewey, which has been of considerable influence upon educationists. The title, *How We Think*, gives an indication of its contents. In it, Dewey elaborated a theory about the mind's activities in solving problems and proposed criteria which govern judgment about success or failure. What is interesting about it in this context is Dewey's proposal that the most characteristic and the highest level activity of the mind is the kind of thinking that occurs when confronting and trying to solve a real problem. Given Dewey's preponderant influence upon educationists, it is not suprising that modern educational theory has been dominated by a problem-centered orientation. At the hands of educational administrators like the life adjusters, this produced sometimes absurd proposals, which Bestor pounced upon with savage glee. But the same kind of orientation toward problem-solving is found in Bestor's position. The task of the school, he says, is to teach how to think and thereby to solve problems as they occur in one's life.

A first observation is to repeat that we do not know very much about how we think. Psychology is too young a science, and the complexities of the phenomena associated with thinking are such that discoveries about the mind's workings may be far off in the future. Given this lack of knowledge, it would seem presumptuous to concentrate the entire burden of schooling within the compass of teaching how to think. We are not in a position to know how to think—not, that is, in accurate detail—and for Bestor's educational doctrine to be workable, that particular kind of knowledge would be a prerequisite, a very first consideration. On the other hand, if we conceive the work of schooling as one of stimulating and encouraging the mind to think, then no presumption of knowing how to think is made or required.

A second observation is that some philosophers have called attention to forces which tend to distort thinking or to throw the mind off the track of objectivity and open-mindedness. Francis Bacon's theory about idols is one of the earlier and more interesting examples. Today, several literatures are replete with more intricate studies of the same kind of mind-distorting influences. One of these is psychoanalysis and the related psychology of mental pathology. Another is found in some portions of sociology: the sociology of knowledge, for example. And still another is found in the psychology of personality. Different kinds of personality exert differing kinds of pushes and pulls upon the mind, some of which are not conducive to seeing clearly nor to encouraging a grasp of the whole truth. If we take seriously a responsibility of the school for stimulating the mind, then these related literatures would seem possibly helpful, and, at the very least, they would help educators to become more sensitive to all the many factors in the human environment which influence the mind and sometimes cause distortions.

I mention this here because, first, Bestor seems innocent or scornful of such considerations, and because, second, the educationists whom he derides have been much more intellectually responsible about the role of the school in promoting thinking. They are conversant with these various literatures, and they have made many proposals about new ways of schooling which are designed to take account of social, psychological, and personality factors that exert pressure upon the mind and influence its development. Since these newer efforts were never a part of schooling in the past, they have been the butt of ridicule and sneers from conservatives and, unfortunately, from humanists whose first reaction to anything new is one of scornful rejection.

Another part of philosophy of mind that could be a resource for educational theory is that which strives to say what the mind's function is—whether it is essentially a problem-solving device or it is something else more universally operative. One difficulty with Dewey's kind of theory is that what is said to be the characteristic activity of the mind—namely, problem-solving—is necessarily discontinuous or intermittent in its operations. Between problems, the mind is presumably quiescent. But if one pays attention to what we usually mean by "mind," then a better conception includes the idea of mind as involving the central regulation of behavior, and central regulation is better conceived as continuous rather than intermittent. If this is recognized, then a theory of mind different from a problem-solving kind may be a better resource.

At this point, I would like to mention my own beliefs about this, not to urge them upon anyone, but simply to illustrate my suggestion that the philosophy of mind is potentially useful for educational theory. It seems to me that the function of the mind is to break down the isolation of experience within a present moment. This is accomplished by providing, through the interpretation of what is given, a background continuity in space and time. Phenomena are interpreted as signifying the presence of enduring objects, and the fleeting moment is interpreted as a place within unfolding events which began in the no-longer-here past and will continue into a not-yet-here future. In other words, the mind brings into each moment a construction of a continuing self within a continuing and public world, in order that desires may be satisfied and plans may be carried into completion. This is the bare gist of a conception which, in the philosophy especially of C. I. Lewis, seems to accord with our usual and prephilosophic ideas of the human mind. Leaving aside for the moment any question about which theory is right, it may appear quickly to any who entertain this conception of mind that it is ideally suited to thinking about education. With respect to the human mind, the responsibility of schooling is to give greater scope for its characteristic operations, and to bring into the mind's constructions a greater degree of refinement and of recognition for a bigger and more complex background to one's immediate foreground. An educated mind is different from an uneducated primarily in its capacity to discern a greater number and range of continuities in the world. The term "continuities" seems appropriate, because it emphasizes the mind's construction of enduring objects which are not immediately experienced as enduring. Continuities include causal connections, temporal sequences, and entities like the state, a corporation, or a gravitational field, which cannot be experienced as sensed objects in the way that a pepper mill, a symphony, or a cloud can be sensed. Much of what is most important in the world, by virtue of its impact upon goal-seeking behavior, has that nonperceptible kind of existence, like "society," such that its nature and its presence must be constructed through the mind's interpretation of events. The work of the school is to assist the mind in its interpretation of experience. One result is that objects and events of apparently small size or limited scope may be perceived as fraught with meanings that greatly increase the number of connections between what is immediately sensed and what is constructed by the mind as an underlying reality.

Materials of the preceding paragraph borrow heavily from philosophy, and philosophy is controversial in a high degree. Where is the necessary nonpartisanship? Well, in choosing anything from philosophy for use in educational theory, one does not argue first that the chosen material is true, or more true than alternative theories with which it conflicts. One develops an argument by appeals to two kinds of criteria. The first of these are considerations bearing upon the capacity of ideas to be faithful to our common experience and to enlighten our intellectual grasp of experience. The second are considerations of utility in the construction of educational theory. If a philosophic theory of mind is employed, the critical question is not whether it is more "true" than rival theories; the question is, how useful does it turn out to be in helping us to think about education. Does it help us to make better sense of what we take the essential nature of schooling to be, and is it fruitful, in the sense that by consideration of it we are made aware of new possibilities for schooling and new ideas to try?

A problem-centered approach to conceiving the work of schooling, like Bestor's, leads to certain anomalies. The presumed virtue of it is that it places emphasis upon training to solve "real" problems of "real" life. But the problems which a student encounters in school are, for the greatest part, problems which are real only in the sense that they are created for him by the school. A learner has a problem, let us say, in learning how to solve equations representing chemical reactions. This is a problem which simply would not exist except as it is set up through artifice to encourage learning. A learner has no way of knowing whether this kind of problem, and the kind of learning which results from having dealt with it, will ever become a part of his subsequent life. If an educator tells him that he is learning how to deal with real-life problems, he may reply that he has no intention of becoming a chemist, but that if he were to do so, *then* he would have good reason to learn about chemical equations, a kind of motivation he does not have *now*. The anomaly resides in issues of motivation, of having or not having good reasons for trying to learn. (By contrast, the interpretive theory of mind permits a much more reasonable account of what it is that ought to motivate a properly sceptical learner to invest intellectual labors in tasks set for him by the school. This claim will have to go unsupported, for it seems inappropriate to elaborate here any more of an alternative theory than has already been set forth.)

The question of how best to motivate students to work hard at school-set learning has always been difficult. In schools dominated by tradition, students are told that they ought to study and learn, because what they are asked to accomplish is in their own interest; if students cannot see any connection of curriculum materials to their interests, they are told that sometime in the future they will come to realize that their teachers had been right. "Some day you will thank me." But it would not be easy to convince high school students that the study of geometry would some day turn out to be valuable. If they realize, as they might, that in all probability they will never actually use any branch of mathematics beyond simple arithmetic, they have every right to be sceptical; and the more thoughtful a person is, the more likely he is to be sceptical. Here we have a characteristic inconsistency of the conservative mentality: students are asked to withhold critical intelligence from consideration of school subject matters and their potential value to learners and to apply intelligence only to studying hard for reasons that they cannot understand. Another kind of motivation that traditionalists have relied upon is ambition and competitive striving. It works, too, for a small percentage of students. Given a bright mind and a desire to get ahead of other people in honors and rewards, a youngster will work as hard as necessary for the realization of ambitions. But, happily, not all persons are so grimly determined to get ahead of others. Therefore, this kind of motivation is, by nature, a kind that can operate for only a minority of students. In traditional schools, the majority of students are simply not motivated. For this condition, conservatives tend to blame the students for lack of ambition.

Throughout much of this century, educationists have tried to employ kinds of motivational force that are compatible with a tendency of learners to be sceptical about what they are asked to accept on blind faith, and that seem likely to work with students of all kinds rather than with only a few. With very young children in elementary school, there are various ways of turning learning into play or into a game. Although these had limitations, they made elementary schools far more cheerful than ever they had been before, and at their best they succeeded in taking away a child's view of schooling as an adult-imposed unpleasantness. But even in elemntary school a certain amount of hard work, or of earnest studying, seems necessary, and the play way was not too useful for the degree of motivation that hard study requires. But the more serious limitation is that it seems to work as a form of motivation only in the earliest years of schooling. The greater degree of difficulty in motivating students appears at the later years when a tougher stance coincides with the troublesomeness of adolescence. Here, the project method could sometimes be used, but it required teachers with more devotion and ability than are usually found, and it was not always entirely honest in the way that motivation was supposed to work. To accomplish their projects, students were often required to take a circuitous route, picking up along the way more of learning than really necessary to reaching the ostensible and desired end result. Nevertheless, it must be said to their credit that the educationists succeeded in placing responsibility for the motivation of learning upon the school, rather than upon out-of-school factors, and that is surely where it belongs in a society which upholds the ideal of educational opportunity.

My point is that we confront a problem for educational theory which cannot be solved by simply returning to academic tradition. If high school teachers of the liberal arts and sciences are asked why their students ought to be willing to study and learn, they can give answers, but answers of a kind that are at least partly phony, like the teacher of geometry who told his students that everyone ought to learn geometry, because geometric shapes are to be found everywhere. The truth is, we inherit a tradition of teaching the liberal arts and sciences, and we are rightfully sure that this tradition is good and to be continued, but we cannot explain precisely and convincingly why everyone ought to learn these subject matters. It is easy to understand why a potential scientist ought to learn, say, algebra and physics, but why should Everyman and Everywoman? Conservatives tend to rely upon rhetoric for answers, but neither students nor educational theorists can be satisfied with that. We need new thinking so that we can be hardheaded, honest, and truly convincing to any sceptic who doubts the value to him or to her personally of much learning in the liberal arts and sciences. We cannot be satisfied to make such learning a requirement for college entrance and letting that be the primary reaason why students learn, even though that is probably the most effective motivator we have at present. Even those for whom this works ought to have a better reason, a reason less apparently arbitrary and less under the control of administrator-gatekeepers. Indeed, there are good reasons, but they remain to be clarified, a continuing problem for educational theorists. And when they are made clear, something else will turn up with them: namely, the discovery that it is truly reasonable for all students to learn only certain aspects, or parts, and amounts of the liberal arts and sciences, rather than that which we expect from a vocational specialist within the various domains. When we achieve clarity about good reasons for learning, we will achieve equal clarity about what to select and emphasize.

One final question: is this problem for educational theorizing a problem of pedagogy; that is, a problem merely of teaching methods? Certainly not. An honest and hardheaded account of good reasons why everyone ought to learn the contents of a liberal education would be not only a theory of how to motivate learners; it would be also, and more fundamentally, a rational justification for schooling itself. It goes to the heart of determining aims for education. I say this, which must seem so obvious, because Bestor would leave in existence within departments of education, if he had the power to destroy, only those who specialize in figuring out how to teach; that is, specialists in pedagogy. He seems never to have noticed that the rational consideration of ends and means must go together.

Iu summary, I have tried to show that the educators whom Bestor attacks are really the good guys from whom any future improvement of education must be expected to come. If not for them, we have only a return to academic tradition, with all of its associated problems that were never solved, and with a defeat for democracy and the ideal of equal educational opportunity.

# Publications of Arthur Bestor on Educational Questions

*A Select List, in Chronological Order*

*Chautauqua Publications: An Historical and Bibliographical Guide.* Chautauqua, N.Y.: Chautauqua Press, 1934.

Editor of *Proceedings of the Middle States Association of History and and Social Science Teachers.* Vols. 36-38. 1938–41.

*Education and Reform at New Harmony: Correspondence of William Maclure and Marie Duclos Fretageot, 1820–1833.* Indianapolis: Indiana Historical Society, 1948. Reprinted in facsimile. Clifton, N. J.: Augustus M. Kelley, 1973.

"The Study of American Civilization: Jingoism or Scholarship?" *William and Mary Quarterly,* 3rd ser,. 9 (Jan. 1952), 3-9.

"Liberal Education and a Liberal Nation." *American Scholar,* 21 (Spring 1952), 139-49. Republished in book form in Hiram Haydn, ed., *The American Scholar Reader.* New York: Atheneum, 1960.

"Aimlessness in Education." *Scientific Monthly,* 75 (Aug. 1952), 109-16.

" 'Life-Adjustment' Education: A Critique." *Bulletin of the American Association of University Professors,* 38 (Autumn 1952), 413-41.

"Anti-Intellectualism in the Schools." *New Republic,* 128 (19 Jan. 1953), 11-13.

"Resolutions concerning Public Education." *School and Society,* 77 (31 Jan. 1953), 68-70.

"Education's Open Door to Tyranny." *Christian Register,* 132 (Mar. 1953), 11-14.

"The Transformation of American Scholarship, 1875–1917." In Pierce Butler, ed., *Librarians, Scholars and Booksellers at Mid-Century.* Chicago: University of Chicago Press, 1953. Published simultaneously in *Library Quarterly,* 23 (July 1953), 164-79.

"On the Education and Certification of Teachers." *School and Society,* 78 (19 Sept. 1953), 81-87.

*Educational Wastelands: The Retreat from Learning in Our Public Schools.* Urbana: University of Illinois Press, 1953. Published Nov. 1953. Reprinted verbatim in the present volume (1985), together with a new preface by the author and retrospectives by two professors of education.

"Future Direction of American Education." *Phi Delta Kappan,* 35 (June 1954), 373-78 and 384.

"The Fundamentals of Education." *Vital Speeches of the Day,* 20 (15 Aug. 1954), 658-59.

"How Should America's Teachers Be Educated?" *Teachers College Record,* 56 (Oct. 1954), 1-4.

"Liberal Education in the Education of Teachers." In *Proceedings of the Twenty-Third Conference of Academic Deans of the Southern States.* Louisville, Ky., 1954.

"Education for 1984." In Leonard E. Read, ed., *Essays on Liberty,* Vol. 2. Irvington-on-Hudson, N.Y., 1954.

"Thomas Jefferson and the Freedom of Books." In Arthur Bestor, David C. Mearns, and Jonathan Daniels, *Three Presidents and Their Books.* Urbana: University of Illinois Press, 1955. Paperback ed., 1963.

*The Restoration of Learning: A Program for Redeeming the Unfulfilled Promise of American Education.* New York: Knopf, 1955.

" 'We Are Less Educated Than 50 Years Ago': Exclusive Interview with Professor Arthur Bestor." *U.S. News & World Report,* 41 (30 Nov. 1956), 68-82.

"Educating the Gifted Child." *New Republic,* 136 (4 Mar. 1957), 12-16.

"Why Liberal Education." *Loomis Bulletin,* 25 (Apr. 1957), 6-7.

"Specialized Libraries and the General Historian." *Bulletin of the Medical Library Association,* 45 (Apr. 1957), 123-38.

"Progressive Education: A Debate [with William H. Kilpatrick]." *New York Times Magazine,* 8 Sept. 1957, pp. 25ff.

"The Education Really Needed for a Changing World." *Harvard Educational Review*, 27 (Winter 1957), 1-8.

"The American University: A Historical Interpretation of Current Issues." *College and University*, 32 (Winter 1957), 175-88.

"What Went Wrong with U.S. Schools: An Interview with Prof. Arthur Bestor." *U.S. News & World Report*, 44 (24 Jan. 1958), 68-77. Reprinted in *Congressional Record*, 85th Congress, 2d Session, 30 Jan. 1958, Senate, extension of remarks (vol. 104, Appendix, part 19), A-833 to A-838.

"School Crisis, U.S.A." Series of 5 articles, May-Nov. 1958. *Good Housekeeping*, May, pp. 67ff.; June, pp. 14ff.; Sept., pp. 18ff.; Oct., pp. 47ff.; Nov., pp. 51ff.

"A Crisis of Purpose." *Vital Speeches of the Day*, 24 (15 Sept. 1958), 723-28.

"The Choice before Us in American Education." In Bower Aly, ed., *American Education: The 32nd Discussion and Debate Manual, 1958–59*. Columbia, Mo.: National University Extension Association, 1958. 1: 65-86.

"Man, an End Not a Means: The Significance of Liberal Education." *Kenyon Alumni Bulletin*, 16 (Spring, 1958), 9-13.

"Achieving the Purposes of the High School." In *Proceedings of the Summer Conferences and Institute*. Western Washington College of Education, 7 Aug. 1958. Bellingham, 1958.

"Education and Its Proper Relationship to the Forces of American Society." *Daedalus*, 88 (Winter 1959), 75-90.

"Education and the American Scene." In Brand Blanshard, ed., *Education in the Age of Science*. New York: Basic Books, 1959.

"And Gladly Wolde He Lerne, and Gladly Teche." *Proceedings of the American Conference of Academic Deans*. 16th annual meeting, Boston, 12 Jan. 1960. Washington, 1960.

"History, Social Studies, and Citizenship: The Responsibility of the Public Schools." *Proceedings of the American Philosophical Society*, 104 (15 Dec. 1960), 549-57.

"Intellectual History to 1900" [a bibliographic essay]. In William H. Cartwright and Richard L. Watson, eds., *Interpreting and Teaching American History*. 31st Yearbook of the National Council for the Social Studies. Washington, 1961.

"Education for Intellectual Discipline." In Philip H. Phenix, ed., *Philosophies of Education*. New York: Wiley, 1961.

"The Contribution of History to General Education." In *Higher Education Re-Examined*. Proceedings of the Pacific Northwest Conference on Higher Education, Seattle, 22-24 June 1961. Corvallis, Ore., 1961.

"Historical Understanding: First Line of Defense of American Democracy." *Teachers College Record* (Indiana State College, Terre Haute), 34 (Dec. 1962), 102-4.

"The Humaneness of History." *Western Humanities Review,* 16 (Winter 1962), 3-9. Reprinted in *American Review* (New Delhi, India), 7 (Jan. 1963), 28-33; also in A. S. Eisenstadt, ed., *The Craft of American History.* New York: Harper and Row, 1966. I: 7-15.

"Historical Scholarship in the Schools." In *The Role of History in Today's Schools.* Conference sponsored by the Council for Basic Education, New York City, 12-14 Nov. 1965. Washington, 1966.

"The Policy-Making Function of the University Faculty." In *The Domain of the Faculty in the Growing University.* Conference sponsored by the Common Ministry Serving Washington State University, 9-11 Sept. 1967. Pullman, Wash., 1967.

"History as Verifiable Knowledge: The Logic of Historical Inquiry and Explanation." In Rolland E. Stevens, ed., *Research Methods in Librarianship.* Urbana: University of Illinois Graduate School of Library Science, 1971.

"In Defence of Intellectual Integrity: A Manifesto for the Contemporary University." *Encounter* (London), 39 (Oct. 1972), 18-25. Also published in book form in Sidney Hook and others, eds., *The Idea of a Modern University.* Buffalo: Prometheus Books, 1974.